HARVARD HISTORICAL MONOGRAPHS

XXXVI

Published under the direction of the Department of History
from the income of The Robert Louis Stroock Fund

Historical Pessimism
in the
French Enlightenment

By

HENRY VYVERBERG

CAMBRIDGE, MASSACHUSETTS
HARVARD UNIVERSITY PRESS
1958

To
Crane Brinton

Contents

Part IV

HISTORICAL FLUX—FACTS IN A
CHANGING UNIVERSE

Part V

THE MEN AND THE DOCTRINES

Historical Pessimism
in the French Enlightenment

Introduction

At first glance this work might seem a labored and sustained paradox. The belief in progress has long been considered the culmination of eighteenth century thought, and any attack upon this proposition will rightly be regarded with distrust. Yet the time for a re-examination of the facts is overdue. What follows in these pages is a sketch, a suggestion, of such a reconsideration—an attempt not only to weigh with special caution the historical philosophies of the French Enlightenment, but also to examine the substructure of thought which underlay them and which often led directly, perhaps inevitably, not to a belief in human progress but to historical pessimism.

It is clear that the eighteenth century saw the development of an idea of progress; clearly, too, there were writers and men of action who generously transformed idea into belief. This study does not, certainly, seek to deny these facts. But how widespread was this belief? Which intellectual factions resisted or ignored the optimistic trend, and why? What disturbing uncertainties and intellectual reservations entered the minds of even the master builders of the Enlightenment as they proposed to draw the blueprints of the future? These questions demand serious study, though doubtless they will never be answered to the satisfaction of all. If, for the moment, a few misconceptions concerning the Enlightenment can be exposed, if here and there an emphasis is significantly shifted, the historian may be permitted to feel that a truer understanding of one vital aspect of the past has been achieved.

The central contention of the present study is simply this: that a belief in progress was neither the exclusive focus nor the one logical consummation of Enlightened French philosophy, and that historical pessimism too had its roots deep in the "philosophical" movement itself. The eighteenth century saw a rich proliferation of intellectual currents, and within this growth lay potentialities immensely dangerous to that rationalistic-optimistic synthesis which too often is assumed to have been the ultimate contribution of the century. The thought of the Enlightenment was neither as disembodied and visionary, nor as simple or oversimplified, as it was once imagined, and as it is pictured now and again in our own day.

If, as I believe, the prevalence and the significance of the eighteenth century belief in progress have been overrated, several roads to misinterpretation are evident. There have been, for example, few thinkers indeed in any age who have not cherished a hope for progress according to their own lights; what has not been fully recognized by historians of the Enlightenment is that the hope for progress need not involve a firm belief in the realization of that progress. In this period, as in others, the most fervent expression of an ideal might be accompanied by skepticism as to its practicality and even its final validity. Man is sometimes less consistent than might be concluded from a rationalistic view of human nature.

Often, in fact, the thinkers of the Enlightenment saw the historical movement of mankind as irregular or cyclical, and often the historian, in his zeal for tracing the development of progressionist theory, has slighted or wholly ignored these significant conceptions of cultural decline. Other thinkers of the period were openly hostile to the idea of progress as then conceived, while still others were simply indifferent to man's progressive development; both groups have been almost entirely neglected by the historian. Moreover, it is commonly assumed, when these supposedly atypical trends are noted at all, that they are part of the negligible clerical, reactionary thought of the eighteenth century. Closer examination, however, reveals not only the utter divergence of historical philosophies among the religious writers of the time, but also the presence of historical pessimism in the thought of the *philosophes* themselves.

"Historical pessimism"—the term admittedly lacks precision, yet it must serve here for lack of a better. It is applied in this study to the acceptance, as realities, of one or more of three historical processes: decadence, cycles, and flux. By the three concepts indicated here, and by the idea of progress, mankind has sought to explain or to describe its temporal existence, and to predict its future as well. But the movement of history is complex and its interpretation offers countless variations; neither the Enlightenment nor any other period of Western thought has shown unanimity in its view of historical change.

Progress, decadence, cycles, flux—these are words representing movement. No philosophy of earthly history has been a philosophy of absolute immobility, for in the world of phenomena change has always been evident. To be sure, the concept of flux may indicate change which is essentially without meaning and often simply fortuitous; such are the so-called "static" views of history. On the other hand, cycles, in the strict sense of the term, necessarily postulate plan, meaning, destiny, inscrutable though these may be.

Value judgments may be implied in conceptions of cycles and of flux, but they are not ordinarily central. These conceptions may indeed dispense altogether with absolute values; a relativistic outlook seems to be peculiarly favorable to their development in modern times. Flux and cycles are commonly seen as facts, natural or supernatural, and their reality is accepted as the teaching of experience or of authority. It hath been, proclaimed the writer of *Ecclesiastes*, and it shall be. No ideal is necessarily involved here, no realization of value, no progress, no decline.

Quite different are the complementary notions of progress and decadence, for these historical processes comprise by definition a movement toward or away from an ideal or a set of ideals. Whether the ideal is precise and final, or simply vague, provisional, and contingent, man's judgment of values is necessary in defining that ideal.

The pages which follow represent an attempt to examine the three elements of historical pessimism within a geographical and temporal unit sufficiently homogeneous to permit fruitful analysis. This unit is France from the Age of Louis XIV to the outbreak of the Revolution. The earlier period is treated with relative brevity; the larger part of the study deals with the years from 1715 to 1789, the period to which the term "Enlightenment" has been more commonly restricted.

Certain limitations and emphases will necessarily be observed.

Only passing notice, for example, will be given to clerical writers, for their work is of far less general interest and originality than that of the *philosophes*. Considerations of a political and economic nature are frequently mentioned, and inevitably so, but are by no means central in the scheme of this study; these matters have been so often the subject of voluminous analysis by other critics that repetition is largely superfluous. Such attention as is given here to the political and economic thought of the Enlightenment largely skirts the vast realm of strictly polemical writing; this is a realm vital to the student of the more conventional history, but much less pertinent for the historian of ideas.

This work will therefore stress concepts of social and moral change, and doctrines of the historical destinies of literature and art. Happily, these three areas of man's development—the sociological, the ethical, and the aesthetic—are fundamental, and often inter-related, in nearly all the historical philosophies of the age. Cognizant of the generally low repute in which eighteenth century French writing, purely as literature, is often held today, the casual student may be suspicious of the emphasis placed here upon aesthetic theory and literary criticism. The emphasis, however, is that of the Enlightenment itself; it is an emphasis found not only in Diderot and Voltaire, but also, surprisingly perhaps, in Montesquieu, d'Alembert, and Condillac. Aesthetic concerns are not an isolated compartment within the thought of these writers, but rather an integral part, quite commonly, of their social-ethical outlook.

The complexities of a study such as this justify, and even demand, a methodology which is not strictly homogeneous. It will be noted, for example, that the first and second sections treat individual thinkers and avoid all but the most brief and tentative generalizations; the later sections, which form by far the major portion of the book, build up a general frame of reference before proceeding to a consideration of individual writers. An attempt to apply the second, or more comprehensive, method to the earlier chapters would have displaced the focus of the work, as announced in its title, and would, I fear, have enlarged the work intolerably.

Similar practical considerations have inevitably been influential in other instances. Thus the first group of chapters examines only a sampling of those seventeenth century French authors who were much read by subsequent generations. Such a sampling, whatever its internal logic, must be by definition somewhat arbitrary; nevertheless the major thinkers, at least, are here.

A further practical consideration has resulted in the decision not to trace in detail the precise lines of influence extending, in the present field of research, from the seventeenth century to the eighteenth, or from the earlier to the later eighteenth. The morbid connoisseur of doctoral dissertations is all too well aware of the enormous expenditure of energy—often futile energy—which is ordinarily required for the exact tracing of a single line of intellectual influence from thinker to thinker. This present work therefore does not attempt to establish such lines; it does assume, however, some knowledge of most of the earlier thinkers by most of the later.

The first of the five major parts of this study thus deals with precursors, with *types* of historical optimism and pessimism in the Age of Louis XIV rather than with precise influences upon later thinkers. In Part II a number of prominent exponents of historical optimism in the eighteenth century itself are studied—writers whose work offers useful insights into the requisite conditions for progressionist theory, and who already point to several restrictions of that theory.

Parts III and IV comprise a topical treatment of eighteenth century historical pessimism and its philosophical foundations. In the first of these divisions the idea of decadence alone is considered—decadence as measured against a rational scheme of more or less absolute values, notably in the fields of ethics and aesthetics. Empirical and relativistic trends in eighteenth century thought, and their repercussions upon notions of progress, are discussed in Part IV. It is, notably, from these trends that a philosophy of historical flux arises, for here is found the incipient ruin of any absolute criteria of progress through subjectivism in the arts and relativism in the study of cultures. Here, too, evolve considerations on the comparative pace of cultural growth and decline, and rudimentary conceptions of a cyclical development within history.

So that the whole body and significance of certain writers' thought can be treated as a unit, the fifth and final part of the work is composed of case studies—studies which serve to test, as those in Part I serve to foreshadow, the principles discussed in Parts III and IV. Such studies have special value with controversial thinkers of the first rank, Montesquieu, Voltaire, and Diderot among them. Of lesser stature, but highly interesting as rebels and nonconformists, are the curious figures of Vauvenargues and Linguet. And finally come the materialists, offspring and potential destroyers of eighteenth century moderate thought—La Mettrie, Holbach, and Sade. In this ominous trio, most important for ages later than its own, there rises a threatening crescendo of indifferentism, mechanical determinism, and orgiastic cultural perversion.

It is evident that, in a study such as this, no mere sampling of opinions, no collection of quotations, can touch the root of the matter. Only upon a consideration of the fundamental structure and of certain basic assumptions of eighteenth century thought can be founded any explanation of the presence of historical pessimism in the writings of the *philosophes*. Moreover, only from such a comprehensive consideration can it be shown that historical pessimism in the Enlightenment was not a freak, a sport, but an authentically organic growth.

Yet for the eighteenth century itself, and for the succeeding century, the belief in progress was the wave of the future. This study thus deals, in the main, with an undercurrent of thought—but with an undercurrent of a depth and force seldom appreciated. In an age of disenchantment such as ours, one may be tempted to find more of the future in the undercurrent than in the main stream.

Part I

The Seventeenth Century

Chapter 1

The Man of Reason—Descartes

Our concern must extend beyond the present day.
(*Discours de la méthode*)[1]

That the historical destiny of mankind has presented itself more than once as an enigma is scarcely surprising. Whether linked with man's supernatural destiny or divorced from any such consideration, the enigma has been solved satisfactorily by few men, by few cultural groups. Even medieval thought, dominated as it was by the imposing Christian synthesis, displayed remarkable diversity in its philosophies of earthly history. Though faith and authority prescribed a basic framework within which all speculation must adjust itself, there remained, from the Fall to the Last Judgment, a long historical period to be charted and explained.

Two vital truths concerning this period were accepted by medieval Christianity: the persistent role of divine Providence, and the central fact of Christ's appearance on earth. The latter entailed two consequences pertinent to the present study. The centuries after Christ had a naturally privileged position, for the way to salvation had become more clear to a widening circle of men. Moreover, for the consistent believer, the conception of strictly recurrent cycles in world history was henceforth ruled out, through the unique event of the sacrifice of Christ on the cross.

It is true that, beyond these central considerations, much of patristic and medieval thought tended to dismiss earthly history, and to concern itself above all with mankind's salvation and the promise of a glorious eternity. The millennium was a very real expectation

[1] *Discours de la méthode* (Evreux, 1927), 202.

for most Christians, and the pursuit of worldly knowledge was often flayed as unprofitable and vain, as the lamentable expression of man's ungovernable pride.

But in the earthly body of Christ, which was the Church, many writers saw a progressive development; above all, the religious understanding of mankind might be expected to increase through the years. Even secular progress on earth was now and then noted. Not always were the arts and sciences considered maleficent, and Augustine himself was capable of high praise for man's technological achievements. Proclaiming the need for a renewal of right learning, Roger Bacon saw a great future for a reformed science. Nor was the idea of progress absent from the fields of government and politics. Pierre du Bois advocated the establishment of a European state for the preservation of peace, and Dante interwove the idea of a universal Roman imperium with his view of the religious and social ends of man.

Yet throughout the medieval period there ran a strong and persistent current of pessimism. Man's sins, it was generally presumed, were multitudinous and vile, and the world would not long remain. The thirteenth century Cluniac monk, Bernard of Morlas, put in memorable form a sentiment widely prevalent:

> *Hora novissima, tempora pessima sunt, vigilemus:*
> *Ecce minaciter imminet arbiter ille supremus.*

> The world is very evil,
> The times are waxing late:
> Be sober and keep vigil;
> The Judge is at the gate.[2]

And in the later medieval period, in the fourteenth and fifteenth centuries, men tended to meditate more and more upon the evil in the world, upon the vanity and corruption of things earthly, upon human decay and death. On the eve of the Renaissance the idea of

[2] F. A. Wright, T. A. Sinclair, *A History of Later Latin Literature from the Middle of the Fourth to the End of the Seventeenth Century* (New York, 1931), 299.

progress was perhaps farther from most men's thoughts than at any time since the Dark Ages.

Though the Renaissance brought, by and large, a far brighter view of the world, no theories of progress were immediately forthcoming; the rediscovery and the emulation of classical antiquity were for a time too predominantly the goals of European intellectuals. Not surprisingly, echoes of ancient notions of historical recurrence, or cycles, were common. At the same time, and as late as the earlier seventeenth century, religious speculation concerning earthly history continued in much the same vein as in the medieval period. Poetic and religious minds still turned, now and then, to the universal decay of nature and to an ultimate release only at the day of judgment. Other apocalyptic writers, in increasing numbers, were more optimistic, seeing even a providential progress of things earthly, a gradual purification before the advent of the millennium.

But it was secular speculation which, before Descartes, was to lead most obviously to a modern idea of progress. As in the medieval period, the reality of technological advance was evident to many observers, and the potentialities of technology were noted by such a prominent writer as Francis Bacon. Other thinkers, such as Le Roy and Bodin, chose to reflect upon the broader historical destinies of nations and peoples, and though they retained something of the cyclical notion their emphasis was clearly upon the upward course of their own civilization.

In the work of René Descartes the doctrine of progress received a sound theoretical foundation. The broad principles of this work are too well known to demand detailed exposition here—his separation of metaphysics and theology; his championing of doubt, not as a counsel of Pyrrhonism but as a road to knowledge; his concept of intuition, by which alone one might gain certainty on basic principles; his emphasis upon deduction, by which one should proceed from the simple to the complex; his belief that only through deductive reasoning could one arrive at a body of knowledge which was certain, absolute, and final. Though Descartes did find, it is true, a place for scientific experiment, he cautioned repeatedly against the misapplication of sense experience. In short, his system was unmistakably rationalistic, not empirical, in essence. There is much truth in that folk wisdom of the French intellectuals which holds that Descartes is the "French" thinker *par excellence*—that is, the most rationalistic, the most systematic, the most clear.

Fully implied in this system, and stated outright in piecemeal form, is a Cartesian doctrine of scientific and philosophical progress. Science, wrote Descartes, may be perfected by practice, and true principles, once discovered, will lead inevitably to others. The illustrious example of competent investigators, the obvious truth and utility of their principles, will cause all men to rally to the support and continuation of these investigations, and this conjunction of efforts will be immensely more valuable than the research of isolated individuals.

Nevertheless Descartes was not unaware of some of the difficulties to be overcome—above all, those difficulties inherent in the organization of scientific research. Current misconceptions, too, in science and philosophy would form a pernicious stumbling block on the road to knowledge, and truth would be elusive indeed. "I well know," he wrote, "that many centuries may pass until all the truths which may be deduced from these principles are so deduced. . . ."[3]

The extent to which Descartes considered scientific method applicable to other spheres of life is not clear, but there can be little doubt that he considered the results of scientific progress valuable in other realms. Science and philosophy, he held, must keep a practical end in view: the general betterment of life. Concerning those many philosophical truths yet to be discovered, Descartes noted "to what degree of wisdom, to what perfection of life, to what happiness they may lead us. . . ."[4] Philosophy must be useful to life. Not only did Descartes contemplate the invention of many mechanical devices promoting man's happiness; he also foresaw the application of new knowledge to medicine so as better to conserve man's health and perhaps even to prevent the enfeeblement of old age—the latter hope remarkably anticipating the great ideal of Condorcet.

[3] *The Principles of Philosophy*, in *The Philosophical Works of Descartes* (Cambridge, 1931–1934), I, 215.
[4] *The Principles of Philosophy*, in *The Philosophical Works*, I, 215.

Such was the noble prospect envisaged by Descartes. Its achievement, he wrote, lay entirely before man, for the new philosophical method must supersede the errors of the past. For him "the past was the era of mere history; only the present, the period after the revelation, was the era of progress."[5] Between past and present there was a distinct break in continuity. Though he did at times warn against inconsiderate major reforms, Descartes seems to have remained a partisan of rational planning *de integro* as against tradition and historical growth.[6]

Serious limitations thus are evident in the progressionist idea of Descartes. Human progress is not the long-maturing fruit of history, but the innovation of a rational reconstruction. Nor does its course seem capable of indefinite prolongation; a finite term is implied in his statement that "many centuries may pass until all the truths which may be deduced from these principles are so deduced." It is possible, though, that it was natural caution which led to this second limitation, rather than any inherent logical necessity.

In any case, one may feel that there existed in the work of Descartes a system admirably suited to the flowering of a doctrine of progress, if not of evolution. The rational basis of the system lends itself perfectly to idealistic, perfectionist thinking, and the existence of absolute standards makes unitary, linear progress possible. History, with its disillusionment and horror, is passed by as largely irrelevant. But already in the seventeenth century Cartesian progressionism was to be shaken from within by Fontenelle, and in the eighteenth it was to be further shattered by the attacks of historical investigation and scientific empiricism. And thus the idea of progress was to lose what might appear to have been one of its greatest opportunities.

[5] Charles Frankel, *The Faith of Reason: The Idea of Progress in the French Enlightenment* (New York, 1948), 28.
[6] *Rules for the Direction of the Mind*, in *The Philosophical Works*, I, 5–6; *Discours de la méthode*, 107, 109–111.

Chapter 2

The Man of God—Pascal

We must strengthen the courage of those timid souls who
dare invent nothing in physics, and confound the insolence
of the audacious who bring forth novelties in theology.
("Fragment d'un traité du vide")[1]

Though almost contemporary and often similar, the philosophical
syntheses of Descartes and Pascal offer no small number of instructive contrasts. In Pascal, for example, the opposition of the scientist
and the devout Christian often becomes a serious matter—a situation
which never arises in the thinking of Descartes. Descartes avoids
theology, while for Pascal the Christian revelation is the central, the
incontrovertible fact of the universe. With Descartes the conquest
of nature and the earthly well-being of man are primary, but with
Pascal it is the destiny of the Christian soul which is most worthy
of meditation. And Pascal ends, in effect, by rejecting the dream
of progress which he once shared with Descartes. To account for this
rejection, one must turn to Pascal's fundamental philosophy.

In his earlier writings Pascal, like Descartes, separates carefully
the realms of reason and authority; indeed his line of demarcation
is even more distinct than that of Descartes. Descartes exempts
religious faith alone from the scrutiny of reason, whereas with Pascal
authority is given a much wider area of action. History, law, geo-
graphy, linguistics, and especially theology, as matters dependent
upon memory, are, according to Pascal, the proper fields of dogma
and authority. He sees this division as leaving to the realm of reason
and experiment the study of mathematics, physics, medicine, music,
sculpture, and other sciences.

[1] *Pensées et opuscules* (Paris, 1923), 77.

In this second sphere, how is knowledge to be attained? Pascal feels that rational certitude can scarcely be reached outside the limits of geometry. To reason he assigns a much more modest role than does Descartes, though he knows well the value of deductive logic. According to Pascal it is not reason which comes into contact with the primary data of existence; reason is a mere agent, a catalyst, a method and an instrument rather than a basic faculty of knowledge. And Pascal has only scorn for ponderous rational systems, for sweeping physical theories.

For in effect Pascal reverses Descartes' position on the comparative roles of experiment and reason in the sciences. With Pascal observation comes before reason, and fact before logical analysis. Experiment is no longer the auxiliary of reason, but its governor. All of which perhaps helps to explain the marvellous sense of the diversity of things which Pascal displays, his sense of the variety and complexity of the real world.

Progress, thought Pascal, is possible in the realm of the sciences, the realm in which reason, observation, and experiment cooperate in the attainment of knowledge. Here all blind respect for the Ancients must be banished; here, by giving full scope to the fecundity of the mind, new advances may follow one another inexhaustibly. If perhaps irregular, the progress of knowledge is none the less continuous. Men, unlike the animals, profit not only by their own experience but also by that of their predecessors. The advance of mankind may be compared with that of a single man who lives forever and learns continually. Thus the so-called "Ancients" in reality lived in the youth of the world; mankind today is more ancient than they.

But, as has already been noted, Pascal saw great difficulties in the attainment of certainty of knowledge in those areas open to rational and empirical investigation. Especially in his later years he came to constrict the bounds of the application of reason and observation, and to emphasize the fallibility of man's rational and sensory nature. In the realms of tradition, on the other hand, certitude was possible; it might come from revealed authority, or it might come from the "heart." The heart was supreme notably in matters of faith, but more and more for Pascal the heart came to take a prominent place elsewhere. Only through the intuition of the heart, wrote Pascal, can man grasp first principles, and "the heart has its reasons, which reason cannot comprehend...."[2] Fundamental axioms are grasped neither by reason nor by the senses, but by the heart or the "natural light"—a Cartesian reminiscence, but not an exact parallel, for neither does the Pascalian intuition partake of the nature of reason nor does it apply itself exclusively to clear and simple ideas.

Even the heart, admitted Pascal, may be subject to vagaries. Absolute knowledge, from reason, heart, or experience, thus may often seem a transitory ideal. Pascal here is not far from that skepticism of which he wrote at times so sympathetically. And so in the *Pensées* he can only lose himself in admiration and awe before the universal enigma, with its solution through the Christian faith. In rich colors he paints the aspirations of man, his helplessness and misery, and his grandeur. Man seeks forever that which he cannot hope to find; he desires and cannot be satisfied. One explanation alone can account for these contradictions: the Fall and the degeneracy of man, who however retains some slight vestige of his earlier glory.

Such in outline is Pascal's definitive view of the state of mankind —a view which comes to color the whole of his thought. In the overwhelming presence of the drama of man's sin and salvation the barrier previously raised between the realms of authority and reason crumbles or is forgotten. No longer does Pascal laud the sciences and their potentialities, for in the quest for sanctity the pursuit of science is vain.[3] And, though here the indications are fragmentary, the very progress of the sciences would seem to be denied in the *Pensées*. All earthly things now are seen as being in flux, and progress is punctuated by decline.[4] "The nature of man is not such as to go forward at all times—it fluctuates back and forth. In fever one both shivers and burns, and the chill shows the seriousness of the fever quite as well as does the heat. In like manner go the inventions of men from age to age. And so too it is with the goodness and malice of the world in general."[5] History for Pascal now appears

[2] *Pensées*, in *Pensées et opuscules*, 458.   [3] *Pensées*, 346.
[4] *Pensées*, 371, 492.   [5] *Pensées*, 491–492.

in but one light—the light of Christian dogma, in which the Fall of Adam and the sacrifice of Christ tower above all other facts. Since the beginning of the world there have been men who have waited for or who have worshipped the Messiah; Christianity has indubitably been the goal of mankind through the ages. "How beautiful it is to see through the eyes of faith Darius and Cyrus, the Romans, Pompey and Herod, all act, without knowing it, for the glory of the Evangel!"[6] And so it was that the eager theoretician of scientific progress became the devout Christian, intent only upon salvation.

As one reviews the development of Pascal's thought—a development doubtless more emotional than logical—several points stand out as deserving of note. His early career, first of all, demonstrates conclusively the compatibility of experimental science and the belief in scientific progress. Yet the whole body of his thought well illustrates the shattering effect upon the progressionist idea which a nonrational outlook may entail in fields other than the scientific. Pascal, unlike Descartes, was not an adherent of rational idealism; Christian authority and the witness of facts about him seemed to show that the world was evil, and that if man was to have a goal it must lie beyond the grave. In the end, for Pascal, the only progress which was really meaningful was man's course of preparation for the other world.

[6] *Pensées*, 648.

Chapter 3

The Churchman—Bossuet

> We must understand that this universe, and particularly the human race, is the kingdom of God, which He rules and governs according to immutable laws. (*Sermon sur la Providence*)[1]

The "Discourse on Universal History" is in many ways patterned after the "City of God." For Bossuet as for Augustine, and indeed as for Pascal, Christianity was the focal point and final goal of earthly history. Moreover, the Bishop of Meaux, like the Bishop of Hippo, elaborated a scheme of historical development based upon epochs in time. But the twelve epochs in Bossuet's history simply form a convenient framework for factual categorization; they do not enter into the inner structure of historical growth as he sees it.

This growth, significantly, does not appear to Bossuet wholly inexplicable, divinely controlled though it may be; indeed the opening words of the preface to the "Discourse" affirm the intelligibility of history, the possibility of discovering cause and effect in man's development through the years. And later he elucidates more clearly his position. "Save for certain extraordinary strokes, when God has wished his hand alone to appear, there has not occurred a single considerable change which has not had its causes in past ages.... The true science of history consists in noting in each period those hidden dispositions which were to prepare great changes, and the important occasions upon which these latter were brought to pass."[2]

But Bossuet tried to avoid oversimplification in the study of his-

---

[1] *Choix de sermons de Bossuet, 1653-1691* (Paris, 1883), 225.
[2] *Discours sur l'histoire universelle* (Paris, 1886), 454.

tory, for he realized that politics is an involved and difficult science, and that civilization is complex. Bossuet, too, faced an additional complication: the tremendous problem of reconciling the divine plan with mundane operations, the Universal Cause with those particular causes which invariably serve divine ends, though the interconnection may be obscure to man. For Bossuet, the rule of Providence became the ultimate theme of history.

There is indeed, he wrote, no human force which can serve its own ends alone, for everything is subject to divine will and divine law—and these are immutable. "We must understand that this universe, and particularly the human race, is the kingdom of God, which He rules and governs according to immutable laws; and we shall now apply ourselves to considering the secrets of those celestial politics which rule all nature and which, enclosing within their order the instability of things human, in equal measure dispose of the varied accidents of individual lives and those great and memorable events which determine the fate of empires."[3] Could man see deep enough it would be clear to him that chance has no place in human history. "Let us speak no more of chance," wrote Bossuet, "or let us speak of it only as a name covering our ignorance. What appears by our uncertain lights to be chance is actually a concerted plan in . . . that eternal design which includes all causes and all effects in one order. Thus all serve the same end, and it is only because we do not comprehend the whole that we find chance or irregularity in particular conjunctures."[4]

In this rigidly determined course of events Bossuet finds ample material for an historical apology for the Christian Church. Against the revolutions of pagan nations and the inconstancy of human affairs in general he sets the constancy of the faith and the eternity of the Church. For, though men err and perish, the Church triumphant will subsist through all the ages until that final day when it is transported to heaven.

Religion, moreover, is not unprogressive. The history of the faith reveals a succession of legal sanctions, from the law of nature

[3] *Sermon sur la Providence,* in *Choix de sermons,* 225.
[4] *Discours,* 566.

through written law to the law of the Gospels, or of divine grace. And it is the Church which must prepare men for eternity and lay the foundations of that celestial city which is the goal of all history. Bossuet, like so many of his medieval forebears, is indubitably an historical optimist, though he sees the ultimate realization of man's spiritual progress in another life and another world.

But, as might be expected from his announced intention of examining natural historical causation, Bossuet also devotes many pages to the study of secular history, and especially to the study of governmental and political development. For together, religion and politics, in Bossuet's opinion, furnish the key to the understanding of human affairs. Not only does he treat empires and their revolutions as unwitting servants of the true religion, but also as discrete objects of historical analysis. In this spirit he discusses the problem of decadence.

He examines, for instance, the decline of the splinter states formed from the empire of Alexander the Great—a decline rooted, in the case of Syria, in softness and luxury, and precipitated by internal strife and the might of Rome. The decadence of Rome he treats at greater length, seeing as key factors the dissension between plebeians and patricians under the Republic, and the uncontrolled freedom of the army under the empire. Various contributory factors also are listed: among them luxury, debauchery, and laziness, the seditious tendencies of an impoverished class which continued to increase in numbers, the barbarian intrusions, and the loose granting of citizenship.

As to secular progress on earth Bossuet's writings are not altogether without their contradictions. At one point he seems to see human inventions as balanced by human forgetfulness.[5] At others— and this appears to be a more typical attitude—he finds himself profoundly admiring the progress of human reason in the arts and sciences. Through scientific investigation and the perfecting of his reason man penetrates the handiwork of God; an understanding of

[5] *Discours*, 30–31.

the world through science and reason helps man to enter into the divine plan and become more like its author.[6] Here certainly is no expression of jealousy or mistrust between religion and science, no warfare between theology and technology. If Bossuet is by no means the rapturous scientific progressionist of the "Treatise on the Vacuum," he does avoid the rigid dichotomies of Pascal, as well as the eventual stifling of reason in the exclusive claims of faith.

As a Christian thinker, and particularly as a commentator on his own day and on the general condition of man, Bossuet bears great resemblance to Pascal. It is quite unnecessary here to insist upon those passages in Bossuet's work which touch on original sin, and the weakness and strength, the misery and potentialities, of mankind. In his sermons the world of his day is flayed mercilessly for its moral abandon, its selfishness and pride, its avarice, complacency, and incredulity. But duty and the search for true happiness may yet lead to a better earth; the philosophy of Bossuet is not one of despair, but one of energetic Christian action, of daring and of hope.

For many decades Bossuet was to figure in France as "the last of the Fathers." The eighteenth century produced no churchman of his stature, and religious thought came to possess such little originality as to be virtually forgotten in later years. Thus Bossuet's main significance lies not in his relationship with the clerical writers of the Enlightenment, not in his reconciliation, for example, of religion and scientific progress, but rather in the influence which he exerted upon men of all persuasions, including those most hostile to the Church. How often in the eighteenth century does one seem to hear repeated Bossuet's words on the rise and fall of empires, "this frightful tumult which makes one feel that there is nothing solid among men, and that inconstancy and agitation are the lot of human affairs."[7] But what with Bossuet was irrelevant or inscrutable was in some cases to become, without the guiding hand of Providence, a central dogma—that of historical flux. And Bossuet's analysis of Roman decline may well have served as the basis of similar studies

[6] *Sermon sur la mort*, in *Bossuet moraliste* (Paris, 1912), 179–180; *Traité de la connaissance de Dieu et de soi-même* (Paris, 1864), 66–70.

[7] *Discours*, 453.

in the eighteenth century, and of examinations of contemporary decadence. Moreover, cannot one detect at times the accents of Bossuet in the determinist godless philosophies of the later age, in their denials of the existence of chance in history? Among the heirs of Bossuet were to be numbered some of the bitterest enemies of the great Christian synthesis for which he stood.

Chapter 4

The Littérateurs—Boileau, Perrault, Fénelon

I rejoice to see that in a way our age has attained the peak of perfection. (Charles Perrault, *Parallèle des anciens et des modernes*)[1]

The century of Descartes, Pascal, and Bossuet was also the century of Corneille and Racine, of Molière and La Fontaine, of Poussin and Mansard. Working, as they believed, in the spirit or from the general principles of classical antiquity, these and other illustrious writers and artists created a neo-classical school the excellence of which has been recognized down to our own day, and not least in the seventeenth century itself. In that age of striking artistic production it was only natural that men should begin to take issue with the doctrine, until then largely uncontested, of the superiority of the Ancients in the realms of literature and art. In the end, this relatively restricted question was to entail a generalized theory of progress of real significance.

Classicism was to remain the more or less official aesthetic dogma until well beyond the period to be covered in this work, and upon it were based many of the theories of artistic progress and decadence which will be studied here. A brief summarization of its leading principles is therefore in order. Though stylized and imprecise, Boileau's *Art poétique* has generally been considered the authoritative expression of Classical doctrine in France, and may serve here as a convenient key to that doctrine.

If the *Art poétique* does not present a rigid system of aesthetics,

[1] *Parallèle des anciens et des modernes, en ce qui regarde les arts et les sciences* (Amsterdam, 1693), I, 67.

2+

it does offer a number of indicative general propositions. Boileau holds, for example, that to achieve distinction in poetry one must be born a poet, but he also insists that genius be regulated by certain universal rules, such as the imperatives of the three unities, of *bienséance* and good sense, and of resemblance to an original model. Yet he also recognizes that upon occasion a vigorous mind may justifiably leap the bounds prescribed by the rules, and that both inspiration and discipline are necessary to the true literary artist.

"Nature . . . is everywhere the same . . ."—such is perhaps the most basic proposition of Boileau.[2] And all art should imitate nature. Nature, to be sure, is rather narrowly conceived by Boileau; it is a nature selected, refined, and idealized, a nature best discovered through already existing models, notably the works of classical antiquity. The beautiful must also be the true: "a thought is beautiful only insofar as it is true. . . ."[3] Moreover, almost inevitably, the good is also made an integral part of the beautiful; art must please, but it must also be ethical in purpose. Vain amusement must give way to more profitable pleasure, and literature must energetically promote virtue.

And to the natural, the good, and the true, must be added the rational; indeed reason is at the foundation of Boileau's aesthetic system. Clear thinking and good sense are among his key injunctions, as are simplicity and clarity of expression. But it is to be noted that by simplicity Boileau does not mean artless naïveté, but rather a simplicity which is intentional and contrived. And from all of this emerges the principle that beauty is basically the same throughout time and space, the product of values which are essentially unchanging and absolute.

Such is the core of the *Art poétique*. The Classicism by which it was inspired and which it helped keep alive for a century and more has sometimes been called "Cartesian," but the qualification is misleading. It is true that reason, clarity, and absolute values do have their place in the writings of both Descartes and Boileau, but it is

---

[2] *Réflexions critiques sur quelques passages du rhéteur Longin*, in *Oeuvres complètes de Boileau* (Paris, 1870–1873), III, 307.
[3] "Préface VI," in *Oeuvres complètes*, I, 20.

difficult to conceive of a more distinct opposition than that between Boileau's principle of authoritative imitation and the anti-authoritarianism of Descartes. To join, though, with Daniel Mornet and others in terming Classical literature "intellectual" would seem to be more justifiable.[4] Certainly the Classical aesthetics was not an aesthetics of sentiment and emotion run wild; it involved a clear conception of rational order, with emotion ordinarily well under control.

These then, though often with less emphasis upon authority, were the general principles and presuppositions of nearly all the prominent participants in the famous "Quarrel of the Ancients and the Moderns." The question of the pre-eminence of the ancient authors had been raised early in the seventeenth century, but the argument became general and heated only in the Age of Louis XIV. With more and more vigor, and more and more general success, the Moderns presented their arguments: man's ability to profit from experience, his growing refinement of taste, his outgrowing of the naïve, his new orientation toward intellectuality and philosophy. And arguments came to be drawn from outside the realm of literature. From that key assumption of Cartesianism and of Classicism, the unchangeability of nature, many came to argue the fixed aptitude of all ages for artistic and scientific production, and the cumulative force of experience which led necessarily to progress. In fairly short order there was general agreement on the superiority of modern science and philosophy over those of the Ancients, but in the fine arts and literature the struggle of the two parties was bitter.

Aside from Fontenelle, whose thought will be treated as a unit later in this study, Charles Perrault was perhaps the most distinguished and most influential partisan of the Moderns. Though Perrault shared the aesthetic preconceptions of the other Classicists and dreamed of an absolute and universal beauty underlying the fleeting tastes of different times and different nations, he also denounced slavish worship of the Ancients and stoutly maintained that they were men like those of his own day.

[4] Daniel Mornet, *Histoire de la littérature française classique, 1660–1700* (Paris, 1942), 62–83.

The unchangeability and inexhaustibility of nature are cardinal points in Perrault's doctrine; the natural genius of one century, he wrote, is as great as that of another, but an increase of experience over the years renders mankind gradually wiser. In fact, mankind may be considered as one man, growing from infancy to maturity. "The advantage which our century has of having come after the others, and of having profited by the good and bad examples of preceding centuries, has made it the most learned, the most polished, and the most sensitive of all. The Ancients had good things to say but intermixed them with the mediocre and the bad, and it could not be otherwise with initiators. But the Moderns have had the good fortune of being able to make choices; they have imitated the Ancients in their good points and have not had to follow them in what was bad or mediocre."[5]

Thus Homer, Aristotle, and Virgil, if born in the seventeenth century, would have escaped the defects of their own age and would have been greater than they actually were. The arts, like the sciences, are based on technique, and the knowledge of technique grows necessarily as the years go by. In short, "all the productions of nature remain the same in general. But the ages are not always the same, and with all other things equal it is an advantage for one age to come after the others."[6]

But here a flaw develops in Perrault's optimism, for all other things, he admits, are not always equal. The ravages of war in the Middle Ages, for example, led to the "ignorance and barbarity" of that period.[7] Thus progress in literature and in the arts and sciences has not been unbroken; some centuries have been enlightened and others ignorant. "One may compare . . . the arts and sciences to those rivers which suddenly go underground, but which . . . finally find an opening and flow out again as abundantly as they entered. The openings through which the arts and sciences return upon the earth are those happy reigns of great monarchs who by re-establishing peace and calm in their states make learning flourish there once again. And thus it is not enough that one age come later than another in order to be more excellent; it must be prosperous and calm, or

[5] *Parallèle*, I, 399–400.   [6] *Parallèle*, I, 402.   [7] *Parallèle*, I, 36.

warfare, if it comes, must be only on foreign soil. In addition, it is necessary that this calm and prosperity endure a long time in order that the age may have leisure to ascend step by step to its final perfection."[8]

And in yet another respect Perrault's embryonic theory of progress falls short of final development: his interests lay primarily in the past, with no more than hints as to the future. "I rejoice," he wrote, "to see that in a way our age has attained the peak of perfection. And just as progress for some years has been much less rapid than before, and indeed almost imperceptible, so too do the days seem to lengthen as the solstice approaches. I am happy to think that in all probability we do not have many things to envy in those who come after us."[9] And again: "Perhaps we are beginning to enter old age, as the distaste which one often has today for the best things would seem to indicate."[10]

In Perrault, then, one finds primarily a theoretician of historical cycles, with even his own brilliant period promising a decline. To place him among the architects of historical optimism is permissible only with reservations, for the progress which he described was progress only in the past. Here one may note a striking contrast with Descartes' disparagement of the past, with Descartes' dream of future progress from a rational reconstruction of thought. The failure of Cartesian optimism and Classical aesthetics to adjust to one another must be a major theme of any detailed study of seventeenth and eighteenth century aesthetics.

One need not linger over such stubborn seventeenth century champions of the Ancients as Father Rapin, for theirs was a lost cause—a cause so indefensible, by the usual standards of the day, that its most illustrious stalwart himself eventually went over, in effect, to the camp of the Moderns. Earlier, in the "Critical Reflections on Longinus," Boileau had loudly decried the disrespectful liberties taken by many petty, ignorant, and proud writers of his time. Unfortunately his supporting argument for the superiority of the Ancients was not strong, and tended to wander into personal invective. "Universal consent" was Boileau's first criterion of value

[8] *Parallèle*, I, 36.   [9] *Parallèle*, I, 67.   [10] *Parallèle*, I, 37.

for a literary production; only the judgment of the ages could clearly establish the worth of a book. Thus one could not equitably judge a modern work, whereas many centuries of admiration had confirmed the superior quality of much of classical literature. At best, then, Boileau could only appeal for respect for the Ancients, and a suspended judgment.

But, in 1700, Boileau admitted that he did, after all, sympathize with the Moderns, though cautiously. However, like Perrault, he rejected continuous progress, though for a different alternative. Instead of seeing great unitary movements of progress and temporary eclipse as did his erstwhile rival, he envisaged a complex movement of varying rates and directions of development among the different arts and sciences. This concept, too, was to figure in the philosophy of the Enlightenment.

And so, from the clamor of extreme partisanship in the Quarrel, there arose influential writers counseling moderation. Such a writer was the aesthetician Bouhours; such were many of the great Classical authors themselves. And such, above all, was François de Salignac de la Mothe Fénelon. Fénelon deserves special attention, not only for the intelligence of his criticism, but also for his introduction of several anti-Classical elements which were to attain prominence in the period from 1715 to 1789.

In his work relevant to the Quarrel, the "Letter to the Academy" of 1713, Fénelon decries the stupidity of judging a literary work by its age alone, and rejects certain exorbitant claims made by rabid supporters of the Ancients. Indeed he expresses the hope, if not the belief, that the Moderns may surpass the Ancients, and points to the considerable literary achievements of the immediate past. Yet his preferences quite clearly lie with the Ancients, who reached their artistic heights, he believes, despite the great handicaps of ridiculous religions and defective moral codes.

But Fénelon breaks with Boileau and the whole French Classical tradition in his reasons for these preferences. He deplores not only the current artificiality and planned sterility of the French language, but also the intrusion of *bel esprit* into French letters, and the antithesis of both of these defects he finds in the naïveté and natural simplicity of the authors of classical antiquity. His appreciation of these qualities, for which Boileau apparently had such little real feeling, was to serve as the basis for an intelligent, reasoned defense of the Ancients.

Fénelon had a compact explanation for the appearance of this artless simplicity in the classics: the simplicity of the life and institutions of that age. A degree of that historical sense lacking in many of his contemporaries told him that, contrary to current theory, nature is not altogether unchanging, whether it be exemplified in plant life or in the evolution of human institutions. "Certain climates are happier than others for certain talents, as for certain fruit...," and different historical circumstances lead to different civilizations.[11] So it is that environment and history set apart the peoples of the world, and affect both their artistic achievement and their governmental institutions. Moreover, absolute perfection in either field has never been achieved by men; even the greatest of the Ancients had their imperfections, and governments their seeds of decay.[12]

One is tempted to see in all this an indication of cultural and aesthetic relativism—a relativism completely foreign to French Classicism. Such roots do indeed lie in Fénelon's work, but several qualifications must be kept in mind. In the first place, Fénelon does not himself draw any forthright conclusions concerning the relativity of taste and beauty; he never assails the Classical concept of absolute aesthetic values. Secondly, he seems to introduce his climate theory simply in order to support his own preference for the Ancients. And, lastly, he retains a rigid ethical system and tightly joins the good and the beautiful, thus introducing a strict absolutism into the heart of his aesthetic theory. Fénelon gives only a slight, though a real, hint of the anti-Classical currents which were to increase in volume during the eighteenth century.

But in that century Classicism retained great strength, and in Classicism the two elements of authority and reason continued to dispute the field inconclusively. Of itself, a belief in the universality

---

[11] *Lettre écrite à l'Académie française, sur l'éloquence, la poésie, l'histoire, etc.,* in *Oeuvres de Fénelon* (Paris, 1826), X, 318.
[12] *Lettre,* X, 394.

of natural law, as held by both Boileau and Perrault, might lead to either one of the opposed ideas of progress or decadence. But with Boileau it was authority, or universal consent, which received the emphasis, while with Perrault it was the progress of man through reason applied to experience. In general progressionist theory it may be argued that the future belonged to Perrault, despite his cyclical notions—yet, by a curious permutation which will be studied later, it was the Boileau of the "Reflections on Longinus" who was to triumph in much of the aesthetic theory of the following years. And in the meantime the aesthetic relativism which had been barely suggested by Fénelon was to threaten the whole fabric of Classical aesthetics, and thus put in question all earlier concepts of progress and decadence in the arts and in letters.

Chapter 5

The Libertine—Saint-Evremond

If we were to make love like Anacreon and Sappho, nothing
would be more ridiculous; like Terence, nothing more bour-
geois; like Lucian, nothing more crude. Every age has its
own character. . . ." (Letter to the Duchesse Mazarin)[1]

The libertinism of which Saint-Evremond was perhaps the outstanding advocate in the seventeenth century was of long and mottled
lineage. Weighting heavily human values as against divine purposes, earthly pleasures as against other-worldly rewards, the libertine tradition reaches back at least to the Epicureans of classical
antiquity. By mid-seventeenth century, libertinism as a term had
come to cover a flexibly wide range of manifestations, from incredulity and materialism to moral freedom and debauchery; perhaps only skepticism, naturalism, and hedonism were constant
components of the libertine climate of belief. This tradition was to
persist from Montaigne to Fontenelle, through the Temple and
Voltaire, across the eighteenth century and down to the present day.

The separation of morality and religion is the basic postulate of
Saint-Evremond. Not theology but nature, he held, must inspire
ethics. Human nature undoubtedly is complex, and the bad is as
much a part of it as is the good. But however mean and petty man's
existence may be, nature and reason show that he must strive for
happiness, and that through pleasure alone can he achieve this
happiness. Saint-Evremond turns away from earthly evil and misery
and preaches the enjoyment of the fleeting present. "To live happily
one must reflect little on life and, so to speak, be freed of oneself;

[1] *Oeuvres de monsieur de Saint Evremond* (Paris, 1740), IV, 88.
2*

one must bury one's ills among the pleasures given by external things."[2]

"Nature," he continued, "moves all men to seek pleasure, but they seek it in diverse ways, according to their particular humor and constitution."[3] From this principle, and from the dictates of his native skepticism, he derived the principle of toleration. For, unlike Descartes and Pascal, Saint-Evremond employed skepticism not in any search for absolute truth, but rather in the hope of shaking dogma, whatever its nature, and of showing the necessity of peace and toleration among all schools of opinion. And opinions, he maintained, should be formed not by abstract rational construction, but by reflection upon experience and historical fact. It was to this feeling for fact—a feeling not circumscribed as it was in Pascal—that Saint-Evremond owed those empirical and relativistic elements which are notable in his thought. In the lives of individuals and in the histories of nations he habitually saw not uniformity but complexity, not a transcendental absolutism of purpose or values but an elastic interplay of contingent facts.

Saint-Evremond stated explicitly and underlined emphatically a theory of man's development which, though not new, had been noted only in passing by other French writers of the seventeenth century. This was the theory of "climate"—the belief that human institutions vary according to different types of natural environment, and that one climate is more conducive to certain human qualities and activity than are others.

Isolated passages seem to indicate that Descartes and Pascal, Corneille, and Boileau, to mention only a few, granted some importance to environment as a factor in historical growth.[4] But what had been to these writers merely an extraneous reference became in Saint-Evremond an integral and fundamental tenet of his philosophical and historical outlook. From such influences as climatic change he

---

[2] *Sur les plaisirs: A monsieur le comte d'Olonne,* in *Oeuvres,* I, 139.

[3] *Sur les plaisirs,* in *Oeuvres,* I, 143.

[4] Marcel Braunschvig, *L'abbé Du Bos, rénovateur de la critique au XVIIIe siècle* (Toulouse, 1904), 51–54; Boileau, *Art poétique,* in *Oeuvres complètes,* II, 347; Descartes, *Discours de la méthode,* 114–115; Pascal, *Pensées et opuscules,* 465–466.

saw arising a whole new world since the days of the Ancients. "All is changed: gods, nature, political forms, taste, manners."[5] Religion and laws, philosophy and ethics, are modified and developed just as are the more superficial manifestations of human emotion and intelligence. And it is not only climate which effects great changes in cultures, but also the passage of time. As an example Saint-Evremond sketches in some detail the "diverse genius of the Roman people under the Republic."[6] Rejecting a unitary climatic or national conception of the Roman character, he traces the evolution of the Roman republican temper from noble austerity to luxurious softness; from love of country to love of self. All nations, as Saint-Evremond sees them, grow and decay, rise and fall, in a series of cycles which seem to leave no place for the general progress of mankind.

Though from his observations on the changes wrought by time and environment Saint-Evremond derives no explicit blanket denunciation of absolute values in politics or elsewhere, his sympathies are clear enough. On the specific matter of taste he expresses the most forthright relativism, and in a passage which, to be sure, is isolated, but which may be indicative of his thought in other realms, he states that "justice is simply a virtue established in order to maintain human society; it is the work of men...."[7] And his apparent abjuration of perfectionism lends an additional tone of relativism to his work. If in the more sophisticated historical philosophies of later centuries relativism has not always ruled out a belief in progress, it will be observed subsequently in this study how unsuccessful were those attempts at accommodation made during the seventeenth and eighteenth centuries. The significance of Saint-Evremond's pioneer correlation of relativism and historical flux can hardly be overrated.

Moreover, Saint-Evremond's historical relativism was not excluded even from his aesthetic theory. Though he seems to have

<hr />

[5] *Sur les poèmes des Anciens*, in *Oeuvres*, IV, 311.

[6] *Réflexions sur les divers génies du peuple romain, dans les différens temps de la république*, in *Oeuvres*, II, 1–102.

[7] *Sur l'amitié: A madame la duchesse Mazarin*, in *Oeuvres*, III, 359.

accepted the current definition of art as an "imitation of nature," this definition came to serve a proposition utterly foreign to the general trend of contemporary aesthetics—the proposition that taste is in no sense fixed through the ages. "Every age has its own character.... It is always a question of man, but nature varies in man —and art, which is simply an imitation of nature, must vary with nature. Our stupidities are not those which Horace mocked, nor are our vices those which Juvenal rebuked; we must use a different type of ridicule and a different type of censure."[8] Homer, like others, was a product of his age, and if born in the seventeenth century he would write admirably in the taste of the new age.

It is then not surprising that Saint-Evremond attacked the eternal rules of the Classicists. "One must admit," he noted, "that Aristotle's *Poetics* is an excellent work—but there is nothing perfect enough to serve as a rule for all nations and all centuries."[9] "We are given an infinite number of rules, made three thousand years ago, to regulate everything done today, and one never considers that it is not the same subjects which are to be treated, nor the same genius to be led."[10] A poet who follows the antique rules, now fallen with all those things which fall in the course of time, can write only bad verse. No rule is perfect, and no rule should be rigidly followed. Reason must not strangle inspiration. Boileau, to be sure, had used similar language, but the words ring more true with Saint-Evremond, who goes on to present alternatives to the rules of the solemn pundit of Classicism. These alternatives are good sense and the natural—qualities vague enough, but in Saint-Evremond explicitly representing a revolt from Classical aesthetics. By these standards he judged the literary works of his own age and of previous ages, and in so doing achieved an individuality and a freedom of criticism rare in his day.

It is not necessary to examine in detail Saint-Evremond's comments touching the dispute of the Ancients and the Moderns. Here his position, like that of Fénelon, was one of moderation. But,

---

[8] *Lettre à madame la duchesse Mazarin,* in *Oeuvres,* IV, 88.
[9] *De la tragédie ancienne et moderne,* in *Oeuvres,* III, 148.
[10] *Lettre à madame la duchesse Mazarin,* in *Oeuvres,* IV, 88.

though he admired many of the writers of classical antiquity, his personal sympathies seem to have lain rather with the Moderns, who by judiciously following the Ancients would be expected to surpass their models, and had already done so in the field of tragedy. Saint-Evremond, however, did not draw from this apparent superiority of modern over ancient literature any general law of progress, and there is nothing in his work to indicate that his literary ideas violate his general concept of historical flux, to imply that contemporary literature and civilization would escape the common fate of all cultures.

Saint-Evremond's historical view, as outlined here, can only be pieced together from several sources, and is nowhere elaborated at length. Central as it is to an understanding of the writer, it does not appear to have been a vital preoccupation with him. Personal happiness was his announced aim in life, and there can be little doubt that his determination to ignore as far as possible the sordid and painful aspects of existence deprived him of a feeling for the great power and sweep of the historical scene. Nevertheless his sense of the factual, his distrust of rational abstractions, and his conception of cultural individuality and flux all give him an important place among the precursors of historical pessimism in the eighteenth century.

Chapter 6

The Critic—Bayle

The world is too little capable of discipline to profit by the
ills of past ages. Each age acts as if it were the first. (*Diction-*
naire historique et critique)[1]

In certain respects Pierre Bayle resembles Saint-Evremond, his older
contemporary. Both authors separate religion and ethics; both are
almost exclusively earth-bound in their views of human life and
destiny. Bayle's ethical system, however, has a surprisingly traditional ring, though it is based not upon revelation but upon men's
passions and those universal principles which, he assures his readers,
conscience reveals to all. For morality, he continues, is basically the
same everywhere; one finds no significant moral relativism in Bayle's
thought.

But the truth which Bayle seeks is, like that sought by Saint-
Evremond, predominantly pragmatic; metaphysical certainty is
seldom his goal. Certainty even of factual knowledge, he feels, is
difficult of attainment, for little of the available evidence relating to
a given problem is reliable. Truth itself can be categorized as necessary, or as contingent and historical—and with Bayle only the most
simple axioms would seem to fall into the first grouping, with the
second category becoming all-important.

Thus history comes to occupy a central place in Bayle's thought,
for from it can be gleaned most of that limited knowledge available to mankind. According to Bayle, historical facts can, after all,
be known with a considerable degree of certitude; historiography
now becomes "a science of human facts established by criticism."[2]

[1] "Abélard," *Dictionnaire historique et critique de Pierre Bayle* (Paris,
1820), I, 61.
[2] Jean Devolvé, *Religion, critique et philosophie positive chez Pierre Bayle*
(Paris, 1906), 229.

Abstract systems must give way to data derived from observation, to facts that are clear, definite, and exact. Facts and experience must found the true science of mankind, not only in the realm of history but also in the world of nature. It is not altogether surprising that Bayle at times seems to wander in a maze of utterly unrelated facts, and that his philosophy of history is one of aimless flux.

Unlike Saint-Evremond, Bayle assigns a prominent place in his writings to the evil in the world. Virtue itself, he holds, may have its harmful effects, just as passion and vice may have their usefulness. The world requires both vice and virtue, and civilization in producing each of these produces the other in a compensatory action. But despite this tendency toward counterpoise, "man is incomparably more inclined toward evil than toward good, and there are incomparably more bad actions than good in the world."[3] Of the various facets of man's nature, there are more than a hundred thousand bad for a single good one. And this evil is an aspect of nature itself; it is by no means the result of the corruption of nature by external agents.

Man, according to Bayle, acts upon the most diverse motives—from passing whim, from the desire of pleasure, from habit, from the most obscure promptings of his inner nature. Against these powerful forces reason, a reason based on observation and experience, seeks in vain to offer any real restraint. Passion and error, custom and habit prevail, and man profits little from the mistakes of the past. "The world is too little capable of discipline to profit by the ills of past ages. Each age acts as if it were the first. Just as the spirit of persecution and of vengeance has attempted up to now to interest rulers in its private quarrels, so it will try to involve them until the end of the world, and one may well apply here the sentence of Solomon: 'The thing that hath been, it is that which shall be; and that which is done is that which shall be done.' "[4]

As to his own age Bayle was not optimistic; folly seemed to be

---

[3] *Nouvelles lettres de l'auteur de la "Critique générale de l'histoire du calvinisme,"* in *Oeuvres diverses de mr. Pierre Bayle* (The Hague, 1737), II, 248.

[4] "Abélard," *Dictionnaire historique et critique*, I, 61.

increasing in proportion to the growing enlightenment boasted by his contemporaries. To be sure, he granted that certain improvements in man's condition might be effected. The theatre of Molière, for example, though helpless against major vices, might aid in reforming minor weaknesses, and even historical studies might have their utility if readers could divest themselves of their prejudices. One can only conjecture as to Bayle's opinion of the utility of his own encyclopedic labors, but it seems probable that erudite curiosity played in them at least as great a role as did expectations of consequent changes, and that he hoped at best for temporary relief from some of the minor stupidities which afflict the human race.

No plan, then, no significant progress or decadence, was visible to Bayle as he surveyed the course of human history. Historical flux, essentially meaningless, was the lesson taught by his investigations. The ages as he saw them might vary one from the other, but variation alone, he implied, could not constitute meaningful movement. History teaches that mankind's fortunes ascend and descend alternately, that men are incorrigible, and that two thousand years from now these changes will not have affected the human heart in the least. Man does not progress morally, and cannot be expected to do so.[5]

And it was ethics which, next to erudition, seems to have most interested Bayle; other matters he ordinarily treated simply in passing. He noted the uncertainty of man's scientific achievements and gave small attention to the sciences in general. Politics, except in certain historical questions, occupied him as little as did science; perhaps his closest approach to a general theory of political development was his dictum that, like religions, political bodies naturally become corrupt as they grow older.[6] Literature too, as such, held little charm for Bayle; a literary work for him was simply a vehicle for thought, not an artistic creation.

On the historical destinies of literature Bayle's position is not altogether clear. He does admit that conditions give a certain advan-

---

[5] "Esop," *Dictionnaire historique et critique*, VI, 284–285; letter to the Abbé Dubos, January 3, 1697, *Oeuvres diverses*, IV, 730–731.

[6] "Ales," *Dictionnaire historique et critique*, I, 439–440.

tage to the Moderns as against the Ancients, and deplores the naïveté displayed in the works of antiquity. But in the most explicit manner, though without long discussion, he states that beauty and taste are relative, that they vary as do individuals, ages, and nations.[7]

Thus Bayle came to see the world as an enormous conglomeration of facts, repetitive or senselessly varying. In his zeal for factual detail—one is tempted to say his cult of fact for fact's sake—he did not speculate widely upon historical causation, nor did he envisage a series of vast regular movements in the history of mankind. For these reasons his view of historical development was both less imposing and less superficial than that of Saint-Evremond. And because he did not share Fontenelle's faith in science and reason he avoided certain inconsistencies of his best known philosophical contemporary in France.

[7] *Nouvelles de la république des lettres,* in *Oeuvres diverses,* I, 171; *Commentaire philosophique, sur ces paroles de l'Evangile . . . Et contrain-les d'entrer,* in *Oeuvres diverses,* II, 396; letter to Basnage, December 28, 1672, in *Oeuvres diverses,* IV, 537.

Chapter 7

The Eclectic—Fontenelle

> Everything in the universe is in movement, and it would
> appear to be true that the human race, at least in Europe,
> has made certain steps toward reason. But such a large and
> heavy mass moves only very slowly. (*Sur la poésie en
> général*)[1]

Through a pithy style and a comprehensive intellectual adaptability,
Bernard le Bovier de Fontenelle became perhaps the most influential
writer of his day. No profound or original thinker, he was a popularizer and an eclectic, and as such could scarcely avoid certain incongruities of thought. Yet, if his philosophy lacks in intrinsic merit,
it is rich in interest as an example of the disintegration of the
seventeenth century Cartesian synthesis—a disintegration effected
both by internal and by external pressures.

For Fontenelle throughout his long career remained basically a
Cartesian, retaining the scientific terminology, much of the cold
rationalism, and many of the philosophical principles of his great
predecessor. Like Descartes he postulates the uniformity and permanence of natural law. Like Descartes he upholds the primacy
of science among intellectual disciplines, and like him he emphasizes
scientific method.

Yet even in elementary matters Fontenelle strays from the spirit
of Descartes. Dubious of the value of metaphysics and of involved
abstract reasoning, Fontenelle questions the absolute intelligibility
of the universe and the attainability of truth which is ultimate and
final. Human reason, to him, appears irrevocably limited, with

[1] *Oeuvres de Fontenelle* (Paris, 1790–1792), III, 195.

certainty in any of the great philosophical problems far beyond its reach. Science and philosophy remain useful, but they are largely studies of probability.

Like Descartes and Perrault, Fontenelle underlines the cumulative fund of human experience which makes possible those advances observable in matters of technique. Progress, he grants, is slow, for it is only gradually that reason perfects itself and experience accumulates. But reason's virtually inexhaustible resources will oblige nature to reveal more and more of its secrets. If human stupidity and error are infinite, reason and truth gradually extend their sway, even as the seventeenth century itself had shown by its increasing enlightenment. And, though knowledge is doubtless only for an *élite* few, this century would certainly be surpassed by later ages. Like others before him, Fontenelle compares the world's development to that of an individual who, always learning, grows from infancy to youth and virility, and who will never enter senile old age. The possibilities of the progress of knowledge are unlimited; such progress has no fixed term or goal.[2]

Fontenelle does not confine progress to the fields of science and philosophy alone, for literature too may be expected to advance in the course of time. It is Fontenelle's particular conception of art which makes possible this extension of his theory. Lacking both in sensitivity and in deep feeling, he belittles the poetry of image and of sentiment and proclaims the advent of the *poète philosophe*. Poetry must be the vehicle of thought—of thought which is clear, exact, and precise. And it is only natural that with the progress of philosophy the art which helps to disseminate it will advance in turn. "Perhaps the time will come when poets will pride themselves upon being more philosophical than poetic, more intellectual than talented . . ."; the day of "agreeable phantoms" will be replaced by the era of philosophy in letters.[3] Yet Fontenelle does not ban imagination altogether from literature, and it is precisely this quality

---

[2] *Digression sur les anciens et les modernes*, in *Oeuvres*, V, 288–290; *Préface de l'Histoire de l'Académie des sciences, depuis 1666 jusqu'en 1699*, in *Oeuvres*, VI, 4.

[3] *Sur la poésie en général*, in *Oeuvres*, III, 191–192, 195.

which he holds responsible for the varying rates of development among the arts and sciences. Imagination and talent ripen quickly, whereas science is the fruit only of multiplied experiment and of infinite pains in logic. The agreeable almost always has the advantage over the solid, as the course of Europe's awakening from medieval barbarity amply illustrates.

Since in Fontenelle's view the era of philosophical literature had already been inaugurated, it is not surprising to find him supporting the Moderns as against the Ancients in the great literary battle of the time. Nor is his conception of "philosophical poetry" his only argument for literary progress. In the opening lines of his "Digression on the Ancients and the Moderns" he presents his most famous thesis upholding the superiority of the Moderns: the historical uniformity of nature. "Nature has in her hands a certain clay which is always the same, which she forms and re-forms in a thousand ways, and with which she creates men, animals, and plants alike. Certainly she did not make Plato, Demosthenes, or Homer of a clay finer or better prepared than that of the philosophers, orators, and poets of today."[4]

If the prevailing tone of Fontenelle's philosophical and aesthetic theory is undoubtedly optimistic, his lapses from optimism are even more instructive. Most commonly these lapses occur when he leaves the sphere of Cartesian rationalism for the unpredictable realms of history and psychology. Science, he notes, concerns itself with the regular patterns of the universe, while "history has for its object the irregular effects of the passions and caprices of men, and a succession of events so bizarre that in former times a blind and extravagant divinity was imagined to be their cause."[5] Here one sees a Cartesian reminiscence, but Fontenelle, unlike Descartes, is often attracted to historical studies and writes of history at some length.

Historical change, Fontenelle seems to feel, lends itself slowly, at best, to rational planning. Ignorance and passion give rise to a series of senseless fluctuations of opinion and conduct; history is "simply

[4] *Digression sur les anciens et les modernes,* in *Oeuvres,* V, 281.
[5] *Préface sur l'utilité des mathématiques et de la physique, et sur les travaux de l'Académie des sciences,* in *Oeuvres,* VI, 70.

a spectacle of perpetual revolutions in human affairs, of births and deaths of empires, of morals and customs and opinions which succeed each other in rapid succession."[6] No past progress which is necessary and inevitable can be reconciled with such a spectacle. And the picture gains in color and depth as Fontenelle writes of the cultural variations among nations and centuries, of the influence of climate, and of the countless other external circumstances which retard or direct the progress of mankind.[7] Progress, if at times real, is intermittent, and interspersed with periods of decline.

Fontenelle's psychological observations create a hardly more encouraging picture than do his reflections on history. Almost in the despairing temper of Bayle he writes that knowledge and happiness do not necessarily go hand in hand, that indeed new pleasures are created only by new needs. Nature gives nothing gratuitiously, and desire and satisfaction must forever remain the two terms of a more or less balanced equation.[8]

Human happiness thus seems to Fontenelle a precarious state of health maintained only by feeble and uncertain medicaments. If reason is the great ideal of man, his actual lot tends rather to be stupidity and folly. Passions, not logic, rule men; it is a stroke of good luck indeed that the passions frequently play a beneficent role in human motivation. Only man's illusions make life endurable, and clear-headed thought can only sadden him and paralyze his powers of action. Chimeras are indispensable to the race, and progress itself, when it occurs, cannot still man's insatiable hunger for a perfection which is illusory and unattainable. Should the actual truths of the universe be made known, all would be lost.[9] If these words of disillusionment were written by Fontenelle as an apologia for hedonism, at the same time they call into question the very foundations of his whole rationalistic theory of progress.

---

[6] *Préface sur l'utilité des mathématiques,* in *Oeuvres,* VI, 69.

[7] *Digression sur les anciens et les modernes,* in *Oeuvres,* V, 281–282, 295; *Vie de Corneille, avec l'histoire du Théâtre François jusqu'à lui, et des réflexions sur la poétique,* in *Oeuvres,* III, 17; *Dialogues des morts anciens et modernes,* in *Oeuvres,* I, 239.

[8] *Dialogues des morts anciens et modernes,* in *Oeuvres,* I, 340–343.

[9] *Dialogues des morts anciens et modernes,* in *Oeuvres,* I, 298, 320, 336–337.

Moreover, the pessimism induced by Fontenelle's empirical observations of man and the world is sanctioned and perpetuated by certain elements in the body of his rationalism itself. Such, in the first place, is his conception of determinism. Chance for him has no meaning—or, more properly, it is simply a name for a hidden order in the universe which one cannot comprehend. Everything in the natural world, including the human will, is determined by a pervasive necessity. And this necessity, in the absence of such well-defined purpose as might be assumed in a universe ruled by divine providence, would seem to be both unfathomable and blind. As such, the logic of universal necessity in its future course is unpredictable in any strict sense; nevertheless it would be only natural to assume that what has been necessary in the past will, in all probability, remain necessary in the future. Fontenelle himself does not specifically draw this conclusion, but it is quite possible that he did arrive at it in private, and that it contributed to that occasional historical pessimism already noted.

A second element in Fontenelle's rationalism was much more directly subversive of progressionist theory. His observation of men had led him to see folly and evil as natural components of man's nature, and now the very argument which he had used in support of the Moderns was to lend additional weight to the results of that gloomy observation. If, as he had said when defending the Moderns, nature is invariable in its laws, and if man is a natural organism, then man's basic nature too is invariable. "Man's clothes change, but that is not to say that his bodily figure also changes. Politeness or crudity, science or ignorance, a greater or lesser degree of naïveté, a serious or playful spirit—these are but the exterior of man, and all of this changes. But the heart changes not at all, and the heart is the whole man. Men are ignorant in one century, but the mode for learning can come; men act according to their interest, but the mode for being selfless will never come. Next to the prodigious number of fairly unreasonable men who are born in a hundred years, nature produces perhaps two or three dozen reasonable ones, whom she must spread over the whole globe—and you can well see that in no place can there be enough of these latter to establish a fashion for virtue and uprightness.... The general order of nature appears to be constant indeed."[10]

And so it is that for Fontenelle true progress, like definitive retrogression, seems to be excluded from the field of ethics. He conceives of progress simply as an accumulation of techniques, and sees technique as central only in the arts and sciences. Nor does he grant unqualified validity even to progress in the latter fields, for it is the moral development of man which is after all the basic standard of human values, and advances in technique are powerless to alter man's moral fibre.

Fontenelle was to live on past the mid-point of the eighteenth century, but his major work was complete nearly seventy years before his death. The link which he himself forms between the two centuries is then perhaps less real than symbolic. He was entirely of the seventeenth century, absorbing the most diverse of its currents; in him one finds significant reminiscences and elaborations of the thought of Descartes, of Pascal and Perrault, of Saint-Evremond and Bayle, and even of Bossuet. To later generations he was to pass on an eclectic synthesis which permeated the mental climate of the mature French Enlightenment. And in this synthesis was a significant strain of historical pessimism.

From Fontenelle, from the several other writers discussed here, what conclusions may be drawn concerning the prevalence and the philosophical ingredients of historical optimism and pessimism in the seventeenth century? None, certainly, but the most tentative— or perhaps none at all. But if these early pages have produced no conclusions, they have perhaps provided several provocative hypotheses.

None of the thinkers thus far considered wrote an unequivocal defense of historical optimism, and none an unqualified defense of pessimism. Descartes, to be sure, laid a foundation for historical optimism—a foundation embracing, notably, an emphasis upon the liberating, expansive effects of knowledge, and a pervasive rationalism coupled with a faith in basic principles which are often absolute

[10] *Dialogues des morts anciens et modernes*, in *Oeuvres*, I, 239–240.

and final. In the mature Pascal, by and large an historical pessimist, one discovers a notable reliance upon sense experience, emotion, and history, together with a belittling of the ultimate value of scientific knowledge. In Saint-Evremond—strange bedfellow for Pascal—historical pessimism goes hand in hand with cultural relativism and individual hedonism.

Leaving aside aesthetic theory and literary criticism for a moment longer, what of the others—Bossuet, Perrault, Fénelon, Bayle, Fontenelle? Here, with more seriously divided loyalties, historical philosophy reveals a less clear correlation with basic assumptions and inclinations. Yet much seems to confirm the logic of those linkages of ideas noted in the case of Descartes, Pascal, and Saint-Evremond. For example, Fénelon, Bayle, and Fontenelle seem to be pessimists insofar as they are historians and cultural relativists, actual or potential. Bossuet is saved by the Christian revelation, both from relativism and from pessimism. Christian determinism, with Bossuet, tends toward optimism; in Fontenelle an implied materialistic determinism may have some relevance to pessimism.

Further elementary correlations are indicated in the question of literary history. A sustained backward look seems to lead, in the seventeenth century, to pessimism or to a most qualified optimism. A belief in absolute aesthetic values may lead either to optimism or to pessimism, but the worship of past authority leads to pessimism. Finally, a belief in the desirability of a philosophical orientation in poetry is coupled with a defense of literary progress.

Are any, all, or none of these many correlations of ideas valid for the age of Louis XIV as a whole? Certainly, for an answer, one would have to go far beyond the scope of the present work. Are any, all, or none of the same correlations valid for the French Enlightenment of the eighteenth century? To find a provisional answer to this question will be a major concern of the remainder of this work.

Part II

Historical Optimism in
Eighteenth Century France

Chapter 8

Religion and Optimism— Lignac and Bonnet

It is true that knowledge of the structure of nature is not the work of a single century. Our investigations of nature will doubtless be faulty, but we shall have done much for our descendants if we begin this great work. They will see our errors and will correct them. (The Abbé de Lignac, *Lettres à un Amériquain*)[1]

In the historical study of an idea it is worthwhile, and often essential, to consider not only its antecedents but also those contemporary intellectual currents which ran counter to that idea. Only such a consideration can place the idea in proper historical perspective; only such a consideration can finally verify or invalidate one's hypotheses as to the intellectual prerequisites for the first appearance and later development of the idea. To study historical pessimism in the French Enlightenment one can no more ignore the optimistic thought of the same period than one can ignore the earlier writings which foreshadowed both the optimism and the pessimism of later generations.

Fortunately the historical optimism of the Enlightenment is too well known, in certain of its aspects, to require extended analysis. Less fortunately, the common interpretation of many eighteenth century thinkers is open to serious question, and no agreement among scholars is in sight concerning the true intentions and ultimate significance of many other writers of the age. Much remains

[1] *Lettres à un Amériquain sur "l'Histoire naturelle, générale et particulière" de mr. de Buffon* (Hamburg, 1751), II, part 4, letter 10, 50.

to be done—and much, perhaps above all, on the historical philosophies of the Enlightenment.

Part II of this study will summarize several approaches to historical optimism in eighteenth century France. Some of the material reviewed here is common knowledge among students of the period; other portions of the treatment are controversial, or concerned with little-studied figures or problems. Throughout this section, as in the preceding one, an attempt will be made to discover the intellectual foundations of each author's historical outlook.

To begin a discussion of eighteenth century progressionist thought with a discussion of two religious writers may seem to be the result of a highly perverse zeal for paradox. Admittedly Lignac and Bonnet played relatively minor roles in the broad pageant of the age, yet each of them, viewed in retrospect, may contribute something of importance to the understanding of his time. It is commonly supposed that eighteenth century religious thought was, as a body, reactionary and antiprogressionist; a study of these two thinkers may serve to point out certain limits to this conservatism and to indicate the wide variety of speculation which can be found in the religious thought of the period.

Though of a different spirit, articulate Christianity of the Age of Enlightenment was basically of the same stuff as it had been in the Middle Ages. History remained the realm of Providence, but, as in the earlier age, much of the detail of history was left to the interpretation of the individual writer. The vanity of earthly things and the goal of individual salvation were emphasized by some, perhaps notably by the French Protestants, still subject on this earth to the persecution of the majority. The millennium, the rule of Christ on earth, was preached on occasion by both Protestants and Catholics, and, in the writings of Paul Rabaut, its coming was seen as imminent.

At the same time, other religious writers were attacking the current concepts of human perfectibility and progress. The Abbé Le Gros, for example, used a refutation of Rousseau and Court de Gebelin as the opportunity for a lengthy discussion of that "singular dogma," the perfectibility of the human race.[2] For after all, wrote the Abbé, man was made perfect at the creation.

Yet Christianity was not incompatible with a belief in progress, and this fact did not go unrecognized in the France of the eighteenth century. The forms which such a belief might take were, of course, varied. For one, the century's most celebrated Catholic journalist, Fréron, was an enthusiast for the sciences and their progress, since he felt that their objects were limited and in no way conflicted with Christian purpose or dogma.[3] But perhaps the ablest and fullest defense of the compatibility of religion and science came from the pen of Joseph Adrien Le Large, Abbé de Lignac.

Well above the average intellectual ability of eighteenth century religious thinkers, Lignac applied the methods of secular philosophy to the ends of orthodox Christian apologetics. Choosing as his special province the demonstration of the freedom and dignity of the Christian soul, Lignac was a champion of human reason, which he saw as the necessary complement of revelation and faith, and a bitter opponent of that skepticism which called into question all certainty of knowledge. Philosophy or "natural reason," he wrote, is to be the handmaiden of religion, for reason, unlike instinct, is naturally Christian. Strict limits must be set to the sphere of doubt, for in the human mind there exist certain absolutely indubitable principles independent of sensation and implanted by God. Not physical sensation but the *sens intime* opens the way to metaphysical truth. In this respect metaphysics is an empirical science; one derives its principles from self-observation. "Metaphysics," wrote Lignac, "is the physics of the mind; it must be treated like natural science. The observations and experiments which every man can make upon himself are its sole true principles."[4]

[2] Charles François Le Gros, *Examen des systèmes de J. J. Rousseau de Genève, et de M. Court de Gebelin, auteur du "Monde primitif"* (Geneva, Paris, 1786), 9–10, 33–58.

[3] Elie Catherine Fréron, *L'année littéraire*, 1754, VII, 100; 1755, VI, 289–291.

[4] Lignac, *Elémens de métaphysique tirés de l'expérience, ou lettres à un matérialiste sur la nature de l'âme* (Paris, 1753), 2.

And clearly Lignac was a devotee, at least in a theoretical sense, of empirical method in the sciences. He condemned various thinkers of his day for their abstract rational method, their substitution of vague hypotheses for observed facts, and their entanglement, for these very reasons, in fruitless petty philosophical controversies. In science, he insisted, the observation of nature and one's own experiments are the indispensable guides.

And thus Lignac, as a great admirer of scientific methodology, came to be an ardent supporter of scientific progress. Such progress, he admitted, must be slow, but its future realization cannot be questioned. Nor is science an independent realm; science and theology go hand in hand. For the pursuit of science shows not only the limits of unaided reason: it also gives man a revelation of the ways of God and excites his desire to know even more concerning his Maker. The study of nature is the way to Christian belief, and the progress of science can only quicken the power of faith.[5]

Such were Lignac's conclusions—conclusions which were the product of both the Enlightenment and Christian orthodoxy. Whether weakening or broadening the basis of the faith, these conclusions mark the intrusion of a decided current of liberalism and limited historical optimism into eighteenth century Christianity. To be sure, Lignac entered upon no discussion of general earthly progress, and presumably he would have found the idea repugnant. It was for writers like the Swiss Protestant Bonnet to sketch a scheme of universal progress.

Charles Bonnet did not conform altogether to the orthodox Calvinist pattern, though the influence of this background is evident throughout his work. The principles of utility and of pleasure so common in his day may be found carried over into his system, where in fact they are established at its very foundations. Convinced of the existence of a benevolent God and of providential necessity, Bonnet developed a system of philosophical optimism based upon a chain of being forever unfolding.

Like all Christian thinkers, Bonnet saw man's ultimate goal as

[5] Lignac, *Lettres à un Amériquain*, I, part 2, 120–123; II, part 4, letter 10, 50–51; V, part 9, 257.

other-worldly. Yet, passing through the concept of a world harmony which is pre-established in its germs but progressive in its development, his view of earthly life could only be one of perfectibility. Mankind, he wrote, gradually perfects itself according to God's eternal plan, nor is this development confined to man alone. Following a scheme of universal rebirth or palingenesis, Bonnet conceived of a vast progressive movement of all sentient beings. The entire universe, for him, is in vital movement—a movement toward happiness and perfection, and toward God.

Thus Christian progressionist theory of the Age of Enlightenment could embrace such divergent terms as the ecstatic though somewhat vague visions of Bonnet and the clear-headed methodology of Lignac. Between these extremes lay countless gradations and variations, of which the academic interest far outweighs the intrinsic worth or the historical significance. At this point one may turn more profitably to the main currents of eighteenth century thought.

Chapter 9

Theories of Regeneration—
Deschamps, Morelly, Mably,
Rousseau

> I point out the ideal; I do not say that it can be attained,
> but I hold that he who nearest approaches it is the most
> successful. (Rousseau, *Emile*)[1]

The idea of regeneration is an ancient one. It has long been basic in most religions, though in these systems it is commonly the renewal and the salvation of the individual which demand primary attention; such hopes for a regeneration of the social body as are voiced at all are ordinarily kept in a subordinate position. But in the eighteenth century the doctrine of regeneration was put upon a broader foundation, so as to embrace both individual and social renewal. In this broader form, notably as exposed in the writings of Morelly, Mably, and Rousseau, the doctrine becomes specifically a theory of progress.

The Benedictine Dom Deschamps affords a curious link between Christian and secular theories of regeneration. His system is almost wholly metaphysical; in it there unfolds a mystic idealism based not at all upon natural or historical observation, but rather upon personal inspiration and a rigid rationalism. By no means an orthodox Christian, Deschamps arrives at a form of pantheism which involves the absorption of the individual into the transcendental Whole, of which the earthly symbol is human society. Nature is constantly being transformed, and it is in this ever-changing earthly

[1] *Emile, ou de l'éducation*, in *Oeuvres complètes de J. J. Rousseau* (Paris, 1885-1905), II, 62.

home that mankind must find the realization of its aims. The destiny of the human race is to undergo three successive states: savagery, the state of laws, and the ethical state. Of these the second, that in which man now lives, is incomparably the most miserable. Man cannot return to the earlier native state, but he may yet be regenerated and thereby enter the third state, in which men will forfeit their possessions and join together in brotherly equality and solidarity. Science and knowledge will become irrelevant, and a tranquil agricultural existence will be the norm. The past with its record of crimes and errors will be forgotten, and mankind will enjoy forever its new and happy condition.

In Morelly the mystic element is lacking, but his regenerative and socialistic theories are not dissimilar to those advanced by Deschamps. "Nature" and reason are the foundations of his system, though neither term is adequately defined. Man's reason, he believed, pursues three objects above all others: truth, personal interest, and happiness. All of these lead equally to public and private well-being, provided that reason direct itself by the light of nature. Natural law is constant, and the ethical principles which it guarantees are simple and invariable, and thus easily discovered. Man is capable of vast improvement, for he is not naturally bad; his current degradation is the product of environment and its artificiality. His problem becomes simply one of returning to natural principles.

The most basic of all natural social goals, according to Morelly, is equality. To attain this enviable state all property must be relinquished and a socialistic regime inaugurated. In addition to those ethical ends which Morelly always keeps uppermost in his mind, political stability too will be achieved through the abolition of property, for property has forever been the source of governmental instability and of the decadence of states. Thus social reform becomes a relatively simple matter. If Morelly does acknowledge that virtue and reason develop but slowly, his ultimate confidence in the efficacy of legislation, both political and moral, is unshaken. Morelly's optimism remains truly utopian.

In most respects the thought of the Abbé de Mably is simply an elaboration of that of his predecessor. He too is basically an idealist, a lover of reason and of "nature." Reason again is preferred to historical research or empirical investigation as the prime tool of philosophy. Though he grants to climate and environment a degree of influence upon society, he holds that there exist certain fundamental ethical and political rules applicable in all lands and all ages. Both the legislator and the moralist must deal ultimately with eternal and irreducible principles.

Like Morelly, Mably considers self-love and the search for happiness as intrinsically innocent, as indeed fundamental to all social organization. The construction of a moral system, humanitarian yet linked with religious sanctions, becomes his first concern. With him ethics and politics become one. Since only the virtuous state can survive, it is for the government to legislate virtue. Mably's whole social and political system has but one aim: the creation and maintenance of a virtuous and happy people.

Nature, Mably insists, is good, and the natural man necessarily shares in this goodness. Here Mably encounters the eternal enigma of the genesis of evil out of good; as a solution he simply asserts that man himself, as contrasted with nature, is the author of evil. Man and society have strayed inexplicably from the bosom of nature and must reintegrate themselves in the natural order. The first model for this reintegration is not savage pre-civilization, but rather the simple and austere republics of antiquity. It is an uncomplicated social life at which Mably aims—a regime based upon non-propertied equality and distinguished by the absence of that avarice and luxury which are inseparable from the pursuit of commercial gain.

The principal agents in the transformation from the actual to the ideal must be education and legislation. But man does not change rapidly, for he is less a creature of reason than one of habit, prejudice, and passion. Often Mably appears in the garb of the bleakest pessimist, despairing of all but the most fleeting and minor ameliorations of the human lot. Integral communism seems to him quite chimerical; one may hope at best for certain modest reforms in the present social structure. Yet even these steps, Mably believes, may be of real value, and certainly despair does not seem to be his last word.

Nor is it the last word of Jean Jacques Rousseau. To be sure, the interpretation of the philosopher of Geneva involves innumerable difficulties; one cannot presume to present in a few paragraphs more than a most limited and provisional analysis of his ideas. But Rousseau's thought is far too influential to be ignored here, and too rich not to excite the temerity of an additional commentator.

Certainly the complexities of Rousseau have not deterred the popularizers. At its worst a popularized summary of his thought might run somewhat as follows. Rousseau's basic outlook is that of "Romanticism," which is a composite of antirationalism and individualism. His ideal is a state of nature which existed far in the past, and in which man was wholly good. Since that golden age, however, man has been corrupted by the arts and the sciences, which are essentially bad. But Rousseau persists, on the one hand, in demanding a return to the state of nature, and, on the other, in advocating, quite inexplicably, various ameliorations in the present social and political structure.

Fortunately our popularizer is fictitious; in recent decades, at least, no scholar has made this complete series of unguarded assertions. Yet the individual components of the series are encountered often enough, separately, in works on Rousseau. A point by point examination, however brief, of this distortion of Rousseau's thought will constitute a convenient guide to his attitude toward progress and decadence.

Rousseau's alleged opposition to human reason is perhaps the most deeply rooted of the popular misconceptions of the man. Reason may be seen, negatively, as the opposite either of empiricism or of emotion; it is from the latter viewpoint that rationalism is usually denied to Rousseau, but it is not irrelevant to note at the same time that rationalism as the alternative to empiricism is the method of Rousseau in much of his work. If at times he does give a large role to experience, as in the field of education, more commonly he prefers the rationally abstract to the factual. Nor does he wish to see reason capitulate to emotion and passion. Though he objects with deep feeling to those philosophies which sacrifice the whole man to the coldness of a ubiquitous rationalism, Rousseau does nevertheless champion reason as a vital guide for human life. It is for reason to vanquish religious superstition, to restrain man's harmful passions, and to moderate those desires which, far exceeding man's powers, are otherwise a continual source of frustration and unhappiness. Reason and natural impulse must cooperate; the insights of nature must be rationally guided and developed, while reason for its part must respect spontaneous sentiment and conscience.

Rousseau's individualism has been the victim of a similar distortion. However strongly he may insist upon physical independence and the individual moral conscience, at the same time he keeps in mind two sources of external constraint: society and universal values. In one field, to be sure—that of art—Rousseau upholds the relativity of judgment. But in all other realms, despite his recognition of the broad though superficial influence of climate and environment upon peoples, he stoutly combats all anarchic concepts of basic values. Above all he holds that men everywhere possess in their hearts the elements of a fundamental moral law which is unchangeable across the centuries, and against which all human actions and all human progress must be measured. Moreover, man cannot live as a unit unto himself; he must find his place within the social body. By nature man is sociable, or at least potentially so, and only in the civilized state can he find full scope for his many abilities.

And Rousseau's view of nature has been the subject of a double misapprehension. In the first place, he does not glorify savagery, the individualistic state of pre-civilization. The savage, with no duties to others, can have no virtues and no vices, and thus is hardly a fit subject for idealization. Rather Rousseau sees the golden age as the earliest and simplest social state, where brutishness has been superseded by reason and innocent happiness. Rousseau even doubts the historicity of his own natural man and prefers to see nature not as an historical fact but as a potential factor in all human life. His definition of nature, to be sure, is elusive; with nature he associates such diverse qualities as liberty, simplicity, and growth. The harmonies of external nature, as Rousseau sees them, are such as to convince him of the existence of God and of a divine plan; out of these concepts emerge the comforting assurances of a modified philosophical optimism. Despite imperfections of detail in earthly life, the whole must be essentially good. "All the subtleties of metaphysics," he writes, "will not make me doubt for a moment ... the existence of a benevolent Providence."[2]

The problem of Rousseau's position on the goodness of man is, however, more complicated, and as such it has been the subject of interminable discussion. At the basis of these interpretative difficulties may lie some confusion in Rousseau's own thinking; it is possible, for example, that he mistook his conviction that man is not naturally bad for a proof of man's natural goodness. Nevertheless his persistence in the affirmation of natural goodness is a complementary fact deserving of emphasis. Human freedom and the misuse of human faculties, he holds, make possible the intrusion of error and evil into thought and conduct; the ultimate generation of this evil, unfortunately, remains an obscure puzzle. In any case he is convinced that evil in man is a late product, and that for this reason eventually it may be subdued the more easily. Goodness consists in the potentiality of right moral development—in that potentiality of fruitful expansion which typifies all natural things.

When considering Rousseau's alleged condemnation of civilization, with its perversion of the natural man, one must again exercise caution. As has been noted already, Rousseau does not damn civilization unconditionally, and still less does he hold that the arts and sciences are unmitigated evils. It is true that, at least in his first "Discourse," he considers them essentially vain in their inspiration and potentially dangerous in their effects. Yet he recognizes the value of those pursuits which do not restrict man's free and spontaneous moral development. Even in the first "Discourse" he expresses his admiration for the philosophy and arts of ancient Greece, as well as for certain modern men of science. The pursuit of scientific knowledge, he recognizes, is good in itself, for in this pursuit the scientist partakes more fully of the divine attribute of intelligence. The arts and sciences undeniably may be useful; it is primarily their abuse which Rousseau decries.

[2] Letter to Voltaire, August 18, 1756, *Correspondance générale de J. J. Rousseau* (Paris, 1924–1934), II, 324.

It is evident that by the return to nature Rousseau does not mean a return to a past age; the arts and sciences of civilization are too solidly established for that, and mankind's youthful innocence perhaps too irretrievably lost. Since the state of nature is less an historical than a psychological fact, man, and hence society, may yet be regenerated, for one need only uncover the original nature of man, so long overcast with the artificialities of a corrupt civilization. Nor is this the final step in the process. Nature is not a static condition, but rather contains the possibility of development; the natural man embodies not petrifaction but perfectibility. And the agents of perfectibility are reason and natural feeling, or conscience.

Thus, far from advocating historical primitivism, Rousseau becomes the champion of human progress; his attitude toward man's future course is not negative but constructive. Like Morelly and Mably, and indeed like Descartes a century before, Rousseau is a prophet of human regeneration, of progress *de novo*. Past and future become the areas of history and of progress respectively and as such are sharply separated. But Rousseau differs radically from Descartes in the type of progress which he envisages, for it is now not the progress of knowledge but the moral, religious, and social progress of man which is primary.[3] "Science, beautiful and sublime as it is, is not made for man; ... he has too limited a mind to make great progress in it, and too much passion in his heart not to make bad use of it. It is enough for him to study well his duties, and every man has sufficient knowledge for that study."[4] And with the realization of moral progress, furthered by the all-important educative process, social and political advances too become possible. Here it is fraternity and a certain degree of equality which are the goals, together with a form of social constraint which disguises itself as liberty. But in all of this it is the individual who remains Rousseau's paramount concern; his politics are ultimately reducible to ethics.

It is true that one may find in the welter of theory which forms

[3] Rousseau also believes in the progress of artistic taste, as allied with morality; "the good is simply the beautiful put into action." *Julie, ou la nouvelle Héloïse*, in *Oeuvres complètes*, IV, 37.

[4] *Réponse de J. J. Rousseau, au roi de Pologne*, in *Oeuvres complètes*, I, 31.

Rousseau's thought a number of fragments inconsistent with optimism on the future of mankind. There are, for example, passages concerning artistic decadence and the degeneration of urban life. Other fragments seem to indicate a belief in the flux of all earthly things, and the degeneration of governmental forms is treated at considerable length.[5] Moreover, throughout his work Rousseau displays no small skepticism as to the efficacy of human reason and conscience when pitted against passion and habit; at times resignation appears to be Rousseau's definitive counsel.[6] Yet, with all this, he remains an incurable idealist. Nor is he dismayed by the indubitable fact that his ideals, notably in education and politics, will not be fully idealized, for their approximation, he feels, will in itself mark a tremendous advance in man's estate. Above all, Rousseau emphasizes the need for hope and for faith; better days must come both in this life and after.[7]

And so Rousseau, like Morelly and Mably, remains a believer— a believer in man's power to shake off the past and to be regenerated both as an individual and as a component of the great earthly society. If for these writers the past is the era of decadence, progress is the keynote of the future. The ideal may be difficult of realization, but one may rely upon the light of universal law and of invariable moral principles to indicate the path which must lie ahead. It is a path which must be cut according to the rules of nature and reason—the rules of the moral and social perfectibility of man.

[5] *Emile, ou de l'éducation*, in *Oeuvres complètes*, II, 27, 315; *Du contrat social, ou principes de droit politique*, in *Oeuvres complètes*, III, 355–358.

[6] *Les confessions*, in *Oeuvres complètes*, VIII, 302.

[7] *Emile, ou de l'éducation*, in *Oeuvres complètes*, 62; letter to Voltaire, August 18, 1756, *Correspondance générale*, II, 323–324.

Chapter 10

The Great Doctrines of Progress—
Turgot and Condorcet

> The day will come when the sun will shine only upon free
> men who acknowledge reason as their sole master—when
> tyrants and slaves, priests and their stupid or hypocritical
> instruments will exist only in history books and on the stage,
> and when one will think no more of priests and tyrants
> save to sympathize with their dupes and their victims.
> (Condorcet, *Esquisse d'un tableau historique des progrès
> de l'esprit humain*)[1]

The appearance of Condorcet's great doctrine of human progress
was an event presaged in its century by the production of a number
of progressionist theories more limited or less striking than his.
Among the immediate precursors of Condorcet in France were
Rousseau and Turgot, and with these a handful of less distinguished
figures whose memory scarcely survives. The names of Saint-Pierre
and Terrasson, of Chastellux and Mercier and Volney, mean little
today, but during their lifetime these men were writers of note and
influence. The essential goodness, reasonableness, and perfectibility
of man were the postulates upon which the Abbé de Saint-Pierre
founded his notion of continuous and infinite progress, and upon
which he based his hopes for the success of innumerable detailed
plans for social improvement. The Abbé Terrasson stressed the
solidarity of human progress, and the profit which the arts would
draw from the infusion of the philosophical spirit. Chastellux, trust-
ing implicitly in the powers of education and legislation, expected a
regeneration of man and a return to the natural order of human
and social life, under which the past might be forgotten and atten-

[1] *Oeuvres de Condorcet* (Paris, 1847), VI, 244.

tion be given only to the greatest happiness of the greatest number. Scornful of past history, Sébastian Mercier constructed a utopia based upon the perfectibility of knowledge and technique. And the Comte de Volney saw eventual human happiness as the inevitable fruit of invariable natural law and the "law of imitation."

But far more remarkable than these schemes is the conception of progress outlined at the mid-point of the century by Turgot, then a young student at the Sorbonne. In this doctrine of progress the irrelevance of the data of the natural world is the first assumption. "Natural phenomena, guided by constant laws, are contained within a system of recurrent cycles; here everything perishes and is born again, and in the reproductive succession of vegetables and animals time forever re-establishes the image of that which it has made disappear. The succession of men, on the other hand, offers from age to age a spectacle forever varying. Reason, the passions, and human freedom ceaselessly create new events. . . ."[2] Not cyclical flux, then, but progress is the law of human development. The human race, like each individual, has its childhood and its progress. "Through alternating peace and strife, well-being and misfortune, the body of mankind continuously strides on toward perfection."[3] And, unlike most of his prominent contemporaries, Turgot discerns the providential hand of God throughout this progressive course of history. Thus it is only natural that he proposes to allow the broadest possible scope for the realization of progress; politics, religion, ethics, languages, arts and sciences are all to fall within its sphere.

According to Turgot, the vital prerequisite for progress, as well as the medium of its propagation, is human communication. Ideas derive from sensations and are developed through the use of signs, pictures, and language, through which in turn human knowledge and experience are transmitted and augmented from generation to generation. Error has shown stubborn perseverance throughout history but at last is being arrested in its course. But errors and mis-

---

[2] *Tableau philosophique des progrès successifs de l'esprit humain*, in *Oeuvres de Turgot* (Paris, 1913), I, 214–215.

[3] *Plan du premier Discours sur la formation des gouvernements et le mélange des nations*, in *Oeuvres*, I, 285.

3*

fortunes, like all other phenomena, have their function in the extension of human experience, and it is experience which prepares instruction. Human passions, too, are useful, for they are activating forces, and without action there can be no progress. Thus it would seem that for Turgot all earthly phenomena must tend essentially toward progress. Yet, upon the basis of certain mental reservations, he does recognize the reality of evil, and the occurrence of decadence as well. Progress, for him, is invariably punctuated by decline, and most obviously so in the history of nations and empires. But he does not dwell upon the misfortunes and aberrations of mankind; rather he prefers to seek out those more solid advances which subsist throughout the troubled vicissitudes of history.

For Turgot seeks in history not the accident but the norm, and for him this norm is the course of reason and of progress. For the fulfilment of this natural course the ages are linked together in a great chain of causality. Yet apparently chance also has its role in human history, and in progress itself. It is often by mere chance that new discoveries are made, and it is by chance that a man of genius is born at a particular time and place. But the reception of discoveries and of genius depends to some degree upon conditions prevalent at their appearance. Turgot separates these conditions into the moral and the physical. The latter include air and "climate"; the former include the state of the government, the patronage of the ruler, the existence of war or peace, and the economic misery or ease of the people. But Turgot asserts that the influence of climatic conditions has been much exaggerated, and notes that upon occasion similar climates have given rise to diverse national characters, while dissimilar climates often have produced nations of the same turn of mind. Of the physical and moral causes which do differentiate peoples, the second are of greater importance and certainly of far greater immediacy than the first.

Yet, dependent though it may often be upon accident or environmental circumstance, progress is guaranteed to mankind. Blind though it may seem, it continues with a momentum which to the reader of Turgot can only appear providential. Nor should it be forgotten that for Turgot truth is more natural to man than is error, and that all truths are mutually dependent. Though often broken by moments of temporary decline, progress is necessary and inevitable when viewed in terms of vaster periods of time.[4] And there can be no break in the continuity of progress; past, present, and future are parts alike of the providential order. Even in the Middle Ages, bleak though they may have been, a considerable amount of commerce, learning, and social organization remained in existence, and at the same time the mechanical arts were gradually perfecting themselves. The Church, far from being the ally of barbarism, was a moderating moral and cultural force. Unlike his contemporaries among the *philosophes*, Turgot viewed Christianity as essentially a civilizing and a progressive force, the champion of learning, peace, and justice.

With what progress is Turgot concerned? It is obvious that in his work the meaning of the term varies according to context, yet equally clear that he considers the advance of knowledge as the most fundamental and most certain of all types of progress. Certainty, he wrote, is possible in mathematics, and a provisional certainty may be attained in the other sciences, despite the fact that these latter are largely dependent upon the haphazard presentation of empirical facts rather than upon rational principles. Time, chance, and effort multiply data and reveal causal connections, and with the linking of mathematics and the other sciences truth eventually is uncovered. Moreover, with the extension of philosophy, or reason, into all scientific realms, the sciences can no longer remain isolated but must be linked in content and methodology. Knowledge, unlike taste, has never been lost altogether by mankind, and the techniques of the mechanical arts progress continuously despite temporary decadence in other realms. The whole course of man's intellectual history falls into three stages, roughly equivalent to the theological, metaphysical, and positivistic eras later to be proposed by Comte. But there is no discernible finite term to this development, for knowledge is as limitless as nature and truth themselves.[5]

[4] *Plan du second Discours sur les progrès de l'esprit humain*, in *Oeuvres*, I, 303.
[5] *Plan du second Discours sur les progrès de l'esprit humain*, in *Oeuvres*, I, 321; *Tableau philosophique*, in *Oeuvres*, I, 227.

In literature and the arts the case is less clear, and progress less certain. Here, to be sure, progress in the past is unmistakable, especially in the matters of diffusion and technique and richness of content. Yet the possibilities of literary and artistic advance seem to be limited, both because of the limitations on the objects normally treated and because of the bounds of human nature itself. But room for progress still exists, notably in technique and in the representation of the complex relationships of life. Like all other pursuits, literature and the arts must undergo countless revolutions and are subject to the play of chance and the pressure of circumstance. Governmental and religious policy and the manners, customs, and moral values of a nation all leave their imprint upon the development and the nature of taste, while luxury and cultural refinement play a particularly important part in aesthetic orientation.

Turgot writes little on moral progress, though one may assume that he believes it follows the same upward spiral which he attributes to the course of knowledge, art, and literature. Certainly he would consider ethical progress measurable, for he agrees with many of his contemporaries in finding moral principles to be largely fixed and universal. Virtue and happiness, he notes, are closely united, but he scarcely mentions social progress and the diffusion of enlightenment and happiness among the masses. Whether at the time of the Sorbonne "Discourses" this omission was intentional, or whether it resulted simply from the requirements of brevity and prescribed emphasis, cannot be known with certainty. Yet Turgot did note the roles to be played by education and legislation, and the orientation of his own later life clearly indicates that he was then to harbor a genuine concern for the immediate social, economic, and political betterment of man's condition.

Condorcet's specific and extensive treatment of mass sharing in progress is one of the several points at which he differs from his older contemporary; in his "Historical Sketch of the Progress of the Mind" he envisages the eventual spreading of enlightenment and well-being throughout the population of the various nations. Another divergence of viewpoint to be noted at the outset arises over the question of religion. Where Turgot respects the Christian religion, Condorcet, himself apparently the vaguest of deists, sees in organized religion the prime enemy of the human race. "Without interruption the world has been the prey of imbecile scoundrels believing everything, directed by hypocritical scoundrels believing nothing."[6] From the hour of the death of Socrates, philosophy has been locked in battle with the obscurantism and superstition fostered by priestcraft. Human progress then is the fruit of bitter struggle, of the continuous effort of reason to rise above the welter of prejudice, superstition, and despotic authority in which it has hitherto been submerged.

For it is human reason which ultimately bears the weight of Condorcet's system. As Secretary of the Academy of Science he was particularly well informed upon current scientific developments and was profoundly moved by the spectacle of man's growing understanding and control of the material world. Scientific knowledge became for him the key to all progress. "Having long been occupied in pondering the means of bettering man's fate, I have not been able to avoid the conclusion that there is actually only one such means: the speeding of the progress of enlightenment." "All errors in politics and in ethics are based upon errors in philosophy, and these latter are tied to errors in physical science. There is not a single religious system or supernatural extravagance which is not founded upon ignorance of the laws of nature."[7] But scientific progress is not simply an accumulation of knowledge; it is also the discovery and adoption of a valid scientific method. Fortunately, the rudiments of this method, such as the accepting of proven truths alone and their separation from probable truths, are also applicable to ethics, politics, and other fields of human action. Wherever method is applied, man replaces haphazard advance by progress which is conscious and controlled. Chance has always had a part in human history, but one day man, guided by methodology, will be freed from its tyranny.

[6] *Notes sur Voltaire,* in *Oeuvres de Condorcet,* IV, 357.
[7] *De l'influence de la révolution d'Amérique sur l'Europe,* in *Oeuvres,* VIII, 30; *Esquisse d'un tableau historique des progrès de l'esprit humain,* in *Oeuvres,* VI, 223.

Condorcet likewise puts great emphasis upon ethics—an ethics independent of all religions and sects and founded upon reason and nature alone. The first postulate of this ethics is the basic goodness of man, the preponderance of altruism over vicious selfishness. The latter deplorable tendency in man is indubitably "natural," since it exists, but it is after all something contingent and exceptional, an irregularity or accident which must, and to a certain extent can, be repressed. Moral goodness, on the other hand, is a necessary component of human nature, and like man's other qualities it is infinitely perfectible. Virtue, happiness, and truth are linked by nature with an unbreakable chain. And behind all of Condorcet's statements on knowledge and virtue lies a tacit assumption of great import: the assumption that man when given a free choice between truth and error will invariably choose truth, even as under a parallel lack of restraint he will always prefer good to evil.

Possessed then of a method, Condorcet requires two prime guarantees of its applicability: the invariability of natural law and the existence of constant rules for the establishment and preservation of social structures everywhere. He is at least as certain of both of these guarantees as his professions of probabilism permit. Dismissing as relatively unimportant the disturbing influences of climate and environment, he asserts the constancy of natural laws and the future progress which this constancy seems to promise. On the invariable prerequisites for social progress he is even more dogmatic. These prerequisites form a typical roster of the social ideals of the Enlightenment: liberty, property, equality, secular rule, enlightened government, international harmony. That it ever occurred to Condorcet to question for a moment the eternal validity of even one of these ideals seems unlikely. For after all, "the principles upon which societies are to be established must be the same for all states."[8] Here then are unshakeable criteria for human progress, as well as reassuring guarantees of its possibility. The great theoretical edifice may now be raised.

[8] *Recueil de pieces sur l'état des protestants en France,* in *Oeuvres,* V, 440.

Condorcet's doctrine of progress is in a sense a doctrine of re-generation; it includes a Rousseauistic protest against the denaturing of man and demands the re-establishment and extension of man's natural faculties. The slow rebirth, to be sure, is not ex-clusively the work of the future, for it began with Europe's awakening from the darkness of early medieval times. Gradually, since then, reason and virtue have been able partially to escape institutional restraints, and though ignorance, unhappiness, and crime still exist they are already mortally wounded. Especially in the ninth of ten epochs, the epoch now ending, the spirit of discord has diminished, and truth and fraternal good will have become potent forces in the world. And in this epoch, as evidence of pro-gress, the idea of the infinite perfectibility of the human race has at last been advanced.

Progress, Condorcet admits, has been difficult, though one may feel that his system does not offer an entirely adequate explanation for the coexistence of persistent error and invincible truth. Theory, he asserts, has preceded popular awakening and social reform, and the desire for truth has always exceeded the capacity for knowledge and justice. The rate of progress has been halting and uneven; the faculties of the human mind have not developed simultaneously, nor has reactionary resistance to progress been equal in all fields. Yet, if Condorcet notes that progress is often punctuated by decline, he dwells upon only one period of decadence, the thousand years fol-lowing the height of Roman glory. Despite reservations, progress for Condorcet remains essentially unitary, both in its composition and in its line of development.

As in science so in other fields, according to Condorcet, progress consists basically of concrete achievement and of an extension of methodology or control. Like the physical sciences, moral science will advance by empirical methods and will attain a high degree of certitude, though its progress will be slower than that of the physical sciences. Social progress is the concomitant of scientific and moral progress. Artistic and literary progress too is closely related to the cultural environment and especially to the state of philosophy and natural science. The much-heralded imminent exhaustion of arts and letters is simply a fable; they can be expected to advance indefinitely as the progress of knowledge and philosophy extends the scope of natural investigation. The arts will become an adjunct to pervasive human reason.

Condorcet's dreams for the new age, or tenth epoch of mankind, are utopian, and his eyes scan not only the immediate future but the centuries far ahead. In his view the perfecting of man and society will become more and more certain, more and more inevitable. Though errors may still arise, their potency will decrease, and though progress at times may be slower than at others, an actual decline will be impossible. Progress will take three major lines: the destruction of inequalities among nations and among individuals, and the perfecting of man himself. International peace and justice will be established, and an enlightened commercial policy and the adoption of a universal language will put the seal upon fraternity among nations. Cooperative scholarship will promote, and education disseminate, enlightenment, while the advance of the mechanical arts will bring new comfort and happiness to the mass of mankind. Finally, the application of new knowledge, notably in the field of medicine, will ensure the perfecting of natural human faculties. Thus future progress is virtually unlimited; human perfectibility has no final term other than the destruction of the earth itself. The horizons of man's understanding will forever advance, and should society ever reach the practical limits of expansion it will have attained such a utopian state that one should see in those limits no cause for chagrin.

Thus Condorcet the theorist became the inspired prophet—the prophet of mankind's tremendous potentialities. His vision, however, was not altogether his own, for it was made possible by the intellectual assumptions common in his day, by the work of many predecessors. Since only a handful of these writers to whom he owed so much have been studied in these pages, any conclusions concerning historical optimism drawn from their writings must be recognized as provisional. Yet before turning to that current of thought that rejected the optimistic tradition one may profitably review the assumptions which by Condorcet's time had made possible his belief in progress.

First of all, in each of the thinkers whose historical philosophies have been summarized in this section, there existed a faith in human reason which to the latter-day skeptic must appear almost boundless. And, consistent with this faith, a strong reliance upon rationalism appears in the methodology of these same writers. At no time does the empiricism of hard facts, outside perhaps the realm of science, seriously challenge the imperatives of rationalistic idealism. In not one of these thinkers is there a shattering skepticism on basic principles; in not one does probabilism receive more than lip service. In short, each of our writers is thoroughly convinced that his rational powers have shown him the true principles and goals of mankind's development.

The concept of "nature" held by each writer (except Lignac, whose idea of progress was the least developed) contributed notably to the same end. Though the eighteenth century was in no agreement in its definition of nature, these writers did agree on one of its attributes: the universality and invariability of its laws. Indeed, few thinkers of the Enlightenment withstood altogether successfully the charms of philosophical simplicity and unity; in the several historical optimists studied here there was virtually no resistance whatever. Mankind, to them, was fundamentally a unit, and should become even more so. Geographical and historical conditions might modify certain superficial characteristics of the group or the individual, but basic values would remain unchanged. Above all, the essentials of morality were timeless; what was good for the Enlightened Frenchman was good for all other ages and peoples. Thus reason was reinforced by nature to provide a measuring stick for mankind's progress or decline.

And nature, to the thoroughgoing optimists, offered a most encouraging indication that civilization would progress rather than decline: human nature was essentially, or at least potentially, good. Under proper conditions, they were convinced, this side of man's nature must inevitably assert itself. These proper conditions were not impossible of realization, for mankind would have at its disposal the marvellous instrument of education. No blind determinism would force men to think and act as in the past; by education according to rational, natural, and invariable principles the best in men would be drawn out and progress would be assured.

Such, at any rate, is the pattern of historical optimism revealed in the few, but important, thinkers discussed in this section. But the thought of the French Enlightenment is not a unit; neither the presuppositions hitherto considered, nor the idea of progress which so often they appear to have stimulated, can alone represent the varied intellectual texture of the age. One must pick up, then, those other strands the genesis of which has already been suggested—those countercurrents of progressionist theory which in the eighteenth century were manifested above all in the ideas of decadence and of historical flux.

Part III

Decadence—Reality Measured against Reason

Chapter 11

Decadence, Reason, and Nature

Philosophy knows only those rules founded in the eternal
and immutable nature of things. (Diderot, *Encyclopédie*)[1]

"People are always crying that this world is in the process of degeneration . . ."—so sighed Voltaire in 1744.[2] And in 1794 Condorcet
could note with amazement the pessimism prevalent in his century,
and the existence of those "numerous partisans" of paradox or
skepticism who had tried to demonstrate the difficulties of attaining and utilizing knowledge. "Endlessly," he wrote, "we have
heard them complain of the decadence of knowledge even when
actually it was progressing. They deplored the misery of the human
race while at the same instant men were recalling their rights and
beginning to use their reason; they predicted the imminent advent
of one of those oscillations which must bring men back to barbarism,
ignorance, and slavery, and this at the very moment when everything concurred to prove that humanity had nothing more to fear."[3]

Here certainly eminent authority is lent to the thesis that the
doctrine of progress was not unresisted in the eighteenth century.
Much of the resistance, of course, came from the camp not of the
philosophes but of their opponents, yet even with many of the *philosophes* progress was a hope rather than a conviction; seldom did it
constitute the basis of a system. More often it was simply an opinion,

---

[1] "Encyclopédie" (*Encyclopédie*), *Oeuvres complètes de Diderot* (Paris,
1875–1877), XIV, 425.

[2] *Nouvelles considérations sur l'histoire*, in *Oeuvres complètes de Voltaire*
(Paris, 1877–1885), XVI, 140.

[3] *Esquisse d'un tableau historique des progrès de l'esprit humain*, in
Oeuvres de Condorcet, VI, 195–196; see also *Discours prononcé dans
l'Académie française le jeudi 21 février 1782 à la réception de M. le marquis
de Condorcet*, in *Oeuvres*, I, 394.

and an opinion which was sometimes at variance with other beliefs held simultaneously. Before considering the integral thought of several significant individual thinkers, a more general analysis must be made of eighteenth century historical pessimism and of its immediate philosophical foundations.

As has been noted earlier, the ideas of progress and decadence presuppose certain standards of value and measurement which often are not emphasized in systems of historical flux. Involving movement toward a certain ideal or away from it, progress and decadence thus are complementary. The close alliance between the two concepts is perhaps most strikingly illustrated by the vicissitudes of the Quarrel of the Ancients and the Moderns, in the course of which the standards which at one time had led to support of the Moderns were later to cause the most stubborn resistance to the idea of progress in the arts.

Today, with more subtlety and a more pervasive skepticism, theorists of progress have tried upon occasion to dispense altogether with criteria of absolute and eternal validity, and have substituted various schemes of evolving values or social accommodation. The thinkers of the eighteenth century, when writing of progress, had not yet achieved this sophistication; they were, as rationalists, much too sure of themselves and of their ideals for this type of evasion. Yet it is true that the rudiments of a revolt from absolute progressionist ideals were already present, above all in the concept of method. Condorcet, like many scientific investigators before him, saw method as a self-nourishing process, forever expanding as it progressively proposed new techniques to be followed and new problems to be met. And scientific method was seen now and again as the model for advance in other fields of human activity. However, for the Enlightenment, method remained predominantly a means and not an end; it was crucial first of all to define, however broadly, the goal to be attained.

Certainly the average *philosophe* was by no means unwilling to announce the standards by which he measured human advance and decline, and the goal toward which he felt that man and society should evolve. Thus one finds the Comte de Mirabeau upholding political freedom as the touchstone of progress, and his father the Marquis proposing an agricultural economy as the goal of society. Buffon saw man's control over nature as the most desirable end, while Condillac and the Encyclopedists glorified the progress of human reason and knowledge, and man's advances in the mechanical arts. Others emphasized progress in virtue, in aesthetic taste, or in international harmony—and all saw human happiness as the fruit of this evolution.

Several instances of the intrusion of rationalistic idealism into a practical context may be profitably noted in passing. The progress, for example, of science itself was scarcely questioned in the eighteenth century, yet the ultimate worth of scientific progress was not accepted with nearly the same unanimity as was the fact, for science might find itself in conflict with the final purposes of man as they were variously conceived. The Church accepted science only when it did not impinge upon dogma or upon the pursuit of the Christian life. Rousseau and many a poet and primitivist deplored the potentialities of science for destroying the element of simple goodness in human nature. Others, among them Vauvenargues and La Mettrie, found scientific advance neither greatly beneficial nor harmful to the race, but rather, in view of man's true ends, merely irrelevant.[4]

The progress of contemporary philosophy did not meet with the general recognition accorded the progress of science, though clearly the *philosophes* approved of the general intellectual trends of their day. Yet certain reservations entered even the main philosophical current, and into the *Encyclopédie* itself there crept an article condemning the current perversion of philosophy. On the eighteenth century this author commented: "One likes to call it the century of philosophy, but, while not denying altogether the assertion, I would prefer to call it the century of half-learning."[5] The great intellectual

---

[4] Cf. Fréron's review of *Examen philosophique de la liaison réelle qu'il y a entre les sciences & les mœurs*, in which the author found that the sciences neither help nor hinder morality, but simply bring out men's natural predispositions. *L'année littéraire*, 1755, V, 58–67.

[5] "Académies (Avantages des)," *Supplément à l'Encyclopédie* (Amsterdam, 1776–1777), I, 97.

revolution wrought by Descartes, Newton, Leibnitz, and the academies had been prostituted, continued the author, by a crescendo of journalism and popularization which had practically banned solid, serious thought and investigation.

Buffon, in a generalization of similar breadth, came to different but no less condemnatory conclusions. "In this century," he wrote, "even though the sciences seem to be cultivated with care, I believe that it is easy to perceive the negligence into which philosophy has fallen—a negligence perhaps greater than in any other century. The arts which one calls scientific have taken philosophy's place; the methods of mathematics, of botany and natural history, in a word formulas and dictionaries, occupy nearly everybody. Men imagine that they know more because they have multiplied the number of symbols and of learned phrases, and they do not remember that all of these arts are simply the scaffolding for reaching knowledge and that they are not knowledge itself. . . ."[6]

Such passages are perhaps symptomatic of those doubts and questionings which at times may have crossed the mind of the eighteenth century thinker. But such doubts were not incompatible with a broader historical optimism; moreover, they were apparently ephemeral, for they very rarely find a place in the works of the leading scientists and *philosophes* of the period. It was of course the *antiphilosophes* who seriously took to task the reigning philosophies and the moral decadence fostered, they believed, by these philosophies.

To initiate here a lengthy discussion of this campaign against the *philosophes* would be to transcend by far the proper limits of this study. The *antiphilosophes* themselves, with the possible exception of Caraccioli, were men of small talents, amply deserving the oblivion into which they have fallen in the course of time. They were not, however, without their moments of lucid good sense, and many of their judgments on the Enlightenment have been re-echoed and elaborated by abler thinkers than they.

Yet the virulent criticisms leveled by the *antiphilosophes* against

---

[6] Buffon, *Histoire naturelle, générale et particulière* (Paris, 1799–1808), I, 64–65.

the reigning thought of their age usually fell short of any generalized philosophy of history; the critique, at least when on rationalistic, absolutist assumptions, has little significance in the history of true historical pessimism. And the assumptions of these writers, it should be noted, were indeed predominantly absolutist—that is, derived from abstract reason and from the revealed authority of religion. For reason had so insidiously pervaded even the camp of the *antiphilosophes* that its weapons were scarcely less used there than in the cause of the Enlightenment. But only in conjunction with a broader historical outlook and a distinctly empirical strain did such criticism now and then have significance for the present study.

Idealistic, absolute standards of progress or decline were applied, of course, not only to the development of science and philosophy but to all fields of human activity. Moral corruption and aesthetic decadence were frequently diagnosed, and often were seen as proceeding hand in hand. On this close relationship the most diverse writers—the scholar Maupertuis, the dour Classicist Rigoley de Juvigny, the devout and pompous Marquis de Pompignan—might find themselves in full agreement.

In this vein the highly articulate Caraccioli formulated an even more sweeping indictment of his age. "Already this century has run more than half of its course, and we have nothing to offer our successors but insipid novels, miserable plays, impious philosophies, and extravagant opinions. How corrosive this degeneration has been! Since the beginning of the century fifty-eight years have passed, and each of them has been a step downward from the worth of our fathers. Our fathers occupied themselves in self-study while we dissipate, they sought only truth while we love only illusion, they drew their arguments from religion while we persist in establishing systems which contradict that religion, they drew from original sources while our knowledge of the ancient authors derives only from citations, they questioned their souls while we are attentive only to our senses, they permitted themselves recreation only as relaxation from arduous labor while we believe that one should live only to enjoy the most criminal pleasures. In a word, they meditated and we talk, they were profound and we are superficial, they reasoned and we wander aimlessly."[7]

It is true that philosophers, aestheticians, moralists, and political theorists of all centuries have frequently tempered their hopes for the future realization of their ideals with sad reflections on the short-comings of the moment; indeed the contrast is indispensable to idealism. One must therefore beware of mistaking temporary discouragement for true historical pessimism. Yet all too often the opposite error has been made—that of dismissing all talk of con-temporary decay as merely perfunctory or fleetingly temperamental. If much captious criticism of their age by Enlightened thinkers can be ignored, other criticism has real significance when it involves a notion of general decline from earlier years, and above all when a parallel is drawn with decadent periods of past history.

For certainly the diffusion and the popularization of the idea of decadence were aided substantially in the eighteenth century by the use of historical analogy. Comparatively little attention was given to the decline of ancient Greece, but the fall of Rome excited great interest, especially after the success of Montesquieu's "Grandeur and Decadence of the Romans." The phenomenon of Roman decay, in the arts as well as in the body politic, was often brought to the attention of the reading public and became indeed a commonplace of eighteenth century history and literature. Almost as generally accepted by writers and public was the fact of medieval decadence. Turgot and Montesquieu here were the sole prominent dissidents, and though now and then as in the preceding century a voice would be raised in praise of the glimmerings of talent, courage, or gentility in the Middle Ages, the general opinion of the medieval period was low indeed. Feudal Europe seemed to be the very anti-thesis of the world envisioned by eighteenth century idealism; in its presumed ignorance, its superstition and intolerance, its barbarity and lack of refinement, its alternate despotism and anarchic disorder, it came to represent decadence at its darkest.

To be sure, some vagueness envelops all these criteria of progress

[7] Louis Antoine de Caraccioli, *La jouissance de soi-même* (Utrecht, Amsterdam, 1759), pp. IX–X.

and decadence. Yet despite that love for misty generalization which one encounters so often in eighteenth century French thought, the existence of basic ideals as the measures of progress and decadence seems clear enough. Upon what foundations were these ideals erected? Above all, as has already been intimated, upon the twin concepts of "reason" and "nature." Before turning to that field in which these concepts led, perhaps, most directly to a discussion of decadence, it may be appropriate to assess provisionally their importance in Enlightened thought as a whole.

In the philosophy of the Enlightenment the primacy of human reason, so often asserted, was frequently challenged by forces both within and outside the individual. On the one hand it was continually shaken by the demands of feeling and emotion, while on the other the external data of observation, experiment, and experience, as well as the imperatives of established and revealed authority, contested its supremacy. Conscious authority in most fields, to be sure, had largely lost its intellectual respectability, but the demands of empiricism and emotion were pressing.

The facts of the eighteenth century revival of feeling, sensibility, and emotion are well known. The imperatives of sentiment now took an important place both in psychology and literature, and in religion as well. Like reason, the light of emotion might serve either as a challenge to progress or as a premonition of decadence; it was only later that Romanticism, as a justification of sentimental traditionalism, became at times a distinctly antiprogressionist force. Yet the fact remains that the predominant tone of the French eighteenth century is clearly rationalistic rather than Romantic. Even organized religion was largely rationalistic, and in secular life neither hypersensitivity nor passionate emotionalism was the cultural norm.

The problem of the relationship between reason and empiricism is less easily dismissed. Unfortunately the existence of the problem was not even recognized by many eighteenth century thinkers, since for them reason and empiricism were complementary and their relationship simple and self-explanatory. D'Alembert, for example, appeals alternately to reason and to experience, asserting that "philosophy is simply the application of reason to those different objects for which it is properly created," and that these objects include empirical facts.[8] Such a position obviously evades the issue, for the most elementary acquaintance with human nature and with philosophical systems reveals that, despite a fairly widespread agreement on the complementary roles of reason and experience, individuals nevertheless do incline toward weighting more heavily one or the other of these intellectual approaches.

Certainly scholarship in the eighteenth century was heir to a strong rationalistic influence, and as late as 1719 one could write that "two things are necessary in the study of the physical sciences—experience and reasoning; we shall start by reasoning."[9] And though in the course of the century deduction in the physical sciences was to be partly replaced by empirical research, the rational analytic habit which had grown up in the meantime was displaced elsewhere only with extreme difficulty. Even the new science of psychology as developed by Condillac followed a predominantly deductive pattern, and like literature and philosophy it sought to deal primarily with ideas which were clear, simple, and unshakeable. Outside the realm of the arts and natural sciences, experience was generally consulted, if at all, only to confirm the answers which reason already had proposed. Such, notoriously, was the case in the political and social sciences, where right was very seldom indeed established upon a solid preliminary basis of fact. As Diderot remarked in the *Encyclopédie*, nearly everybody was convinced that he possessed a self-evident knowledge of "natural rights," so familiar had the usage of that term become.[10]

Reason in the eighteenth century also came to refer to a sort of common-sense criticism which at the same time relied heavily upon an everyday empiricism. Actually this type of reason often was thoroughly mingled with its more intuitive counterpart, but whatever the precise components of reason as applied in a particular situation, the essential simplicity of the data and of the problem at

---

[8] *Essai sur les élémens de philosophie, ou sur les principes des connaissances humaines,* in *Oeuvres de d'Alembert* (Paris, 1821–1822), I, 126.

[9] Denyse, quoted by Daniel Mornet, *Les sciences de la nature en France, au XVIIIe siècle: un chapitre de l'histoire des idées* (Paris, 1911), 81.

[10] "Droit naturel" (*Encyclopédie*), *Oeuvres complètes de Diderot,* XIV, 296.

hand was almost always postulated. This assumption of simplicity, added to the widespread belief in the ultimate rationality and unity of the universe, inevitably created systems of simple, rational values which were not subject to change. Reason and the values which it upheld were seen as constants, and that which the average *philosophe* hesitated to term theoretically absolute became absolute in the force of its application. Human nature, truth and justice were commonly assumed to be fundamentally the same in all ages and in all nations, and the constant characteristics of these qualities were of course precisely those which the Enlightenment itself had discovered. And so arose those unassailable aesthetic, ethical, and social ideals the existence of which has already been noted, and which guaranteed the possibility, the detection, and the measurement of progress and decadence.

If the possibility of real progress and decadence thus was guaranteed, the choice between the two remained open. Was progress more natural than decadence, or was the opposite true? Here the attitude toward the goodness of nature and of man becomes relevant. While most thinkers shared Rousseau's view of a developing nature, by no means all of them agreed that nature was essentially good. Buffon at times indeed saw the natural world as possessing an almost malignant quality; for him nature is the enemy of man, a force to be subjugated and transformed and which forever threatens to reassert its primordial power. Only a most precarious progress was compatible with this view of nature. And, on the other hand, the philosophical optimism which might result from a belief in the absolute goodness of nature was hardly more conducive to a belief in progress. Unless, as with Charles Bonnet, an evolving rather than a static chain of being was envisaged, one had to accept the obvious impossibility of bettering an already perfect world.

More directly relevant to the formation of a doctrine of progress or decadence was the position taken on the natural goodness of man himself, though a belief in man's original goodness, instead of leading to an optimistic view of his developmental possibilities, might give rise simply to dirges on the corrupting influence of civilization and to a nostalgia for primitive or rustic life. Yet if man is naturally good and if evil is simply an artificial accretion, a strong presumption would normally be created in favor of the ultimate triumph of his good qualities, and of human progress in general. And clearly the eighteenth century did take a somewhat more favorable view of human nature than had the preceding periods of Western history. The Fall and the consequent corruption of man were scoffed at by every writer in the main current of thought, and literature and psychology alike proclaimed the potentialities for good which are contained in the passions.

Yet there were few thinkers who took the crucial step of asserting that goodness is natural, and evil unnatural, to man. The point deserves emphasis, for misunderstanding here is all too common. With certain reservations, Rousseau and Condorcet both held to this ultimate and basic goodness of human nature, but their position was regarded with little enthusiasm by their most prominent contemporaries. Throughout the French Enlightenment there runs a strong current of skepticism on man's nature; confidence in his potentialities for right living is forever countered, with varying intensity, by recognition of his parallel potentialities for evil. Like Montesquieu and Vauvenargues somewhat earlier, neither Voltaire nor Diderot, Helvétius nor Holbach, could believe in the essential integral goodness of man. Good and evil alike, they held, are proper to human nature; man is born neither good nor bad but with a capacity for the development of both of these qualities. And, in an age when morality and knowledge were in close union and when goodness thus was more than a simple moral quality, truth and error too were seen as equally natural to the human race.

Thus progress and decadence alike became conceivable to the eighteenth century mind. If many of the great *philosophes* harbored real sympathy for the doctrine of progress, they did not ordinarily do so because they believed in the ease of eradicating an unnatural corruption from human nature, or because they found in man an inherent and invincible inclination toward the good. Here, however, one crosses the vague line between rationalism and empiricism; the discouraging results of many *philosophes'* observation of the world about them can best be discussed, in later sections of this study, as elements in the empirical approach to man and society.

Is it true, however, that the historical philosophy of the Enlightenment, when operating strictly in the realm of absolute values and rationalistic ideals, turned as readily to pessimism as to optimism? For it would appear, on the face of things, that such might well be the case. Yet to this question one can only answer with a categorical negative.

The explanation of this persistent optimism is not difficult. First of all, rationalistic idealism is almost inevitably positive, constructive, and hopeful. Secondly, the theoretical assumption of the goodness of human nature was never combatted by an equally theoretical assumption of its badness; rather the Enlightenment had to turn to empirical observation to discover the mixture of good and evil in the human race, thereby of course transcending the limits of strict rationalism. It is clear then that the question posed above is in itself misleading: actually the historical philosophy of the Enlightenment seldom operated "strictly in the realm of absolute values and rationalistic ideals." Not only did the *philosophes*, even the optimists discussed in the last section of this study, quickly discover that actuality did not measure up to ideal, but many of them came to the conclusion, on philosophical and historical grounds, that it would never do so in the future. Others, still more extreme, were to question the very existence of the absolute ideals which they found so tempting.

Yet in one field absolute values still, for many writers, remained supreme, and in that field—that of literature and the arts—it was decadence, not progress, which was most widely proclaimed. An analysis of this phenomenon demands a separate chapter.

Chapter 12

The Aesthetic Norm

Taste is by no means arbitrary: it is founded upon incontestable principles. And the necessary consequence of this fact is that there should be no work of art which cannot be judged by the light of these principles. (D'Alembert, *Réflexions sur l'usage et sur l'abus de la philosophie dans les matières de goût*)[1]

The late seventeenth century had seen the construction of a well defined theory of progress in literature and the arts; Perrault and Fontenelle had sketched a system of aesthetics which augured well for progressionist doctrine in the following century. Yet in actuality the main current of the Enlightenment saw not a broad extension of the doctrine of artistic progress, but rather a fairly general diagnosis of decadence. What lay behind this curious reversal of historical optimism?

It is true that in two respects the doctrine of progress in literature and the fine arts now appeared to be on even firmer ground than before. First of all, increasing emphasis was put upon the moral content of artistic production. The amorality of the Classical French stage was the special target for criticism as eighteenth century aestheticians came to emphasize more and more the ethical aim of art. Pleasure, it was generally agreed, must not be the sole fruit of the arts; "the purpose of poetry," declared Marmontel, "is to make men, if possible, both happier and better...."[2] In the *Encyclopédie* a marked moralistic and utilitarian theory of art appeared under the

[1] *Oeuvres de d'Alembert*, IV, 327.

[2] *Eléments de littérature*, in *Oeuvres complètes de Marmontel* (Paris, 1818–1819), XIII, 443.

name of the German Sulzer. It is for art, he wrote, to make vice repulsive and virtue attractive; "the true end of the fine arts is the inculcation of a lively feeling for the true and the good."[3] Honest sentiments and useful ideas are the proper fruit of art, wrote Dupont de Nemours, while for Batteux, the most influential Classical aesthetician of the century, the good and the beautiful were so thoroughly mingled as to become indistinguishable.

And so, quite in line with the absolutist tradition of earlier French Classicism, yet another fixed standard for aesthetic judgment came to be widely accepted. For though the immutable Christian ethics of a Fénelon might give way to the philosophical imperatives of the Enlightenment, moral absolutism was scarcely less predominant on that account. "All the civilized nations of the world," wrote the Chevalier de Jaucourt in the *Encyclopédie*, "are in agreement on the essential points of ethics."[4] And D'Alembert added that "ethics possesses rules which are fixed and final"; a complete moral science may be deduced from the need for co-operation among men in society and from the mutual duties imposed by this need.[5] Thus the primary principles of the new code, which incidentally bore a striking resemblance to the old, became not only the infallible standard of human conduct but also an indispensable measure of the arts which were to influence that conduct.

And if the new ethical orientation was thought to permit further literary and artistic progress, the beneficent influence of Enlightened philosophy upon letters was likewise noted by a number of commentators. This role of philosophy in literature had been one of Fontenelle's crucial principles, and it was now defended, with more caution, by no less a figure than D'Alembert. Though D'Alembert granted a certain place to pure poetry, to art for sheer enjoyment's sake, at the same time he pointed out the greater merits of a poetry allied with philosophy. Poetry for him was to be whenever possible the vehicle of ideas, and should treat nothing to which the ordinary

[3] "Esthétique," *Supplément à l'Encyclopédie*, II, 872.
[4] Louis de Jaucourt, "Morale," *Encyclopédie, ou dictionnaire raisonné des sciences, des arts et des métiers* (Paris, Neuchâtel, 1751–1765), X, 702.
[5] *Discours préliminaire de l'Encyclopédie*, in *Oeuvres de d'Alembert*, I, 42.

4+

prose style was not equally applicable. Philosophy, as the ultimate synthesis of all phenomena, would be necessarily omnipresent, yet must leave to genius and to the arts their entire original freedom.

These views of D'Alembert, as shared by Sulzer and Marmontel among others, helped keep alive a certain interest in the old dispute for supremacy between the arts of the ancient and the modern world. If the Abbé Dubos raised an influential voice in praise of classical antiquity, the general trend perpetuated the moderate stand initiated by Fénelon and by Boileau himself in the later stages of the great Quarrel. From Chaudon and Pompignan to Marmontel, Grimm, and the Chevalier de Jaucourt came condemnations of the exclusive cult of either Ancients or Moderns, and exhortations to seek out beauty wherever it might be found. Yet even among the majority, it should be noted, the imitation of antique taste was still held to be the only sure route toward continued progress.

Thus the rivalry between ancient culture and modern artistic achievement lost much of its earlier significance. Gradually the axis of aesthetic comparison shifted in the eighteenth century as the great French age of Classicism became more and more distant. Increasingly the spirit and the works of classical antiquity became identified with those of the Age of Louis XIV, and with the firm establishment of this parallel the critics found themselves comparing the productions of their own day not with those of antiquity but with the more accessible works of the century before their own. Moreover, despite those progressionist elements in eighteenth century aesthetics which already have been noted, the comparison between the two centuries was nearly always unflattering to the later of the two. In the arts, therefore, the work of the seventeenth century Moderns became the bulwark of the eighteenth century conservatives, with the earlier victory of Modernism by now becoming a prominent support of the doctrine of decadence.

And so, as in contemporary England, talk of a decline in letters and the fine arts became loud. The decadence of painting was frequently remarked both by the *philosophes* and by their opponents, by Dupont and the *Encyclopédie* as well as by Clément and Rigoley. As to literature, since the day of Perrault himself a falling away from the heights of the great Classical school had been noted. An occasional commentator took refuge in a plea of mere dissimilarity between his own and the earlier age, but most writers could not escape a decisive value judgment. Even D'Alembert was forced to admit the comparative inferiority of his own century in certain types of literature, despite the rare merit of a number of contemporary writers. Marmontel bowed to a similar necessity, while upholding the continued progress of taste in matters of speculation rather than imagination. Both emphasized the exhaustion of talent after the seventeenth century outbursts of creativity, and the current abuse of that great heritage.

With D'Alembert and Marmontel came a host of lesser commentators deploring the pernicious innovations of their day and announcing the definitive decadence of literary taste. Fréron, Charpentier, Aquin de Chateaulyon, Gilbert, Rigoley, Pompignan, Clément, Sénac de Meilhan—each of these and many more added to the gloomy diagnosis. "The utter degradation of poetry," "the end of good taste," "the complete ruin menacing French literature from all quarters"—such are the typical phrases of this conservative school.[6] The best that can be hoped for the future, wrote Rémond de Saint-Mard, is the survival of pure taste in a few isolated writers, as during the decadence of ancient Rome.

Nor was this critique based upon that Romantic tint which in the course of the century came to color the Classical literary complexion. It was pre-eminently the disorder of eighteenth century literature which was condemned, and the loss of the clarity and simplicity, of the reasonableness and regularity of the standard Classical style which was regretted. For despite Diderot and the pre-Romantic movement—phenomena reserved here for later discussion—Classicism remained the established aesthetic dogma in France throughout the eighteenth century. Theory and practice alike

[6] Nicolas Joseph Laurent Gilbert, "Préface de l'auteur," in *Oeuvres complètes de Gilbert* (Paris, 1823), 3; Pierre Louis d'Aquin de Chateaulyon, *Satyre sur la corruption du goût et du style* (Liège, 1759), 29; Jean Jacques Lefranc de Pompignan, letter to an unknown person, January 19, 1750, quoted in François-Albert Duffo, *J. J. Lefranc, marquis de Pompignan: poète et magistrat, 1709-1784* (Paris, 1913), 476.

attested its continued power as the basic if not the unmodified aesthetic framework of the century; the works of André, Batteux, and Marmontel retained their popular appeal despite the attacks of a Dubos or a Diderot. And it was from the standpoint of the most orthodox Classicism that the literary and artistic decadence of the century was frequently measured.

With heroic obstinacy eighteenth century Classicism continued to assert the existence and validity of absolute aesthetic values. Here Marmontel, it must be said, was not decisively clear, though his belief in the possibility of a complete and regular system of poetry, submitted to one simple law which should be the common origin of all particular rules, denotes an aesthetic temperament which certainly is Classical in essence. Batteux was even more insistent upon the immutability of aesthetic laws and the existence of one unchangeable, ideal standard of beauty. And among the amateurs D'Alembert was no less definite in his position. "Taste," he wrote, ". . . is founded upon incontestable principles"; all works of art must be submitted to them for judgment.[7] Universal rules of aesthetics may be, and have been, formulated for all times and all places. At the same time, he continued, it is a matter of common observation that tastes do vary according to nation and age, but there is no question here of essential beauty, which is independent of all the variants of mode and convention.

The "imitation of nature" retained its place beside immutable values as one of the fundamental doctrines of eighteenth century Classical aesthetics, despite no small confusion as to the exact meaning of the term "nature." In many cases this "imitation of nature" was doubtless a simple formula with little real meaning, while upon occasion, as in the commentary of D'Alembert, the term took on a certain psychological precision. Yet the infinite richness and diversity of phenomena which "nature" embraced for the Abbé Dubos were utterly foreign to conventional Classicism; as in the seventeenth century it was a nature carefully chosen and embellished which was the norm—a nature best grasped through the study of earlier monu-

---

[7] *Réflexions sur l'usage et sur l'abus de la philosophie dans les matières de goût*, in *Oeuvres de d'Alembert*, IV, 327.

ments of art and literature. Countless plaints of decadence which was caused by this scorn for models are to be found in eighteenth century writings, with the models now of course including not only the works of antiquity but also those of the Age of Louis XIV.

Beauty as conceived within the main current of eighteenth century French thought comprised three vital qualities: the intellectual, the *sensible*, and the ethical. The place of morality, as noted above, was definable in relatively simple terms, but the balance between intellect and feeling was a matter of infinitely greater delicacy. As an issue between the respective claims of rules and genius, this problem had been met by the seventeenth century and had received a rough pragmatic solution which gave a role both to the flights of genius and to the sensible restraints of rules founded upon reason. And so the question rested also in the eighteenth century. But new complications now pushed to the fore—complications introduced by the alleged abuse of reason irrespective of rules.

Such were the questions of the *bel esprit* and the loss of naïveté which were often said to be hastening the decadence of literature. Naïveté, as with Boileau, certainly did not represent the totally artless; it was considered to be a calculated effect. It represented a legitimate use of reason, whereas *bel esprit* was seen as rationalism corrupted by the effeminacy and mannerism of current social behavior. *Bel esprit* was the precious and superficial brilliance which passed for a refined reason; it could only be summarized, in Clément's opinion, as "frivolous jargon," or in D'Alembert's words as "the childish art of making things appear more ingenious than they really are."[8] And its prevalence in eighteenth century letters was pointed out again and again and branded as a sure sign of decadence.

But the question of the abuse of reason in literature and the infringement of the rights of inspiration and feeling went deeper than the issue of *bel esprit*. What could be the proper role of philosophy itself in literary works?—or was it to be excluded entirely from

---

[8] Jean Marie Bernard Clément, *Nouvelles observations critiques, sur différens sujets de littérature* (Amsterdam, 1772), 304; D'Alembert, "Elocution," *Encyclopédie*, V, 524.

imaginative writing? That the century was not lacking in defenders of the beneficent role of philosophy has already been pointed out. But this foundation for a theory of literary progress was challenged not only by the pre-Romantics but also by many of the most orthodox Classicists whom the century could muster. This number, curiously enough, included some of the worst offenders against literary purity, but the formal opposition to philosophy in letters is rendered on that account perhaps all the more significant.

Even D'Alembert, who had so warmly championed the right use of philosophy in creative literature, did not hesitate to score its abuse. "The philosophical spirit," he wrote, "has spread into belles-lettres themselves; it is claimed that it is harmful to their progress, and indeed one must recognize the truth of that fact. Our century in its tendency toward analysis and synthesis seems determined to introduce cold didactic discussions into matters of feeling." Philosophy must beware of applying to aesthetic matters "principles which are true in themselves, but which have no relevance to those matters."[9] And Marmontel, also, tended to differentiate the realms of speculative and imaginative taste.

It is hardly surprising that the conservative opponents of the Enlightenment were particularly virulent in their attacks upon the pernicious introduction of philosophy into imaginative literature—a perversion for which the original responsibility of Fontenelle was widely assumed. The death of a poetic school which reasoned on the sublime was predicted, while the imaginative flights of earlier years were contrasted with the rational sang-froid which now was invading belles-lettres. "Poetry," wrote Clément, "abhors the jargon of pedants and the technical language of the sciences."[10] And Clément went on to sketch a general rule of literary decadence, in reference to a poem by Silius Italicus: "What characterizes it is a certain taste for philosophizing and moralizing which is common

[9] *Discours préliminaire de l'Encyclopédie,* in *Oeuvres de d'Alembert,* I, 78; D'Alembert, *Réflexions sur l'usage et sur l'abus de la philosophie dans les matières de goût,* in *Oeuvres,* IV, 331.

[10] Clément, *Observations critiques, sur la nouvelle traduction en vers françois des Georgiques de Virgile* (Geneva, 1771), 286.

enough among writers in decadent ages—writers who prefer to think rather than to feel, to reflect rather than to move."[11] Here, in a defender of rational aesthetic rules, in a writer saturated with the Classical dogmas of clarity and simplicity, the link with Romantic doctrine is clearly evident.

And the literary decadence of the day was demonstrated from a wide variety of other approaches. Throughout the discussion it was French works which above all were under consideration, but it is clear that for the average commentator the decadence of French literature, the standard of all European literature, was felt to be of universal significance. The translation into French of countless foreign works, good and bad, was branded by Fréron as an outstanding cause of the current depravation of taste. The ever-vigilant Clément was particularly alarmed by the English influence upon the French stage—an intrusion for which he held Voltaire largely responsible. To be sure, Voltaire did not adopt "all that theatrical filth which so delights the English public; but he imitated the multiplicity of incidents and extravagance of plot of the English authors, the disordered and continuous movement which they call action and which only causes confusion and turmoil, and that emphasis upon spectacle, décor, and pantomime which amuse the mob, for whom sight is the whole mind."[12]

If pernicious foreign influence was held to be a cause of French literary decline, the neglect of the great works of earlier ages by the reading public was considered to be a significant symptom of that decline. And the current pettiness prevalent in literary circles was seen as both cause and symptom. "The greatest misfortune of letters," wrote D'Alembert, "is not the scorn of those who ignore them, but rather the degradation caused by the very writers who cultivate them."[13] For cooperation and public spirit the literary world

[11] Clément, *Essais de critique sur la littérature ancienne et moderne* (Amsterdam, 1785), I, 75.

[12] Clément, *De la tragédie, pour servir de suite aux Lettres à Voltaire* (Amsterdam, 1784), I, 16–17.

[13] *Réflexions sur l'état présent de la république des lettres pour l'article "Gens de lettres,"* in *Oeuvres et correspondances inédites de d'Alembert* (Paris, 1887), 77.

had substituted caprice and jealousy, the use of satire and calumny, and the petty rivalries of exclusive sects.

The relationship of author to reading public was also seen by some as a factor contributing to the decadence of letters. In earlier years, sighed Marmontel, the lettered public was small and select, and the example of great talents favored good taste. Now, with an extension of the public, "it is the multitude which dominates the few, and the contagion of bad taste is spreading among all estates. If this revolution be carried through, the ruin of arts and letters will be complete."[14] Clément saw the problem as a constant one in all civilized ages and nations, in each of which the writer had to face the fact that the many were ignorant and crude, and that the persons of taste and discrimination were few indeed. "Evidently the degree of perfection reached by the arts among these different peoples has depended upon the relative complaisance of the artists for the taste of the many. . . ."[15] So it was that, according to some critics, quantity rather than quality had become the predominant goal of authorship. The mania for prolific writing was denounced from many quarters, and the advent of the "age of paper" was proclaimed.[16]

Finally, there was the question of criticism and creation. Criticism, Boileau had declared long before, is easy, but art difficult. The aesthetic wealth stored up in earlier years, wrote D'Alembert, had created a great fund of critical principles, while the brilliant Age of Louis XIV had nearly exhausted creative possibilities for the moment. Criticism, it was asserted, was replacing original flights of genius—and so yet another negative point was recorded on the aesthetic tally sheet of the century.

Thus current literary and artistic decadence was widely diagnosed by the Classical school of eighteenth century aesthetic criticism. Voltaire himself, as will be seen in a later chapter, contributed not a few lines to the critical chorus. And it seems clear that this criticism was not simply fleeting, not simply accidental, but rather inherent

[14] Marmontel, *Eléments de littérature*, in *Oeuvres complètes*, XII, 83.
[15] Clément, *De la tragédie*, I, 18–19.
[16] Clément, *Petit dictionnaire de la cour et de la ville* (London, 1788), II, 120.

in the very structure of Classicism. To look back with nostalgia to the past, to deprecate the relative shortcomings of the present, is virtually the inevitable fate of any philosophy which is based upon rigid, absolute principles, and which at the same time is historically minded and fundamentally authoritarian in its outlook. The Classicism of the seventeenth century, in its vigorous creativity, had never wholly succumbed to authoritarianism; the Classicism of the following decades submitted to it quite consciously, and so was doomed.

In aesthetic theory, then, one finds perhaps the clearest example of the failure of intellectual authoritarianism in the eighteenth century, and a striking illustration of the inadequacy of the revered principles of "nature" and of "reason." But new currents were to flow into the literature and arts of the Enlightenment, and indeed into the whole intellectual atmosphere of the age. Romanticism, empiricism, relativism—these were to challenge more and more imperiously the regnant Classicism, rationalism, and intellectual absolutism of the century. The revolution which they wrought in the major fields of cultural endeavor, and in historical philosophy as well, will form the substance of the fourth major division of this study.

Part IV

Historical Flux—Facts in a Changing Universe

Chapter 13

The Two Empiricisms

Only facts are interesting; all the rest is error and lies.
(Grimm, *Correspondance littéraire*)[1]

If the French Enlightenment contributed little that was novel to the eternal epistemological problem, this problem remained much in the minds of the serious thinkers of the age. After the mid-point of the century the discussion of the origin of ideas and the methods of knowledge and its limits commonly took the form of a commentary upon the system of Condillac, who in 1746 had published his important "Essay on the Origin of Human Understanding." But the simple acceptance of sensation as the foundation of knowledge did not by any means clear away all practical difficulties surrounding the nature and the processes of human understanding. And so in the eighteenth century as in many other ages a perpetual difference, latent or overt, existed between the advocates of three potential modes of cognition: observation, reason, and feeling. Nor did an acceptance of all of these modes by any one writer clarify his position significantly, for the vital question of proportionate emphasis remained to be answered. Such attempts as were made by D'Alembert and others to categorize the respective realms of application for the three methods must be regarded with suspicion, for in practice the same writers seldom maintained rigorously their own distinctions.

Reserving for a later section the role of sentiment and imagination, one may return to the persistent problem of rationalism and empiricism. The crucial role of reason in eighteenth century thought

[1] Friedrich Melchior Grimm and others, *Correspondance littéraire, philosophique, et critique* (Paris, 1877–1882), V, 468.

has already been noted; the restrictions placed upon reason remain to be summarized. For here lie several of the determinants of the historical philosophy of the period.

Indifference or hostility toward the great rational, abstract systems of the seventeenth century arose in the course of that century itself; the mature Enlightenment simply perpetuated and elaborated the approach of a Saint-Evremond or a Bayle. Despite their conviction of the reality of an orderly and rational world, the *philosophes* were equally convinced that man could not systematize phenomena by the light of pure reason alone. The latter conviction was the basis for Grimm's insistence on the importance of "facts," for the attacks of the *Encyclopédie* upon ancient Greek philosophy, and for Condillac's criticism of seventeenth century thought. No abstract system, according to Condillac, could possibly embrace all the many facets of a question, since no abstract system could avoid altogether the pitfall of mistaking vague words for precise realities. And wrote D'Alembert several years later: "The taste for systems, more proper for flattering the imagination than for enlightening the mind, today has been almost completely banished from good philosophical works. One of our best thinkers, the Abbé de Condillac, seems to have administered it the final blows."[2] Both Condillac and D'Alembert saw observation and experience as replacing the spirit of system, the futile quest for ultimate principles, in science and philosophy.

Thus, while its role remained of great importance in the eighteenth century, reason was commonly held to be efficacious only in conjunction with observation and experience. And though empiricism and reason were held to be practically synonymous, in cases of evident conflict in the realm of scientific method it was reason which was ordinarily forced to give way. This situation was accentuated in the course of the century as the natural sciences and the empirical method became familiar to a growing segment of the educated public.

The implications and techniques of empiricism were numerous, but sensationalism was its fundamental philosophy. Sensations, according to Condillac, are the sole ultimate source of knowledge;

[2] *Discours préliminaire de l'Encyclopédie*, in *Oeuvres de d'Alembert*, I, 77.

through the senses, and especially through the sense of touch, man knows the external world, and through them, by progressive modification, his understanding, his passions, and his actions are made possible. "The only method of acquiring knowledge," wrote Condillac, "is to go back to the origin of our ideas, to follow their generation and to compare them from all possible angles; this is what I call analysis."[3] And on these broad principles the *philosophes* of the second half of the century were to be in general agreement.

Sensationalism, then, explained man's knowledge of things and of values as deriving ultimately from the action of external stimuli upon a passive yet receptive mind. This plastic quality of the human mind became responsible for mental and ethical growth and was, for a number of writers, the guarantee of intellectual and moral perfectibility. Education became the key to progress, for in its broadest sense education was the sum of all sense experience. Helvétius above all drew this sanguine conclusion, and for him and for many of his contemporaries right education might be instituted by the action of enlightened legislation. Education and legislation became all-important in the development of the individual and the progress of the race.

The technique of progress thus became for some thinkers both well-defined and practicable. But a grave difficulty lurked in the sensationalist scheme: would rigid control over the presentation of sensations be possible? In the ordinary course of events the occurrence of sense impressions seemed to be simply fortuitous. If men were completely the product of environment, could they deliberately change this environment, and indeed could they want to do so? Seldom if ever did the average *philosophe* face these questions squarely; rather he seems to have simply assumed that his own exceptional insight would penetrate the artificiality and error of bad environment, to arrive at last at the valid components of experience. It was widely held that if man could understand his environment, he could change it. Knowledge, in other words, was power.

---

[3] *Essai sur l'origine des connoissances humaines,* in *Oeuvres de Condillac* (Paris, 1798), I, 111.

But this answer to the sensationalist-environmentalist question was unsatisfactory. That this fact was at least dimly perceived is indicated by a widespread but uneasy tendency toward a drastic alternative: universal determinism. Yet an explicit doctrine of unqualified mechanical determinism was rarely proposed and was in no sense typical of the age. Condillac himself vehemently denied any association with the doctrines of mechanism and fatalism, but his system undoubtedly swayed other thinkers in those directions. Grimm, D'Alembert, and even Helvétius revealed deterministic leanings at times, and in La Mettrie, Holbach, and Sade determinism became a central dogma. And this determinism of natural law extended inevitably from the external world to man himself, for man was inextricably a part and product of the natural world. In a later chapter the divergent potentialities of this system will be discussed; for the moment one need only note that, as with Fontenelle, determinism might well serve to underline the inevitability of error and evil and thus run directly counter to that perfectibility by education and laws which from another viewpoint sensationalism had seemed to guarantee.

Thus the theory of human perfectibility through environmental reform involved major logical difficulties. But the optimism of sensationalism was challenged not only by internal theoretical contradictions, but also by the data of direct experience. The observable error, folly, and misery in the world at times gave pause even to the most hopeful of *philosophes*. Here was a direct and immediate empiricism, as contrasted with the second-hand, and in effect largely theoretical, empiricism of a sensationalist philosophy which ordinarily permitted contact with reality only after a heavy growth of deduction, analysis, and synthesis had been penetrated. In Condillac himself one can find both the direct and the indirect types of empiricism; "our sole object," he wrote, "must be to consult experience, and to reason only from indubitable facts."[4] Despite his own *a priori* methods and despite his frequent relegation of fact to a distant background of original sensations, Condillac remained in theory a proponent of the experimental method.

---

[4] *Essai sur l'origine des connoissances humaines*, in *Oeuvres*, I, 25.

Yet unquestionably a vast distance separates the spirit of Condillac and that of such a natural scientist as Buffon. The work of the latter consists primarily of a mass of descriptive data; the direct observation of facts and the description of individual phenomena are his method. Similar observation and description, on a less grand scale, became the preoccupation of many a lesser scientist and the amusement of many a wealthy amateur in the eighteenth century. Whether this direct empiricism involved experiment, observation and experience, or simple common sense, a point of contact with factual reality was invariably maintained.

Undoubtedly a direct empirical approach in the natural sciences might remain a self-contained compartment in one's intellectual life, isolated from one's general world-picture. More often, however, observation in the natural sciences seems to have come into conflict with general habits of abstract rationalism, and increasingly such observation appeared to be allied with historical, sociological, and psychological studies. A clear example of the application of empirical observation to these studies may be found in the pessimistic reflections which upon occasion in the eighteenth century followed from the observation of the ways of man and the world.

Now, pessimism is certainly not the sole and inevitable consequence of a realistic study of the world, as the continued appearance of optimistic realists amply demonstrates—yet it is true that while abstract philosophical systems are nearly always idealistic and optimistic, the realism of hard experience contains vast potentialities for pessimism. The study of contemporary man and society, and of past history, may only serve to emphasize those constant elements of frivolity and folly, perversity and evil-doing, which continually threaten the optimism of the abstract idealist; history, sociology, and psychology reveal not only truth and virtue but also error and vice as vital determinants of man's earthly course. Among the successors of Bayle and of Fontenelle was numbered not only Voltaire but also the Marquis de Sade.

Nor was the pessimistic empirical current of the Enlightenment unrelated to the ancient Christian tradition. If from the Fathers to Pascal and Bossuet the evil and perverse qualities of man had been often demonstrated by the light of faith and by experience alike, the traditionalists of the eighteenth century generally took a no less pessimistic view of human potentialities.

But it is in the circle of the scientists and of the *philosophes* that the more significant conclusions were drawn in this respect. In Voltaire and Vauvenargues, in Grimm and Madame du Deffand, pessimism on human nature was an outstanding intellectual feature. And the disillusionment of Buffon, the exact observer of man and his environment, is peculiarly interesting. Imbued with a high sense of man's real dignity and convinced even of his ultimate perfectibility, Buffon could evince only horror and dismay before that persistent tendency toward evil which he had noted in man throughout history. "How much," he mused, "man could do to better the lot of his race if only he would always direct his will by his intelligence! ... It appears that from time immemorial man has devoted less attention to reflection on the good than to the pursuit of evil. Both of these trends are comprised in every society, and since fear is the most potent of all mob emotions it was the great malefactors who at first most forcibly struck the imagination of man. Later those who brought diversion to man were most highly considered, and only after long centuries of serving these idols of false honor and sterile pleasure has man recognized that science is his true glory, and peace his true happiness."[5]

To be sure, Buffon's conclusion here is optimistic; he seems to have held consistently to a doctrine of ultimate progress, though it was a progress punctuated by many discouraging lapses. Such too in general was Condillac's position, and in his "Ancient History" he noted sadly that "time, which destroys everything, is slow in destroying prejudice."[6] "Doubtless," he wrote elsewhere, "we are far indeed from that enlightened century which could guarantee all posterity against the possibility of error. In all probability we shall never reach that age; we shall come closer as the centuries pass, but it will always escape our grasp. For the philosopher, time is a vast

---

[5] Buffon, *Histoire naturelle, générale et particulière*, IV, 41–42.

[6] *Histoire ancienne*, in *Cours d'études pour l'instruction du prince de Parme*, in *Oeuvres de Condillac*, X, 150.

racecourse: truths are scattered here and there, embedded in the mass of errors which fill the whole. The ages pass, errors accumulate, truth is elusive, and the athletes compete for prizes distributed by a blind spectator."[7]

In the work of Buffon and Condillac the hope for progress is genuine, but because of man's observable and persistent tendency toward error and evil they see his upward climb as slow and uncertain. These *philosophes* differ perhaps more in degree than in kind from Turgot and Condorcet, but the difference remains real. Other writers, and especially those with deterministic leanings, were to be much less confident of the reform of man than were Buffon and Condillac.[8]

But, one may ask, how significantly did historical empiricism contribute to this restriction of optimism? How important, indeed, was history in the formation of the eighteenth century mind? Certainly the period has been widely reproached, and justifiably in certain respects, for its lack of an historical sense. Many an Enlightened thinker would have agreed substantially with the severe dictum of Marcel Proust: "The muse which has gathered together everything which the higher muses of art and philosophy have rejected, everything which is not founded in truth but which is simply contingent, though to be sure it does reveal certain laws of its own—this muse is History."[9] This Proustian conception is essentially Cartesian, and so too is the common eighteenth century view of history as an accumulation of error which must in the future be superseded. Condillac's cosmic racecourse served to pictorialize a conception of history which is frequently encountered in the works of the French Enlightenment. History was in general a gloomy panorama before the eighteenth century eye, and for many writers past and future were clearly discontinuous.

Yet for the Enlightenment history was not totally valueless or irrelevant, nor was the belief in historical discontinuity by any means unqualified. Voltaire, who indeed was exceptional in this respect,

[7] *Traité des animaux*, in *Oeuvres*, III, 448.
[8] See esp. chapters on Montesquieu, Voltaire, La Mettrie, and Sade, below.
[9] Marcel Proust, *Albertine disparue*, in *A la recherche du temps perdu* (Paris, 1919–1927), VII, 164.

was often inclined to see human error as the link between past, present, and future. Turgot and Condorcet, on the other hand, discovered the growing strength of reason in the historical past, and saw the future as promising the continuation and acceleration of this happy trend. Perhaps a more general view than either of these, though often allied with the second, was the recognition of past errors and of the pressing current need for their suppression, together with the conviction that these very errors would be a useful guide for man in the future. Such was the view, for example, of Condillac and D'Alembert, of Dumarsais and Helvétius; history in their opinion was the teacher of mankind, the great transmitter of human experience. Wrote Condillac: "I consider history to be a collection of observations offering to citizens of all classes the truths relative to them. If we learn to draw upon those elements useful to us we shall become more wise through the experience of past ages."[10] "The reading of history," asserted Dumarsais, "is very useful for giving us experience; it teaches us facts and shows us the happy and unhappy events which were their outcome."[11]

Thus recognizing the great practical importance of the study of history, the *philosophes* devoted a large portion of their efforts to historical labors. The mathematician D'Alembert gave history his occasional attention, and more than half of the collected works of the psychologist-philosopher Condillac are historical studies. An investigation of the contents of a cross-section of late eighteenth century libraries has revealed that over a quarter of their books were works of history.[12] Certainly, in the restricted sense of the time devoted to the reading of history and to historical investigation, history was far indeed from being neglected in this period. Yet it was very often a particular type of history which was emphasized. "Historical science when not enlightened by philosophy," wrote D'Alembert, "is

[10] "Discours préliminaire," in *Cours d'études pour l'instruction du prince de Parme*, in *Oeuvres de Condillac*, V, pp. xlv–xlvi.

[11] C. Chesneau Dumarsais, "Expérience," *Encyclopédie, ou dictionnaire raisonné des sciences, des arts et des métiers*, VI, 297.

[12] Daniel Mornet, "Les enseignements des bibliothèques privées (1750–1780)," *Revue d'histoire littéraire de la France*, XVII (1910), 449–496.

the lowest ranking of all realms of knowledge."[13] One should concern oneself, he continued, with the useful in history, with those historical figures who have aided mankind in its search for knowledge; the history simply of rulers and governments is often the mere record of man's misfortunes and crimes.

Despite this typical preoccupation with the practical and immediate value of history, many eighteenth century writers did view history at times in a more detached manner. The methods of historical scholarship which had been so far advanced by seventeenth century erudition were still generally respected, especially before the polemics of the last pre-Revolutionary decades came to dominate literature. Like Bayle, later historians indubitably delivered themselves over from time to time to the luxury of examining facts for facts' sake, and an Abbé Dubos certainly possessed a considerable feeling for the past, quite apart from its relevance to the problems of his own day. But whatever might have been the peculiar orientation of the various writers of the Enlightenment, one cannot deny them a true sense of the dynamism of history; whatever their view of the historical course of mankind, movement always characterized this course. Whether or not this movement appeared to be purposeful, almost invariably there remained an impression of a world in the making, and of a world which, in its dynamic complexity, stubbornly refused to adjust itself wholly to the neat, abstract principles championed by the Enlightenment.

Thus the empiricism of history and of science, together with an inscrutable philosophical determinism, came to challenge the beautiful simplicity of historical optimism. Since often these trends appeared simply to underline the incorrigibility of mankind, human perfectibility as presumed by an uncomplicated sensationalism became difficult at best. Rationalistic idealism, if never completely destroyed, was forced again and again to modify its position. Moreover, the very bases of a rational measurement of progress and decadence were to be shaken in a most disturbing fashion by the

[13] *Mémoires et réflexions sur Christine, reine de Suède*, in *Oeuvres de d'Alembert*, II, 119.

data of experience. Sensationalism, like the older rationalism, sought primarily to establish knowledge on the sound foundation of indubitable and immutable principles. Direct observation and historical study, on the other hand, brought into question the adequacy of abstract rules and simple sensations as the measure of man's development. Complexity and indeed confusion characterized the new trend; historical and sociological facts received new weight, and the way to subjectivism and relativism was thrown open.

Chapter 14

The New Aesthetics

> One might say that each region has been able to produce
> but a single harvest, and that, once the soil has been
> exhausted by its own fecundity, its fertility can be renewed
> only by centuries of lying fallow. (Marmontel, *Eléments de
> littérature*)[1]

Much has been written, and few indisputable conclusions drawn,
concerning the breakdown of Classical aesthetics in the French Enlightenment. With the very nature of the pre-Romantic movement
so radically in question one can hardly anticipate conclusive quantitative judgments as to its effects. At best one can simply point out
certain qualitative changes brought about by the new aesthetics, and
show that these were not without their significance in the changing
eighteenth century conception of mankind's artistic and literary
development.

Already mention has been made of the growing skepticism with
which the Enlightenment came to view the earlier search for
absolute values and final causes in the realm of science and philosophy. This caution of the *philosophes* did not limit significantly
the range of human progress as they saw it, nor did it restrain them
from envisaging certain ethical and political ends which were virtually immutable and beyond criticism. It is probable, however, that
this scientific and philosophical anti-absolutism, together with the
study of history, did have its part in the gradual eighteenth century
breakdown of absolute values in literature and the fine arts.

Certainly the transitional character of the aesthetics and the
creative arts of the Enlightenment is undeniable; especially toward

[1] *Oeuvres complètes de Marmontel*, XII, 70.

the middle of the century the reign of Classicism was challenged vigorously. If the old rules, the imitation of classical antiquity and of the Age of Louis XIV, were still upheld by the majority, more and more these rules were both neglected in practice and undermined in theory. The transition is symbolized perhaps best of all by Marmontel, who doubtless owed much of his popularity with his contemporaries to his eclectic mediocrity, to his ability for appearing simultaneously in all aesthetic camps. Temperamentally a Classicist, as has been noted above, Marmontel at the same time initiated a cautious attack upon the ancient rules and the eternal infallibility of antiquity. Increasingly the eighteenth century shifted its aesthetic emphasis from externally imposed standards to the dictates of artistic inspiration, from objective rules to subjective genius, from things to men. As Bury has pointed out, the reigning doctrines of psychology made man the measure of all things; the older abstract imperatives lost much of their appeal.[2]

In short, a revolt from the strict ties of tradition and rationalism was due. The great Classical artists had not been devoid of feeling, sentiment, or passion, but the eighteenth century chafed against the old restraints which once had been borne so gracefully. More and more after 1750 the weight shifted in the uneasy balance between genius and rules. Observed one critic in 1768: "Genius, enemy of constraint, loses ardor and soars less high when it is denied free flight."[3]

Somewhat earlier a greater critic had written in the *Encyclopédie*: "Rules and aesthetic laws seek to shackle genius, but it escapes to soar to the sublime, the pathetic and the great.... There are few errors in Locke and too few truths in Shaftesbury; the former however is simply a broad, penetrating, and correct thinker, while the latter is a genius of the first order. Locke saw, and Shaftesbury created and built. To Locke we owe certain great truths coldly ascertained, methodically developed, and dryly announced, while to

---

[2] J. B. Bury, *The Idea of Progress: An Inquiry into its Origin and Growth* (London, 1924), 161.

[3] Louis Charpentier, *Causes de la décadence du goût sur le théâtre* (Amsterdam, 1768), I, 10.

Shaftesbury we owe various brilliant systems which are often ill founded but full of sublime insights—and even in his moments of error he pleases and persuades by the charm of his eloquence."[4]

Not analysis, then, but feeling and insight mark the true work of genius, according to Diderot. His approach, which will be examined in more detail in a later chapter, was by no means uncommon in his century, nor were he and Rousseau the lone French heralds of Romanticism. The Abbé Dubos had seen the excitation of artificial passions as the mission of art; for him, as later for Buffon and D'Alembert among others, taste and creativity derived primarily not from reason but from feeling. But clearer cases even than these are the number of creative writers who throughout the century maintained the literary rights of the emotions and of *sensibilité*: such for example were Marivaux and Nivelle de la Chaussée, the Abbé Prévost and Bernardin de Saint-Pierre.

These movements in literary theory and practice left their mark in the historical philosophy of the Enlightenment, difficult to define though this effect may be. With those rare writers who, largely under English and German influence, delivered themselves over to despair and melancholy during the latter part of the century, a variety of rustic primitivism became the cultural ideal. But this anti-progressionist ideal seemed, at least on the surface, to be more than countered by the new optimistic concept of the expansion of art introduced by the enemies of Classicism. On the stage, for example, the gradual crumbling of the old rules made possible other genres than the traditional tragedy and comedy, and the *drame* offered a hitherto unsuspected field for progress.

And the new aesthetics made progress possible in many other matters of artistic technique. Classical aesthetics, devoted to fixed principles and standards, had defined progress in terms of increasing efficiency in the use of established techniques, notably through the application of experience and of ethical and philosophical principles. But for the opponents of Classicism there were wider fields to be conquered; nature was still to be imitated, but not in its former unrealistic and restricted form. Increasingly, nature came to be viewed

[4] Diderot, "Génie" (*Encyclopédie*), *Oeuvres complètes*, XV, 37–39.

as approximating the complex diversity of man's actual environment, and more and more fields were opened to the ambitious author.

It is significant that the new aesthetics was less violently critical of Classical literature than one might expect. If there was little talk, among the pre-Romantics, of the decadence of contemporary Classicism, this virtual silence was doubtless occasioned not only by indifference but also by the simple fact that they possessed few solid standards for judging decadence. Of course some working standards were maintained, such as the desirability of promoting morality through the arts. Dubos, Marmontel, and others sought to establish the relative merit of works of art and literature by gathering the relevant opinions of all ages and all nations. The common opinion of mankind through the years became the new standard—a provisional standard, but a standard nevertheless. Clearly, however, this was not a basis of judgment altogether applicable to contemporary works.

The pre-Romantics, then, saw an expanding field open before the arts. But, with their dearth of objective aesthetic values, could they demonstrate that this expansion denoted progress and not simply change? Could expansion be considered good by definition alone? To these questions one searches in vain for a conclusive answer. But a significant trend may be noted in the thought of the opponents of Classicism—the trend toward historical relativism.

Already, without the trappings of historical analogy, an aesthetic relativism was implied in the growing emphasis upon individual creative inspiration. This relativism took on historical garb when consideration of the individual was supplemented by an empirical and historical approach to the art-producing civilization. Here the effect of the cultural environment upon the arts came to be considered, and here the artistic idiosyncrasies of each civilization were explained as far as possible by the broader characteristics of that civilization. From this study there could result no conception of simple or linear progress or decadence in the arts, but only a kaleidoscopic picture of cyclical or fluctuating development.

The clearest and most original eighteenth century exposition of this historical relativism of aesthetic phenomena was produced in

1719 by the Abbé Dubos—thus demonstrating, incidentally, that chronological distinctions here are by no means rigid, and that the "new aesthetics" was in large part contemporary with the old. The three volumes of "Critical Reflections on Poetry and Painting," despite their literary deficiencies, form one of the most important, and most undeservedly forgotten, works of the eighteenth century. One may still say with D'Alembert that "the Abbé Dubos is one of those men who possess more merit than reputation."[5]

An empiricist and a sensationalist in the manner of Locke, Dubos approached aesthetics from a position differing basically from that of his contemporaries. Aesthetics for him, to a high if not an exclusive degree, was a question not of abstractions and dogma but of experience and contingent facts. He deplored the current substitution of speculative reason for practical experience, "the best master which the human race has ever had," and turned to observation and history in order to discover the nature and destiny of literature and the fine arts.[6] For his day his historical sense was unusually well developed; no French writer of his generation, save possibly his younger contemporary Montesquieu, had his feeling for the diversity and uniqueness of the various ages of history.

Dubos explains the differences among the cultures of the world, and hence the reasons for the varying nature and fecundity of artistic production, as stemming from two major groups of circumstances, the "moral" and the physical." As moral causes of variation he lists those circumstances which affect the developmental pace of the arts without involving any basic change in the nature of artistic genius. Such, he states, are the general state of the nation in question, the attitude of the ruler and the public toward the arts, and the excellence of living masters who may instruct the younger writers and painters. But Dubos, after stating these conditions, gives little attention to them, for he considers them of relatively minor importance.

Much more space in the "Critical Reflections" is devoted to the physical background for cultural variations, for Dubos holds that

[5] *Eloge de J. B. Dubos*, in *Oeuvres de d'Alembert*, III, 203.
[6] Jean Baptiste Dubos, *Réflexions critiques sur la poésie et sur la peinture* (Paris, 1755), II, 477.

the physical factors normally outweigh the moral. In many ages and nations, according to him, letters have not flourished despite the most favorable moral circumstances, and while sometimes the fine arts and letters make sudden progress though the moral factor has not changed, at others they decline despite the strongest efforts to sustain them. Dubos then goes on to discuss the operation of the physical factors. He commences with the individual; taste, he writes, is the product of personal circumstances. "Our taste depends upon our physical organs, our present inclinations, and the condition of our mind. When our taste changes it is not because someone has persuaded us to change it, but because some physical change has taken place in our bodies." "Genius is . . . a plant which, as it were, grows by itself, but the quality, like the quantity, of its fruit depends a great deal upon the method of cultivation."[7] And as in the cultivation of plants, so in the cultivation of minds the climate is of vast importance. Thus Dubos adheres to the tradition of Fénelon and Madame Dacier, and contributes to later aesthetic theory, in advancing the theory of "climate" to help account for historical variations in artistic taste and productivity.

Unlike Dubos, most of the later eighteenth century aestheticians were to emphasize the potentialities for moral advance which resided in art and literature; one need only recall the tone of Diderot and Rousseau in these years. And this emphasis upon ethical values, fixed and authoritative in essence, was to restrict to some degree the relativism that was invading the arts. In the work of Dubos, however, this restraint is largely absent. Eternal rules of taste became for him an absurdity, for under any given circumstances the type of artistic creation depended, he believed, upon time and place, and upon the human characteristics imparted by these influences.

Dubos' aesthetic iconoclasm, in theory, was extreme indeed, and was combatted vigorously by Batteux and other aestheticians of the century. Yet he was much read; it is probable that he influenced Montesquieu, and Marmontel in his perpetual indecision strongly echoed at times the theories of Dubos. Though Marmontel seems to have retained his faith in the existence of an essential, immutable

[7] *Réflexions critiques*, I, 516; II, 45.

standard of beauty above all the fleeting vagaries of time and place, here and there in his work one finds the most unqualified assertions of the great role of climate. "The climate above all," he wrote, "determines the degree of energy, activity, sensitivity, and warmth in the character of men, and hence their natural inclinations."[8]

And upon one occasion Marmontel seems to have denied unequivocally any permanence of taste or, in fact, of any values. Taste changes, he then stated, even as the "natural" changes, and "the natural is composed of those qualities and those accidents which vary according to the age, to conditions and climates, to the forms of society and the various peculiarities implanted by that society upon men's minds and characters. So it is that truth differs from truth, not only from one people to another or from one age to another, but also in the same place and time from one man to another, and in the same man according to the influence of passions and of external events."[9]

In view of those Classical tendencies evident elsewhere in his work it would appear unwise to take those words of Marmontel altogether at their face value. The relativist position of Dubos, on the other hand, is seldom seriously compromised. And, except in the case of the natural sciences, which he saw as progressing by the simple accumulation of facts, the measurement of human progress across the ages became with Dubos an impossibility. Each age, for him, possessed its own standards of value, and even these might vary from decade to decade. Productivity as well as taste was subject to rise and decline, and history became the scene of endless cyclical fluctuation, in the arts as in nearly all other fields.[10]

However, the belief in cyclical fluctuation was by no means peculiar to Dubos, nor even to the relativist tradition in general. Frequently the concept of decadence according to a standard of absolute aesthetic values was combined with an historical view of artistic decline. The point may be illustrated by the doctrine of the necessary exhaustion of the arts—a doctrine widely discussed in the

---

[8] *Eléments de littérature*, in *Oeuvres complètes de Marmontel*, XIV, 264.
[9] *Eléments de littérature*, in *Oeuvres complétes*, XII, 31.
[10] Dubos, *Réflexions critiques*, II, 335.

eighteenth century in England as well as in France, and comprising elements both of historical relativism and of the most dogmatic value judgment.

It was a truism of the Classical school of aesthetics that "everything has its limits."[11] In nearly all quarters analogies with the passing of all natural phenomena were drawn in support of the view that the arts flourish in one period only to decay and die; regularly the fear was expressed that the periodic exhaustion of the arts was an inevitable law of nature. Neither in the fine arts nor in literature could the counter-current of optimism silence the persistent assertion of the necessary exhaustion of subjects and of methods of treatment. The noontide of French genius and taste, wrote Bricaire de la Dixmerie, was reached in the great Age of Louis XIV, but "every day has two parts. Our fathers enjoyed the first, while we enjoy the second. In their time they picked certain flowers which have lost for us a part of their bloom; we harvest those fruits which then had not reached ripeness."[12]

And Marmontel carried the parallel farther. The best subjects for literature, he wrote, are limited; after a great period of artistic production the field is less easily cultivated, and letters decline for centuries. "One might say that each region has been able to produce but a single harvest, and that, once the soil has been exhausted by its own fecundity, its fertility can be renewed only by centuries of lying fallow.... Under the magnificent reign of Louis XIV the vast field of poetry, which for ages had been lying uncultivated and gradually storing up strength, resembled a new and fecund territory where vegetation is impatient to recompense the first efforts of cultivation.... Today, with this rich surface exhausted, one must dig deep; and, following a cycle which is entirely natural, the season of preparing new growth is succeeding the season of harvesting."[13]

Other writers, such as Sénac de Meilhan, saw the problem in terms

---

[11] Nicolas Bricaire de la Dixmerie, *Les deux âges du goût et du génie français* (The Hague, 1769), 525; cf. Louis de Jaucourt, "Sculpture," *Encyclopédie, ou dictionnaire raisonné des sciences, des arts et des métiers*, XIV, 839.

[12] Bricaire de la Dixmerie, *Les deux âges du goût*, p. liv.

[13] *Eléments de littérature*, in *Oeuvres complètes de Marmontel*, XII, 70; *Poétique françoise* (Paris, 1763), I, 32.

of the replacement of originality and freshness by uninspired imitation. His own age, he declared, was producing "more enlightened critics and amateurs, and fewer men of great talent," than the preceding century. "Impotence, admiration of the past, the self-love which comes from age and from the insensitivity of a withered soul, and finally the lust for money—all these seem to portray the sexagenarian character of the century."[14]

The critic Charpentier, like Sénac, stressed the inevitable exhaustion of talents, but now with the support of specific historical analogy. "The Greeks were original in the arts and sciences; all paths seemed to be open to them, and the methods which they employed appeared to them to be the fruit of their own research and their own meditations. This high idea of themselves kindled their genius, and unlike their successors they did not have to take precautions against resembling earlier writers. . . . There has never been an author who has not felt more ease and more fire when approaching new subjects than when using those which have already been treated.[15]

And Charpentier compared the literary and artistic productions of the Romans most unfavorably with those of the Greeks. "It appears," he concluded, "that such is the fate of those peoples who succeed each other without break and who consider the works of their predecessors simply as objects for imitation. . . . The interval between the Greeks and the Romans was too short."[16] Imitation, he felt, was always a constraining force, though it might have its value when many centuries had passed between model and imitator. In this latter case, "the changed circumstances furnish new and happy applications as well as different interests and new situations which take objects out of their original setting and thus denature them somewhat, so as to efface those traits of resemblance which otherwise would be too evident."[17]

In this judgment, with somewhat less emphasis upon external

---

[14] Gabriel Sénac de Meilhan, *Considérations sur l'esprit et les mœurs* (London, 1787), 58.

[15] Charpentier, *Causes de la décadence du goût sur le théâtre*, I, 10–11.

[16] *Causes de la décadence du goût sur le théâtre*, I, 9–13.

[17] *Causes de la décadence du goût sur le théâtre*, I, 14–15.

than upon internal causes, Condillac concurred. As taste progresses, he wrote, so does enthusiasm for the arts; when taste reaches the limit of its development, the enthusiasm for creative work declines, and we "apply ourselves more to the discovery of faults than to the appreciation of beauty.... Aesthetic analysis closely resembles chemical analysis: both destroy the object while reducing it to its components. Thus we find ourselves between two perils: if we simply abandon ourselves to the impression which beauty imparts, we feel it without understanding it, while if on the other hand we attempt to analyze it, it is dissipated and our warmth of feeling is cooled.... Thus taste declines as soon as it has made such progress as it can make, and its decadence occurs precisely in that age which considers itself the most enlightened. For in that age one reasons better on the beautiful, and on that very account feels it less."[18]

Changes in literary tastes, according to Condillac, parallel the growth and decline of language. Those forces which sustain life and movement in letters lead ultimately, even in writers of talent, to a ruinous quest for novelty of expression. "The ease of copying their defects soon persuades mediocre minds that they too can attain similar reputation. Then it is that is born the reign of subtle and denatured thought, of precious antitheses and brilliant paradoxes, of frivolous turns, unnatural expressions, and words created unnecessarily—in a word, the reign of the jargon of *beaux esprits* spoiled by defective metaphysics. The public applauds, and frivolous and ridiculous works of the moment increase in number. Bad taste passes into the arts and sciences alike, and talent becomes more and more rare."[19]

The diagnosis of contemporary artistic decline offered by D'Alembert, for the moment a Classicist, is not dissimilar. "Taste and the art of writing make rapid progress in a short period of time, once the true route is opened. Scarcely does a man of great genius glimpse the beautiful but he perceives it in its whole breadth. The imitation of *la belle nature* seems to be confined to certain limits quickly reached in one or two generations, and the following generation

[18] *Traité de l'art d'écrire*, in *Oeuvres de Condillac*, VII, 396–397.
[19] *Essai sur l'origine des connoissances humaines*, in *Oeuvres*, I, 452–453.

can only imitate its predecessors. But it is never content with this sharing of glory; the riches already acquired excite the desire to increase them. And thus the new generation wishes to add to its heritage, and in so doing, far from surpassing this heritage, it simply overshoots its mark. At a single time, then, there exist more good critical principles, greater knowledge, more good judges, and fewer good works; no longer does one say of a book that it is good, but rather that it is the work of a man of cultured mind. So it is that the age of Demetrius and Phalerius immediately follows that of Demosthenes, the age of Lucan and Seneca that of Cicero and Virgil, and our age that of Louis XIV."[20]

Contemporary taste, continued D'Alembert, is in imminent danger of falling into complete barbarism; a false *bel esprit* is irresistibly taking over the realm of letters. But, he added, this barbarism will be its own remedy. "For everything has its regular fluctuations, and darkness will give way in time to a new century of light. We shall be all the more dazzled by the new daylight for having been in the darkness for some time. This darkness will be in itself a most destructive sort of anarchy, yet it may have its useful consequences."[21]

Historical analogy, as in the comments of Charpentier and D'Alembert, was frequently drawn upon to buttress these diagnoses of aesthetic decay. Though it was with the literary decline of Greece and Rome that the contemporary state of the arts was most commonly compared, Marmontel, among others, went somewhat farther; for him, France after Louis XIV was comparable to Greece in the days of the Sophists, to Rome after Augustus, and to Italy after the age of Leo X. This fourfold classification of the great ages of literature and the fine arts had been made long before by Dubos. "The four happy ages when the arts have attained a perfection not to be found in the others are as follows: the age which began ten years before the reign of Philip father of Alexander the Great, the age of Julius Caesar and Augustus, that of Julius II and Leo X, and

---

[20] *Discours préliminaire de l'Encyclopédie*, in *Oeuvres de d'Alembert*, I, 78–79.
[21] *Discours préliminaire de l'Encyclopédie*, in *Oeuvres*, I, 81–82.

finally that of our monarch Louis XIV."[22] This listing soon became commonplace in the eighteenth century, and was upheld by writers of the most various backgrounds and sympathies.

These four ages, then, became for many writers the high points of the history of the arts—a history which can only be described as fluctuating or cyclical in its course. To be sure, the cycles were viewed somewhat loosely; certainly they were not made to follow any fixed plan of time or of sequence. Historical relativism, the analogy of development in the natural world, the disillusionment caused by man's apparently ungovernable propensities toward error and evil, and even the most rigid aesthetic Classicism—all of these elements contributed, in varying proportions, to this notion of fluctuation in the history of the arts, as against a linear conception of artistic progress or decadence. Taste and glory alike, it was sometimes said, last but a day; "everything here below tends toward its own destruction and renewal."[23] As Fréron wrote, "The arts and sciences have their beginnings, their progress, their revolutions, their decadence, and their final fall just as do the empires of the world. Talents die and are born again without guiding the course of philosophy or being guided by it. ... This is what experience demonstrates, what history teaches, and what our contemporary philosophy would try to deny."[24]

And the views of the critic of the *Année littéraire* found their parallel in the writings of those same *philosophes* whom he heralded as the executors of ruin in the arts. Marmontel, Condillac, and D'Alembert all detected a certain rhythm of creative artistic productivity in history. The arts, wrote Condillac, perpetually go through their succession of "childhood, progress, and decline," while D'Alembert observed that the literary like the material world has its "necessary revolutions, about which it would be as unjust to complain as about the changing of the seasons."[25]

[22] Dubos, *Réflexions critiques*, II, 141.
[23] Bricaire de la Dixmerie, *Lettres sur l'état présent de nos spectacles* (Amsterdam, 1765), 5.
[24] Elie Catherine Fréron, *L'année littéraire*, 1755, I, 247.
[25] Condillac, *Traité de l'art d'écrire*, in *Oeuvres*, VII, 392; D'Alembert, *Discours préliminaire de l'Encyclopédie*, in *Oeuvres*, I, 79.

Historical optimism thus was cheated of victory in the realm of art and literature for the second time in the course of the eighteenth century. The first defeat had been the one dealt to that Classical Modernism which had emerged triumphant from the great seventeenth century Quarrel. At the conclusion of the Quarrel the defenders of the Ancients had been vanquished, and the arts had seemed about to receive additional support from their alliance with rationalism and philosophy. But literary optimism was rudely shaken by the widespread reaction against the intrusion of these new elements, and a decline from the great age of Louis XIV was diagnosed by many. Yet, despite this temporary setback, the very diagnosis of decadence left room for future recovery and progress. In the meantime, however, those same factors of observation and feeling which had contributed to the reaction against philosophy in letters were combining with historical studies to deliver an even more crushing blow to optimism. This was of course the attack of historical and aesthetic relativism upon the older standards of artistic growth. In a somewhat incongruous alliance with certain elements of the conservative idea of decadence, this form of relativism brought into question all concepts of universal progress in literature and the arts.

Such a schematization of course does considerable violence to chronology, and is not intended to represent a clear progression of events. Nor does it represent a consistent trend discernible in all eighteenth century literature; it seeks to point out only a few trends among many. But it was not only in literature and the fine arts that historical optimism was modified or directly combatted; other aspects of man's development were also to be examined, with very much the same resultant disillusionment.

Chapter 15

Historical Interaction

We acquire hardly any new knowledge without losing an agreeable illusion; our enlightenment almost always comes at the expense of our pleasures. (D'Alembert, *Réflexions sur l'usage et sur l'abus de la philosophie dans les matières de goût*)[1]

No era of recorded history has been without its specialists in the various fields of intellectual endeavor; the specialist has become as essential to the life of thought as to the life of action. In the eighteenth century, as in other ages, numerous investigators worked assiduously and quietly to extend, if only minutely, the bounds of knowledge and of ideas within a single realm of study. After absorption within the general intellectual current, or rejection from it as erroneous or insignificant, the work of these industrious specialists has almost invariably been forgotten, for centuries or forever.

Dangerous though all sweeping judgments in such matters may be, one may hazard the observation that the thought of the Enlightenment offers a pattern of survival which differs, at least quantitatively, from the norm of other ages. For the eighteenth century was perhaps as free from the narrow pedanticism of the ivory tower as had been any previous period of "modern" history, and certainly far more free than any subsequent period. Conversely, there has seldom been an age which has so incautiously given itself to bold but frequently shallow generalizations; the great libraries of today offer astonishing, gloomy perspectives of dust-laden volumes from the French Enlightenment, most of them not solid though limited

[1] *Oeuvres de d'Alembert*, IV, 333.

contributions to knowledge, but rather attempts, generally abortive, at broad synthesis. Such is the case not only in the realms of aesthetics, of psychology and ethics and politics, and of various combinations of these fields, but in all types of historical writing as well.

For the trend of eighteenth century historical studies was clearly toward the universal in time, place, and topic. If the Enlightenment's approach to history often today may appear oversimplified, certainly the age was not one of restricted and narrow historical interests, of either topical or temporal specialization. And in the new universal history it was ordinarily not the particular but the universal in man's behavior which was the preponderant concern. Though losing in richness, the historical spectacle thereby seemed to the eighteenth century mind to gain immeasurably in intelligibility.

In the quest for universal human behavior it is only natural that the eighteenth century sought to describe general developmental trends in history. Such trends might include the grand progress envisioned by Condorcet or the cyclical fluctuation seen by the Abbé Dubos. But whatever the trend, its analysis almost inevitably occasioned, or was the result of, a certain amount of theorizing upon the constant relationships among the various components of the culture. Seldom was any one realm of activity viewed in isolation. The effects of governmental institutions, or of moral or economic conditions, upon the progress or decadence of a civilization aroused considerable discussion, as did the question of the solidarity of cultural progress or regress.

It was ordinarily admitted that, though progress in one field tends to be accompanied by progress in others, and decadence in one with decadence in others, the developmental rates of these changes are not the same. For example, the view was expressed by many writers of the French Enlightenment, as by the great Italian, Vico, that the arts developed in primitive mankind prior to philosophy and the sciences; Condillac enlarged this assertion into a general theory of the more rapid development of the arts in any progressive culture. To this theory Marmontel agreed, for he saw the insight of genius as independent of cumulative research. At the same time he pointed out that after a lapse into barbarism the sciences may suddenly be rediscovered in all their purity, while the recovery of taste is a matter of gradual education.

Among the genres of literature, as among the various fine arts, Condillac and others saw considerable uniformity of development, and a similar link was presumed to exist between literature and the fine arts in general. "Who is there who does not know that the perfection of literature contributes to that of the fine arts?"—so queried Bricaire de la Dixmerie rather belligerently.[2] D'Alembert and Dubos, too, stressed the developmental solidarity of all the arts, while admitting certain irregularities in the course of that development.

The effect of external pressures upon the arts was also widely noted. Patronage and protection, inevitably, were said to influence artistic development, though it was mainly in *antiphilosophe* circles that this influence was emphasized. Genius and talents, stated Rigoley de Juvigny, "languish and die when they are not protected," and protection itself might be unenlightened and tasteless.[3] And commentators of all schools united in pointing out various indirect effects of governmental institutions and policies upon artistic production. Governmental encouragement of prosperity, the further-ance of justice and education—these and other factors, according to Dupont de Nemours, augment human knowledge and aesthetic discernment. Condillac saw the government as influencing national character, the national character as influencing language, and language as the agent for literary progress. While the malignant effect of tyranny upon the arts was being decried in many quarters, and the calm of peacetime held necessary for their progress, Marmontel and others ventured to suggest that war and strife might at times stimulate human faculties.

Science too was presumed to have its effect upon the rise and fall

[2] Nicolas Bricaire de la Dixmerie, *Les deux âges du goût et du génie français*, p. xlvii.

[3] Jean Antoine Rigoley de Juvigny, *De la décadence des lettres et des mœurs depuis les Grecs et les Romains jusqu'à nos jours* (Paris, 1787), 25.

of the arts, though the estimate of this effect varied widely. As has already been noted, some writers insisted that scientific knowledge is an aid to taste; others preferred to emphasize the abuse of knowledge within the proper sphere of imagination. On the effect of science and philosophy upon the happiness and morality of a people, a similar lack of unanimity may be found. It is important to recognize that there were frequent exceptions to the much publicized belief of the Enlightenment that learning and knowledge must lead inevitably to virtue, happiness, and intellectual competence.

Such exceptions, to be sure, are more often found in the writings on the periphery rather than at the center of the Enlightenment—in a Vauvenargues, for example, or an Abbé Dubos. Dubos granted the progress of the sciences, but denied that this progress had any necessary effect upon man's general understanding. "It is true," he wrote, ". . . that the natural sciences . . . are more perfect today than they were in the day of Augustus or that of Leo X, but that is far from saying that we reason better or possess more accurate judgment than did the men of those earlier days. . . . The sole cause for the gradual perfecting of the natural sciences . . . is our good fortune in knowing more facts than did our predecessors. . . . If we see a larger part of the truth than did the Ancients, it is not that our eyesight is better than theirs, but rather that time has revealed more truth to us."[4] Science, for Dubos, guaranteed progress neither in the arts, in intellectual judgment, nor in moral behavior.

Agreement was more general upon the existence of a positive relationship between moral conditions and the advance or decline of the cultural unit or of its other component elements, such as the arts. The Marquis de Mirabeau saw the degeneration of morality as the concomitant of the decadence of the state, while Condillac stated flatly that "flourishing ages have their natural limits, beyond which moral corruption inevitably brings about the decadence of society."[5] Ethical conditions, continued Condillac, influence lan-

[4] Jean Baptiste Dubos, *Réflexions critiques sur la poésie et sur la peinture*, II, 478–479, 510.
[5] Victor Riquetti de Mirabeau, *L'ami des hommes, ou traité de la population* (Paris, 1883), 229–274; *Histoire ancienne*, in *Cours d'études*, in *Oeuvres de Condillac*, X, 391.

guages, and languages conversely have their effect upon morality. Moreover, "just as intellectual revolutions produce parallel ethical revolutions, and as the latter produce governmental changes, so too are governmental forms influenced by moral behavior."[6]

Governmental action and political conditions were likewise presumed to play a role in general progress or decadence. "The progress of reason is never retarded save by the vices of government"—so wrote Condillac in an unguarded moment.[7] And the whole philosophical school demanded at least a certain degree of freedom of discussion and of printing as a prerequisite for progress. Though war and internal troubles were commonly held to be the signal for general decadence as well as for artistic decline, other writers saw these disasters as a challenge to human effort, and hence as agents of at least a limited progress.

If the various relationships within the cultural unit thus far treated were seldom subjected to systematic or lengthy consideration, the relationship between luxury and general decadence was one of the topics most widely and heatedly discussed in the eighteenth century. The question was not, of course, without its complications and contradictions. It is difficult to reconcile the position of some writers on luxury with their general philosophical and social outlook; still others, like Raynal, were apparently torn between the attractions of the simple life of "nature," and the virtues of an advanced society nourished by commerce and luxury.

Diderot, to be sure, achieved a compromise which was both sensible and moderate for his age. He held, first of all, that many writers had mistaken mere contemporaneousness for causal connection in the growth of luxury and the decay of states. "In the constitution and the administration of states," he asked, "have there not been faults and defects which, quite independently of luxury, have brought about the corruption of governments and the decadence of empires?"[8] He admitted, nevertheless, that luxury beyond a certain point does give rise to selfish, anti-social passions; the problem is

---

[6] *Histoire ancienne*, in *Oeuvres*, IX, 3.

[7] *Histoire ancienne*, in *Oeuvres*, X, 72.

[8] "Luxe" (*Encyclopédie*), *Oeuvres complètes de Diderot*, XVI, 9.

therefore the determination of this point. Luxury is advantageous when it consumes a certain minor proportion of a nation's agricultural and industrial wealth, but beyond this limit it becomes pernicious both to private morality and to civic health.

Though this counsel of moderation was repeated here and there in the eighteenth century, French writers commonly preferred to launch diatribes against the evil effects of luxury, rather than to examine calmly the precise consequences of luxury in given situations. The prevalence of an avaricious self-interest which was presumed to follow from the commercial pursuits of the age was loudly deplored, in general terms, by such writers as Clément. The following lines convey well the usual spirit of the attack.

> *O siècle de trafic, d'usure et d'injustice!*
> *O mélange inouï de luxe et d'avarice!*
> *Le mal est-il au comble, et peut-il croître encor?*
> *Notre unique vertu, notre seul Dieu, c'est l'Or.*
> *L'intérêt fut longtemps une lâche foiblesse;*
> *Le sordide intérêt passe enfin pour sagesse:*
> *Loix, politique, honneur, tout se règle par lui.*
> *Les vices d'autrefois sont les mœurs d'aujourd'hui.*
> *Il n'est plus de richesse infâme, illégitime;*
> *La seule pauvreté désormais est un crime;*
> *Et fussiez-vous souillé par les plus noirs excès,*
> *Soyez riche, et l'argent va blanchir vos forfaits.*

Our ancestors, concluded the poet, were nobler than we, though they lived less luxuriously:

> *Le François étoit gai, brave et peu raisonneur,*
> *Aimant son roi, sa dame, et, plus que tout, l'honneur.*[9]

But it was by no means the *antiphilosophes* alone, nor Rousseau alone among the *philosophes*, who decried luxury, who waxed nostalgic over the old days of simplicity and frugality, and who scented decadence as the concomitant of the new luxury. Holbach, D'Alembert, Condillac, and the Marquis de Mirabeau among others were

[9] Jean Marie Bernard Clément, *Satires* (Amsterdam, 1786), 8, 15.

5*

very specific on this point. Luxury, cried the Friend of Man, softens the body and hardens the heart; it corrupts the soul and weakens the intellect. It breaks all natural ties and, by exalting the parvenu, destroys the whole social hierarchy. It enfeebles both industry and agriculture and arouses all sorts of artificial needs and desires. It causes the degeneration of the arts, which flourish only upon that true beauty which is "as simple as it is noble and elevated."[10] Condillac referred bitterly to the "fatal poison" of luxury, and declared that "it is a clear case of fact that only the simple life can make a people rich, powerful, and happy."[11] And Marmontel wrote that "luxury does more than enervate the body: it softens and corrupts the soul."[12]

Philosophes and *antiphilosophes*, then, were in broad agreement on the ruinous effects of luxury upon the individual and the social body alike. Often the parallel of the decline of Rome was adduced in support of this opinion, as was the authority of "the wise men of both the ancient and the modern world." "Luxury," wrote Chaudon, "is not only the corrupter of virtue but also the destroyer of empires."[13] Or, in the words of Pompignan, "the presumed utility of luxury is a paradox condemned by experience as well as reason, for luxury redounds to its own benefit alone. Prodigal rather than liberal, it enriches only those arts which it produces and which are its support; its superfluities satisfy the needs neither of the cultivators nor of those workers usually employed."[14]

Widespread indulgence in luxurious frivolity, wrote Condillac, can only sap the foundations of society. "Luxury . . . will take workers from the most useful arts and cultivators from the plow; it will increase the price of the necessities of life, and for the small number of citizens who will live in opulence the greater number

---

[10] V. R. de Mirabeau, *L'ami des hommes*, 311.

[11] *Le commerce et le gouvernement, considérés relativement l'un à l'autre*, in *Oeuvres de Condillac*, IV, 286, 287.

[12] *Bélisaire*, in *Oeuvres complètes de Marmontel*, VII, 123.

[13] Louis Mayeul Chaudon, *Anti-dictionnaire philosophique* (Paris, 1775), II, 18.

[14] Jean Jacques Lefranc de Pompignan, *Discours sur cette traduction*, in *Oeuvres de M. le marquis de Pompignan* (Paris, 1784), IV, 63.

will descend into poverty."[15] Luxury, above all, ruins agriculture, in Condillac's opinion, and it dries up the general circulation of money which is vital to general prosperity. Sooner or later, then, "luxury ruins those nations into which it has insinuated itself."[16]

With varying vehemence many eighteenth century writers gave vent to similar sentiments, despite such counter-attacks as those delivered by Voltaire. For some, the effects of luxury were but one illustration of a general rule of cultural compensation—a rule not infrequently encountered in the writings of the time. Luxury, ran the argument, was the outcome of industry which in itself was honest and fruitful but which later became canalized, perverted, and mischievous; similarly progress in other fields might be followed or accompanied by decadence in a natural compensatory reaction such as that noted many years before by Fontenelle. An elementary and loose form of this thesis might be found in the common assertion that every age has both its advantages and disadvantages, its merits and defects, or in the view of the normal accompaniment of truth by error.

A clearer development of the compensatory theory was offered by D'Alembert. "We acquire," he asserted, "hardly any new knowledge without losing an agreeable illusion; our enlightenment almost always comes at the expense of our pleasures. Our ancestors in their simplicity were perhaps more strongly moved by the monstrous plays of our older theatre than we are moved today by our most beautiful theatrical works. Nations less enlightened than our own are not less happy on that account, for with fewer desires they also have fewer needs, and they are content with less refined pleasures than are we. Yet we would not care to change our enlightenment for their ignorance or for the ignorance of our ancestors. If this enlightenment reduces our pleasures, at the same time it flatters our vanity, and we applaud ourselves for having become difficult, as if doing so were meritorious. The most stubborn of our feelings are pride and self-love...."[17]

[15] *Le commerce et le gouvernement*, in *Oeuvres de Condillac*, IV, 274.

[16] *Histoire ancienne*, in *Oeuvres*, XII, 305.

[17] *Réflexions sur l'usage et sur l'abus de la philosophie dans les matières de goût*, in *Oeuvres de d'Alembert*, IV, 333.

Condillac, from somewhat the same premises, likewise stated a theory of compensation, and with similar gloomy conclusions. All progress, he wrote, must bring new needs. If these needs are not entirely disadvantageous—for they do develop man's intelligence and sensitivity—there is, nevertheless, a serious danger in this development: the danger of frivolity and dilettantism. A people comes to worship change for its own sake; "such a people follows its habits, opinions, and prejudices in haphazard fashion, and never thinks of reforming itself, for it sees no need for doing so. Preoccupied by its illusions it sees everything indifferently—order and disorder, laws and abuses alike. Thus its delusion is such that it sees its prosperity in those very things which prove its decadence." [18]

The connection between decadence and prosperity was of course not in itself a theory new in Condillac. The Abbé Dubos, for example, had stated the general rule in his "Critical Reflections" of 1719. The decadence of art, he asserted, frequently has coincided with a period of general prosperity, happiness, and refinement; such was the case in seventeenth century Italy, as well as in Hellenistic Greece and in Rome after the reign of Augustus. [19] In much the same vein Condillac wrote of luxury and of the decline of nations: "The centuries of atticism, urbanity, and elegance, the polished centuries which are considered to be the most flourishing of all, are ... the epoch of the decadence of morality and of states. Luxury then reigns ..., and because arts and letters are in bloom, men have collections of paintings which they do not appreciate and libraries of books which they do not read. Because it is fashionable to be seen abroad, they take their ennui from establishment to establishment, to exchange it for the ennui of others." [20]

Thus it was that the unitary development of an age came to be subject to serious question in the eighteenth century, though in many respects the various elements of the cultural unit were seen as developing in close alliance among themselves. Nevertheless, if

---

[18] *Le commerce et le gouvernement*, in *Oeuvres de Condillac*, IV, 330.

[19] Dubos, *Réflexions critiques*, II, 182–248.

[20] *Histoire moderne*, in *Cours d'études*, in *Oeuvres de Condillac*, XVI, 397–398.

one can determine with some certainty the position of individual thinkers such as Condillac and Dubos, any attempt to define a general eighteenth century stand on developmental relationships within rising and declining civilizations meets insuperable obstacles. The greatest difficulty facing the student of the period is that few thinkers saw the problem as a whole; therefore one is obliged to construct a synthesis of isolated fragments—a synthesis which to some degree undoubtedly forces the thought of the writer in question.

Yes, despite the vagueness of many eighteenth century comments upon cultural relationships, these comments are not without their significance. For they are evidence not only of a genuine interest in the problem of historical change, but evidence also of sporadic attempts to get beyond purely abstract generalizations and into a consideration of actual historical mechanics—a consideration which, though broad, was basically empirical. Above all, these comments are an indication of the serious attention given to historical studies in that century. If these studies were by no means entirely factual and objective, they were seldom wholly abstract fabrications formed from the prejudices of the age.

Chapter 16

The Cultural Unit

The character of a nation consists in a certain spiritual disposition which is habitual and which is more common in one
nation than in another. (D'Alembert, in the *Encyclopédie*)[1]

It has been seen that many an eighteenth century thinker, equipped
with a lively sense of historical change and with an inquisitive, at
least partially empirical turn of mind, well realized that in the
history of mankind there were countless vicissitudes, countless challenges to interpretation. Some of the attempts of such thinkers to
apply historical analysis to individual cultures have been reviewed,
with emphasis upon the factors contributing to the decadence of
these cultures. Already the term "cultural unit" has appeared in
these pages—but can one justly use the term within an eighteenth
century context? Though the vagueness surrounding much writing
of the period on the subject precludes use of a too rigorous terminology, it is undeniable that many of the *philosophes* and their contemporaries did consider the almost organic developmental relationships in history as creating roughly unitary cultural groups, or
individual civilizations.

But what was the nature of these civilizations? Did the average
eighteenth century writer think in terms of nations or groups of
nations in the political sense, or was his conception less spatial than
temporal? In the case of classical antiquity the answer is clear
enough; in other cases no definite answer is at hand. Often in a discussion of these matters the writer refers specifically to France, but
the predominant position of that nation in contemporary Europe was

[1] "Caractère des nations," *Encyclopédie, ou dictionnaire raisonné des
sciences, des arts et des métiers*, II, 666.

such as to make its destiny of far more than narrowly national significance—a fact which was recognized, and indeed overestimated, in the French literature of the day.

This recognition of the existence of various temporal and spatial groupings of mankind could only result in a structural view of world history which was not, basically, established upon the abstract, rationalist assumptions common in the French Enlightenment. Historical investigation, bound at least in large part to an empirical approach, was now the prime guide to the general study of civilizations, and this form of investigation was supplemented, in the absence of anything resembling precise sociological method, by reports of life and travel abroad. The results of neither of these two types of research could be such as to encourage notions of cultural uniformity throughout the ages.

The interest in contemporary foreign peoples which reached a new height in eighteenth century France was of course not without its precedents in earlier years. The Age of Louis XIV had received tidings of foreign lands from such diverse heralds as Saint-Evremond in England and the Jesuits in China, and a vogue for travel and for travel narratives came into being in the later decades of the reign. To be sure, the veracity of the reports which reached France might be of a low degree indeed, especially when they involved exotic peoples who were less sophisticated than the French. But sentimental utopian exoticism was matched upon occasion, in both the seventeenth and the eighteenth centuries, by saner narratives; serious studies, for example, were made of Chinese history, thought, and institutions. Whether idealized, vilified, or described with some objectivity, foreign nations came to be more and more widely known in France, and educated Frenchmen became increasingly aware of the existence of a wide variety of cultural patterns outside their own.

The pursuit of historical studies tended to produce similar results. If historical works commonly presented the past with a marked eighteenth century bias, not even the most distorted view could altogether hide the fact that not every age had conducted itself upon eighteenth century principles. The work of Dubos and Montesquieu gave real insight into the Middle Ages, and here and there, as earlier with Saint-Evremond, a certain feeling for the uniqueness of the various ages of history was aroused. It is difficult to treat historical development in the abstract, and though the Enlightenment in some instances strove to do precisely that, the diversity of history always remained somewhat intractable. Some recognition of cultural complexity was inevitable, and at times this complexity was emphasized quite deliberately.

Thus the French eighteenth century was by no means unaware of the patent differences between cultural units, whether defined as nations or groups of nations or as temporal historical periods. In this respect the *philosophes* and their opponents were in substantial agreement. Even the most hasty glance at the various nations of contemporary Europe revealed vast discrepancies in institutions, cultural well-being, and general spirit.

D'Alembert, among others, ascribed to each long-established nation a definite character. "The character of a nation consists in a certain spiritual disposition which is habitual and which is more common in one nation than in another, though this disposition may not characterize all citizens of the nation. Thus the French character comprises such elements as sprightly superficiality, gaiety and sociability, and love for monarch and monarchy. In all nations which have long existed there is a basic character which has changed not at all through the years."[2]

D'Alembert did not, however, always assert so confidently the unchangeability of national character. That the characteristics of the ages of history, and especially of the successive centuries of Western civilization, did vary was a fact generally recognized in the French Enlightenment. Comparisons were frequently made between the seventeenth and eighteenth centuries; the former, thought D'Alembert at one point, was the age of genius and taste, while the latter was the age of enlightenment, tolerance, and practical knowledge. This distinction found quite general assent among other writers of the day, but did not exclude other bases of comparison among these and other centuries. The poet Dorat saw the spirit of his own age as consisting in a taste for subtle combinations,

[2] "Caractère des nations," *Encyclopédie*, II, 666.

as against the bold conceptions of the age of Louis XIV. Marmontel saw each of the many past ages as having qualities peculiarly suited to the development of certain art forms. Le Roi, in the pages of the *Encyclopédie,* noted that each century might be characterized pithily; thus one might speak of the age of chivalry, the age of the arts, the age of philosophy, and so forth. Caraccioli found it possible to apply a convenient adjective to each of a number of centuries; thus "the tenth century was ignorant, the eleventh barbarous, the twelfth superstitious, the sixteenth fanatical, the seventeenth luminous, and ours irreligious and frivolous."[3] Chaudon sought to distinguish the peculiar religious orientation of each century; his listing included such manifestations as monasticism, pilgrimages, crusades, revolt and independence, and finally irreligion.

From this view of the individual characteristics of the various nations and ages it was only a step to the assertion that man is a product of his cultural environment. Such, already, was the clear implication of the regnant sensationalist philosophy. Throughout the Enlightenment there ran a distinct current of general environmental determinism, if only seldom a determinism of a rigid philosophical nature. Though on occasion the emphasis upon environmental influences was challenged by the implications of the uniformity of the productions of nature, a compromise was always reached—and a compromise almost always upholding the reality of environmental influence.

The question of the development of natural genius may serve to illustrate this point. Agreement was nearly unanimous upon the fixed rate of production of genius across the centuries, while at the same time it was generally admitted that certain circumstances favor, while others stifle, the development of such genius. Condillac, not unexpectedly, saw a proper degree of linguistic perfection as the prerequisite for the flowering of natural talent. D'Alembert and others were willing to grant even to the much scorned medieval period a production of natural genius quite equal to that of their own day, while scorning the sterile atmosphere of ignorance and dogmatism which gave no opportunities for growth to that genius.

[3] Louis Antoine de Caraccioli, *La jouissance de soi-même,* 224.

In explaining these cultural differences among the nations and ages of the world, eighteenth century thinkers frequently turned to theories of "climate." Dubos, as has been seen in an earlier section, gave a central position to the role of climate in molding the artistic expression of an age, nor did he limit the operation of climatic influences to the arts alone. In noting the influence of climate upon culture, Dubos had been preceded by many other writers, Fénelon among them. It is noteworthy that the progressionist theories of Turgot and Condorcet had little room for climatic speculations; both writers asserted that the influence of climate often had been exaggerated, and that climate was relatively unimportant in the formation of civilizations. Helvétius, who likewise was an optimist concerning mankind's destiny, took a similar stand. Yet one must hesitate to establish an invariable correlation between progressionist theory and opposition to doctrines of climatic influence. Condillac, who often was something of an historical pessimist, depreciated climatic influences, and substituted for them the omnipotence of linguistic development.

The gloomy optimist Buffon granted that man is influenced by climatic conditions, though "man can modify the influences of his climatic environment."[4] D'Alembert held that the general character of a given people could not depend upon governmental forms which were always changing, and that this character thus seemed attributable only to long-range climatic changes. In the *Encyclopédie*, Diderot offered a specific instance of climatic influence as then understood: in his article on the philosophy of the Egyptians he noted that the miracle of the annual fecundation of Egypt was a standing invitation to superstitious beliefs and practices in that land.

Moreover, the climatic environment was widely assumed to have a certain influence upon the moral code of a nation or an age. The basic ethical absolutism of the eighteenth century has already been noted; this absolutism was, however, modified, though seldom if ever destroyed, by the inroads of climatic theory. But if the eternal validity of the most basic moral principles was only rarely brought into doubt, it was quite impossible to ignore the variation of moral

[4] Buffon, *Histoire naturelle, générale et particulière*, IV, 30.

custom from age to age and from people to people. Marmontel ascribed this variation partly to climatic differences—that is, to changes in the natural environment, which in turn affect the bodily organs. Climate, he wrote, determines such qualities of character as energy, warmth, and sensitivity. In cold climates men tend to be serious, laborious, firm, and courageous, while warm climates encourage ardor, ambition, and the extremes of vice and virtue.

Marmontel believed that not only climate but also such factors as institutions and occupational pursuits affect the peculiar character of a people. Diderot listed an even greater number of determinants of this character. Of ethical forms he asserted that "their variety among the different peoples of the globe depends upon climate and religion, laws, and government—upon needs, education, manners, and example. According to the strength with which one of these causes may act in each nation, the others give way to it in similar measure."[5]

Governmental conditions, in the broadest sense, were often seen as playing a prominent role in forming the moral character of a people. Even D'Alembert, despite his lines on the inability of fleeting governments to mold popular character, felt that long-established governmental forms would eventually change that character; despotism, for example, would gradually make a people vain, lazy, and frivolous. Montesquieu preferred to emphasize the reverse of this process and asserted that governmental forms should be made to suit the character of the citizens. In similar fashion the Chevalier de Jaucourt stated that governmental forms "should be extremely dependent upon the climate and locale, as well as upon the spirit, character, and physical extent of the nation."[6]

Thus, at least in part, each civilization, age, or nation came to be considered by some writers as a natural unit with its own unique character. Could the many units so conceived be accommodated within a scheme of linear historical development? Undoubtedly the question must receive an affirmative answer—but with reservations. First of all, each historical or cultural grouping had become partially

[5] "Mœurs" (*Encyclopédie*), *Oeuvres complètes de Diderot*, XVI, 120.
[6] Louis de Jaucourt, "Gouvernement," *Encyclopédie*, VII, 790.

explicable, partially justified, in terms of itself alone. More basically, with their emphasis upon environmental determinism, many eighteenth century thinkers were forced to accept a disturbing relativism of values in some or all of the major fields of human achievement. Since, as has already been noted, the century arrived only infrequently at anything like a standard of social accommodation as the measure of progress, some writers found themselves in the uncomfortable position of being unable to define "progress," and thus proportionately inclined to write simply in terms of change or historical flux. Other writers, more conventional, persisted in speaking of progress and decadence, but of a progress and decadence so rapidly succeeding one another that history could only offer a disheartening spectacle of fluctuation. Most commonly of all, the two types of historical flux might become confusedly entangled in the thought of a given writer. Those doctrines of flux, the culmination of eighteenth century historical pessimism, deserve separate treatment.

Chapter 17

The World in Flux

> In all ages to come the savage will advance step by step
> toward the civilized state, while civilized man will return
> toward his primitive condition. (Raynal, *Histoire philoso-
> phique et politique*)[1]

Before turning to still other effects of historical studies upon
eighteenth century philosophies of history, one must note in passing
an important contemporary reinforcement to pessimism. For, if
historical investigation in that century was the most powerful
opponent of any linear conception of progress or decadence, the
parallel seen between human history and the development of the
natural world also contributed significantly to the atomization of
the historical picture.

Another parallel—that between individual development and the
collective development of mankind—was of course not new in the
eighteenth century; Augustine had clothed in providential garb a
comparison between the childhood, youth, maturity, and old age
of the individual and similar stages in the whole life of mankind.
But when, in this way, the entire history of man was compared to
that of a single individual, the difficulties were considerable. Though
Augustine had asserted that the old age of mankind was not a
period of decay, and though Fontenelle had expected mankind to
avoid old age altogether, there were those who questioned the good
sense of holding to a general principle with such egregious exceptions. Among these critics, for example, was Fréron, who pointed

[1] Raynal, *Histoire philosophique et politique des éstablissements et du
commerce des Européens dans les deux Indes* (Geneva, 1780–1781), V, 20.

out that man and all natural things grow and decay alike, and, by implication, that the human analogy could not serve as a support for a theory of general progress.

Thus the eighteenth century was not satisfied with the analogy between general historical development and the development of the individual. However, a second parallel did come to be accepted by many writers—the parallel between the course of civilization and that of the natural world in general with its diverse phenomena. States and cultures now were seen, to some degree, as the equivalent of other natural units or organisms. An explicit denial of the validity of the analogy came from the pen of Turgot, but he was not commonly followed in this denial. The increasing consciousness of the natural world, through the growing passion for empirical natural studies, doubtless contributed in some measure to the popularity of the new analogy. In any case, the writers of the day from Fréron and Caraccioli to Condillac and Mirabeau made wide use of the parallel. "All creatures," wrote Caraccioli, "have their beginnings, their growth and their period of perfection, but since by nature they are defective and variable they decline necessarily as soon as they reach a certain point. Thus also do the ages of history have their progress, their beauty, and their decadence."[2]

Marmontel's analogy was more specific: he proposed at one point to compare poetry to a plant which flourishes in one soil and not another, and which, after it has flourished, necessarily declines and dies. Yet he recognized the inexactitude of the parallel, and ended in typically confused fashion by rejecting it in effect.[3] Condillac took a much more decisive position: "In all moral things as in the physical world there is a final period of growth after which decline is necessary."[4] In his opinion progress and decadence, change and succession, are the natural attributes of duration, and duration the attribute of all created things. And in the same vein the Marquis de Mirabeau declared: "There is a cycle prescribed for all moral things as for all natural phenomena—a cycle of birth, growth,

---

[2] Louis Antoine de Caraccioli, *La jouissance de soi-même*, 226.

[3] *Eléments de la littérature*, in *Oeuvres complètes de Marmontel*, XV, 1–2.

[4] *Essai sur l'origine des connoissances humaines*, in *Oeuvres de Condillac*, I, 431.

maturity, decline and death. So it is with the days from morning to evening, with the years in their solar revolution, with the life of man from cradle to grave, and with the course of states from their foundation to their fall."[5]

The clearest instance of this cyclical flux was found in the destiny of nations and governments. The fact that governments decay and are transformed, that nations rise and fall, certainly has been before the eye of all ages, yet it is also a point of fact that this repetitive occurrence of corruption and decline has not aroused equal interest at all times. In some cases, in the eighteenth century, a direct parallel was drawn between the vicissitudes of the state and those of the natural organism, man. D'Alembert, for example, noted that "empires, like men, have their growth, decline, and death."[6] Wrote Grimm: "The condition of societies is an imposed condition in which action and reaction are continuous; . . . it is as absurd to wish to assure empires of permanent tranquillity, with a cessation of reaction, as to certify to a man that he will never be unjustly injured by the general mass, or that he can negotiate at will with that mass."[7]

Studies in history as well as interest in the natural sciences contributed to the eighteenth century concern with the phenomenon of decadence. Well before the appearance of Gibbon's distinguished treatment of Roman decline and fall the problem of decadence had occupied many of the best minds of France. Montesquieu, Condillac, and Voltaire gave it major attention, and such thinkers as D'Alembert and even Helvétius recognized the existence of the problem. Helvétius took a conventional view of the link between decadence and moral corruption, and saw the weakness and cowardice of the citizens of a despotic state as the cause of that state's fall when confronted by external enemies. D'Alembert was more cautious. The inevitable decline and fall of empires, he confessed, "often has had mysterious causes which the night of time

---

[5] Victor Riquetti de Mirabeau, *L'ami des hommes, ou traité de la population*, 317.

[6] *Éloge de Montesquieu*, in *Oeuvres de d'Alembert*, III, 448.

[7] Friedrich Melchior Grimm, *Correspondance littéraire, philosophique, et critique*, VI, 428.

hides from us, and which in their impenetrability or apparent insignificance sometimes were hidden indeed to the eyes of their contemporaries."[8]

It was Montesquieu who developed at length a theory of the corruption of governmental forms, but his system had been anticipated in certain respects by Fénelon and others. "As long" thought Fénelon, "as human nature remains feeble, imperfect, and corrupted, all forms of government will always carry within themselves the seeds of an inevitable corruption, and of their own fall and ruin." No particular machinery of government, he continued, can serve as a panacea for the ills of governmental bodies, for these ills are not only inevitable but, in the end, fatal. Even the best type of government may permit the abuse of sovereign power, and thus it too will fall sooner or later. "The political body resembles the human body: a fever, a cold, or the slightest accident may carry off the healthiest and best built body as well as the feeblest and most deformed. . . ."[9]

With Montesquieu the theory of governmental corruption from within was developed much more fully, and it was upon this doctrine of the corruption of political forms that the Chevalier de Jaucourt drew most heavily, in the *Encyclopédie*, for his discussions of decadence. The doctrine was applied by Jaucourt to the fall of Athens, which had abandoned its noble patriotic ideals for the pursuit of pleasure and riches—a change which had been encouraged, inevitably, by the development of the state. And again in the case of Rome Jaucourt saw political decadence as arising from within, and notably from the futile attempt to govern a large nation by laws which were appropriate only for the governing of a small republic, though these very laws had encouraged territorial expansion.[10] If on the possibilities of future evasion of this rule Jaucourt

---

[8] *Eloge de Montesquieu*, in *Oeuvres de d'Alembert*, III, 448.

[9] Quoted by Ramsay, *Essai philosophique sur le gouvernement civil*, in *Oeuvres de Fénelon*, X, 137, 138.

[10] "République d'Athènes," *Encyclopédie, ou dictionnaire raisonné des sciences, des arts et des métiers*, XIV, 151–154; "République romaine," *Encyclopédie*, XIV, 154–158.

was not altogether clear, it appears that he did foresee the eventuality of enlightened manipulation of political institutions within a broadly inevitable course of development.

Yet Jaucourt held fast to his assertion of the intrinsic tendency of all governments to crumble and decay. "The best constituted governments, like the best formed animal bodies, bear within themselves the principle of their destruction. . . . After their early growth, states then tend toward decadence and disintegration; hence the sole means of prolonging the life of a flourishing government is to guide it on every favorable occasion back to those principles upon which it was founded. When these occasions present themselves frequently and when they are skillfully seized, governments are more happy and more durable than otherwise; when these occasions are rarely offered or when one does not take advantage of them, political bodies wither and perish."[11]

It is clear that here Jaucourt was seeking to establish a general rule for the rise and fall of governments, and indeed of nations. "On this earth," he noted, "there does not exist a single perfect government, and however perfect it may appear in theory, as carried out in practice by men it will always be subject to instability and vicissitudes. Moreover, as long as it is men who govern men, even the best government will destroy itself."[12]

D'Alembert asserted that there exists a "profoundly meditated history which has as its object the development in principle of the causes of the growth and decadence of empires."[13] He admitted, however, that the problem of ascertaining true causes is difficult. Buffon noted that empires rise and fall as climatic changes cause the centers of civilization to displace themselves. Thus, though somewhere on the earth's surface the flame of organized culture is forever burning, in any given geographical location a century of civilization is followed by many centuries of barbarism.

Marmontel, more hopefully, implied that it is not an invincible fatality which decrees the decline and fall of empires. "I am well

[11] "Gouvernement," *Encyclopédie*, VII, 791.
[12] "Gouvernement," *Encyclopédie*, VII, 790.
[13] *Réflexions sur l'histoire*, in *Oeuvres de d'Alembert*, II, 7.

aware that all things perish, including states themselves, but I do not believe that nature has traced the exact circle of their existence. There is an age when man is obliged to renounce life, but there is never a time when one should renounce the possibility of saving an empire. Doubtless a political body is subject to convulsions which shake its foundations, to long illnesses which gradually consume it, to sudden attacks which reduce it to extremities . . . , but none of these accidents is fatal. One has seen nations rise again after the most desperate straits, and re-establish themselves, after the most violent crises, with more strength and vigor than ever. Their decadence then is not prescribed as is the decline of our years, their presumed old age is but a chimera, and there remains infinite range for that hope which sustains man's courage."[14]

The Marquis de Mirabeau was somewhat less sanguine on man's ability to arrest the ultimate decay of states, for nature, he wrote, prescribes limits to the development of states, and all states must decline and die as do all natural things. But, he continued, "who can tell how long a state might exist if it were always wisely governed?" As in the case of man's health, one should try to maintain a state by following a healthful regimen. "Of the great number of men who are born each year, how few reach old age! Accidents foreign to our natural constitution age us all prematurely, and so also it is with states. No known people has traversed its full cycle: careless-ness, incompetence, or political vices have destroyed them all. The superior statesman is he who knows first of all at what point of the cycle the machine of government has arrived. For in effect the regimen which would save a man in middle-age might kill a younger man."[15] And Mirabeau saw the France of his day as a nation not in its old age but in its maturity, and hence still capable of an extended life.

Most, if not all, of these conceptions of the decline of nations and governments seem to have involved much more than political decadence; the whole life of the individual culture was often seen as being at stake. To many an eighteenth century thinker such

[14] *Bélisaire*, in *Oeuvres complètes de Marmontel*, VII, 87.
[15] V. R. de Mirabeau, *L'ami des hommes*, 317.

would appear to be the inevitable conclusion to be drawn from historical example, from the analogy of the natural world, and from an embryonic conception of the organic structure of cultures. Similar composite views of cultural decay had made possible the cyclical theories proposed by the writers of the ancient world, but these theories had since fallen into disfavor, at least insofar as they envisaged a strict form of perpetual recurrence.

Italy, to be sure, offered in the early eighteenth century the surprising spectacle of Giambattista Vico, in whose work can be found something approximating the ancient idea of eternal return. Certainly Vico's feeling for the complex interconnections of causes within a cultural unit is unusually acute; this unit, for him, becomes an organic whole possessing a unique character, and fundamentally independent of other cultures. Yet the growth and decay of each culture follows strict, eternal laws. The historical-factual must serve the eternal-Providential, and Vico often finds himself putting the rule before the fact, the rational before the empirical. Thus, despite an impressive historical and philological apparatus, Vico falls into much the same rigid, rationalistic methodology which marks the thought of such theorists of progress as Descartes and Condorcet.

There is a certain truth to the common assumption that Vico was a unique figure in his century; certainly no other thinker elaborated a cyclical system as complete and as absolute as his. Yet, as has already been noted in this study, the French eighteenth century saw the appearance of a number of nonlinear conceptions of history which contain cyclical elements. Less elaborate and less dogmatic than the system of Vico, their basic principle is not so much one of strict cyclical movement as of cyclical fluctuation or, more simply, general historical flux. If less grand in conceptual scale than Vico's magnificently ordered course of civilizations, the historical panorama as seen in France took on characteristics which were more familiar to the casual but intelligent observer of history. Historical investigation, it is true, retained many rationalistic presuppositions—presuppositions which frequently went into the making of full or embryonic theories of progress. But the idea of historical flux, when it appeared, was based in most instances not upon abstract systematization but upon those historical studies which could only underline the complexities of man's historical development.

The Christian religion, in its emphasis upon the vanity of earthly things and despite its conception of a transcendent Providence, had long inclined toward such a view of eternal flux in mundane affairs. Caraccioli in 1759 re-echoed a theme long familiar: "This flux and reflux of events, which at one moment darkens the universe and at another embellishes it, proves the instability of mortal things, as well as our mad insistence upon tyrannizing, upon self-aggrandizement and self-corruption."[16] But this attitude, applied to the whole civilization as well as to empires and the arts, is also found not infrequently in the works of less pious and better remembered writers of the century.

The importance of Dubos has already been underlined in these pages and need only be reaffirmed at this point. His doctrine is by no means simply one of the fluctuating courses of the arts but also of the rise and fall of those entire civilizations of which the arts are but a part. Each nation, according to Dubos, has its unique characteristics, yet each people goes through a succession of changes which affect its rise and fall as well as its general outlooks. These changes, however, follow no absolute plan as in Vico's system, but are the result of physical changes in the environment.

One must admit that the method of Dubos is not invariably that of careful observation, and that the precise influence of climate upon civilizations in concrete situations is seldom examined in his writings. Be this as it may, Dubos upholds the empirical fact of cyclical flux as the general pattern of history, and this without formulating a detailed and fixed order of development and without pretending to fathom the divine motives behind the eternal fluctuation revealed by history. With Tacitus, he can only conclude that "the world is subject to changes and vicissitudes of undiscoverable duration, but which in successive revolutions bring back refinement and barbarism, the talents of the intellect as well as force of body, and consequently the progress of the arts and sciences, their apathy and

[16] Caraccioli, *La jouissance de soi-même*, 161–162.

their decadence, just as the course of the sun brings back the seasons in their turn."[17]

These are words written in the earlier years of the eighteenth century, but the following decades saw many a repetition, at least in part, of the theories of Dubos. Shortly before the Revolution a minor but not insignificant critic, Sénac de Meilhan, was to suggest that his generation was approaching the peak of a cycle of historical development, with decline perhaps not far distant. As enlightenment increased, he wrote, men would become satiated with knowledge and intellectualism, and "in this state of languor into which man must be drawn by the natural course of things, there will perhaps be no other recourse, in ten or twelve generations, than a deluge which will again plunge everything into ignorance. At that time, new races will be occupied with following the circle along which already we are perhaps further advanced than we think."[18]

In the meantime, powerful voices proclaimed the more discouraging lessons of history and of nature. Marmontel saw the world as the scene of great revolutions in empires, laws, ethics, religion, customs, war, politics, arts, and sciences, but unlike Vico he envisaged these revolutions as invigorating agents for the general advancement of mankind. Buffon, while retaining a large confidence in ultimate human advance, saw history above all as the record of man's frequent lapses from reason, of the reassertion of the brute forces of nature and barbarism over civilization, and of the rise and fall and displacement of empires.

Raynal's "Philosophical History of the Two Indies" contains a categorical statement of the eternal fluctuation of peoples between civilization and barbarism. "Man," he stated, "cannot deviate willfully from the laws of nature without doing damage to his happiness. In all ages to come the savage will advance step by step toward the civilized state, while civilized man will return toward his primitive condition. From this the philosopher will conclude that there exists in the interval between these states a point at which the felicity

---

[17] Jean Baptiste Dubos, *Réflexions critiques sur la poésie et sur la peinture*, II, 335.

[18] Gabriel Sénac de Meilhan, *Considérations sur l'esprit et les mœurs*, 44.

of the race must lie—but who will establish this point? And if indeed it is established, where will be the authority capable of directing man to it and of halting man's course when it has been attained?"[19]

D'Alembert, in reference to the arts but with broader implications, stated that revolutions are the law of the world, and that barbarism and anarchy must succeed enlightenment and civilization. He added that "barbarism lasts for centuries and seems to be our natural element, while reason and good taste are but passing phenomena."[20] And this phrase appears not in an obscure work, but in the very manifesto of the French Enlightenment, the "Preliminary Discourse" of the *Encyclopédie*.

Condillac wrote at some length concerning the fluctuating course of human history, and in fact stated that his historical framework would be a succession of periods of varying length, each of them culminating in a revolution. Each period for him offered elements common to other cyclical periods, with "the history of Greece in a way a résumé of all possible cycles."[21] Yet the various nations, he asserted, are not isolated units; they make contact on the intellectual plane. "Empires follow one another, and whole nations are buried beneath their ruins, but opinions remain. . . . Even when an intellectual revolution seems to occur, often this revolution is less the introduction of a new opinion than that of an old opinion in disguise."[22]

Condillac joined D'Alembert in seeing barbarism, not civilization, as the norm of man's condition. "Born from the womb of barbarism, the arts and sciences have enlightened successively a small number of privileged nations. These arts and sciences are a light hidden from the many while it reveals itself to the few—a light which brightens only a very limited horizon. It is capable of only a certain intensification, and it begins to dim as soon as it can no longer grow brighter. It becomes dimmer by degrees, and revives again only to repeat the same cycle." And he adds that "there are . . . two

[19] Raynal, *Histoire philosophique et politique des établissements et du commerce des Européens dans les deux Indes*, V, 20.

[20] *Discours préliminaire de l'Encyclopédie*, in *Oeuvres de d'Alembert*, I, 82.

[21] *Histoire ancienne*, in *Cours d'études*, in *Oeuvres de Condillac*, IX, 83.

[22] *Histoire ancienne*, in *Oeuvres*, X, 2.

kinds of barbarism: the barbarism which follows the enlightened ages and that which precedes them. They bear no resemblance to one another, though both presuppose great ignorance; a people which has always been barbarous is not as vicious as a people which has become barbarous after having known luxury."[23]

This distinction between the two kinds of barbarism is reminiscent of one made earlier by Vico; Condillac developed the distinction at some length, and like Vico he considered the dark period after the fall of Rome as the model for the new barbarism. This barbarism, he wrote, is marked by the prevalence of avidity and the spirit of false glory; not even the most exceptional spirits can escape its influence in those ages when it reigns unchecked. And Condillac treats elsewhere of the persistence of barbaric elements, if not of barbarism itself, in new civilizations, including that of his own day.

I distinguish two types of ignorance: that of barbarous ages and that of refined ages.

The ignorance of barbarous ages is a state of stupidity in which man, unguided by rules or inventions or arts and incapable of learning from his own experience, acts only according to his prejudices and does not know how to observe those causes which make him act. . . . Finally we have emerged [from these barbarous centuries] and find ourselves in the ignorance of those centuries which are refined or at any rate less stupid than the earlier ones. . . .

For, as a matter of fact, if we have attained a certain amount of knowledge, we do not know how we attained it; we do not know how to observe either its foundations or its methods, and we prefer to think ourselves inspired geniuses rather than solid minds learning by observation and experience. In our former centuries of barbarism nothing startled us; in our refined ages we startle ourselves and wish to startle others. . . .

We think ourselves learned without having pursued any studies; this is the high point of the ignorance of refined centuries.[24]

One of the most striking résumés of eighteenth century historical pessimism may be found in the writings of Friedrich Melchior Grimm, the indefatigable critic and correspondent. If Grimm was

[23] *Histoire ancienne,* in *Oeuvres,* IX, 2.
[24] *La langue des calculs,* in *Oeuvres,* XXIII, 200–202.

not a truly original thinker, his meditations upon the course of history are none the less significant as a reflection of the intellectual currents common to his day. And, perhaps because he had become a professional student of the culture of that day, he falls quite indisputably into the empirical, not the abstract-rationalistic, current of the Enlightenment. Indeed in certain respects his intellectual position is in advance of others of his temperament, most notably in his reiterated assertion of ethical relativism.

Like other nonsystematic thinkers, Grimm did not sustain an altogether consistent view of history. At times, for example, his enthusiasm for contemporary philosophy and its progress is great; at others he is darkly pessimistic. Yet, even recognizing those temperamental vicissitudes to which nearly all men are heir, it appears undeniable that Grimm's pessimism is less a matter of temporary mood than of genuine intellectual sympathy. There is an authentic accent of sincerity in his admission that "one begins to doubt that reason and truth are made for man," in his qualification of enlightened historical epochs as "excessively short," or in his statement that the cycles of enlightenment "seem to me to be periodic."[25]

Grimm's essay-letter of January 15, 1757, is almost a codification of disillusionment concerning his own age and its place in the general scheme of history.[26] Every age, he wrote, has seen itself at the peak of civilization, whether because the age is blinded by self-esteem or because the present always works more powerfully upon men's minds than does the past. The eighteenth century has a peculiarly high opinion of itself, and with some justification, but enlightenment will not endure forever. "The easier and nearer this perfecting [of reason] appears, the more we must see this presumed advance as illusion and chimera. What can the efforts of a few wise men accomplish against the unregulated imagination of that multitude which boldly, profanely, and ceaselessly establishes prejudice and disorder beside justice and truth? It is singular that history has not

[25] Grimm, *Correspondance littéraire, philosophique, et critique*, VI, 377, 378.
[26] *Correspondance littéraire*, III, 327–337.

long ago disabused us of the chimera of an ideal perfection and wisdom which men unfortunately will never attain. One has only to read the annals of all peoples to be convinced of this sad truth."[27]

Every nation, continued Grimm, has had only a short period of civilization before its destruction. "I am therefore very far from imagining that we are on the brink of the age of reason, and indeed I almost feel that Europe is menaced by some sinister revolution."[28] "Even," he concluded, "if human reason is as advanced as some would want us to believe, how little will it take to plunge us again into darkness!"[29]

Such are some of the indications in eighteenth century French thought of an historico-empirical conception of fluctuation in the course of man's collective development. Just how seriously all of these indications—and some of those indications to be discussed in the final section of this study—should be taken is a question not easily answered. How many of these passages, for example, are simply polemical weapons rather than firm convictions? It is probable that often the polemical motive was not absent, yet it seems clear from the study of the nature and background of these conceptions that they were not mere extraneous and irrelevant accretions upon a body of philosophy which otherwise possessed a certain unity. It is difficult to imagine how the relativism of the Abbé Dubos could have led to any other system than one of flux; it is easy to understand that Buffon in his studies of the evolution of man rejected any system of linear human progress, and that Condillac in his moments of empirical historical study was struck by the growth and decay of civilizations. But the notion of historical flux was no more the exclusive logical outcome of eighteenth century thought than was the idea of progress; the seeds of both conceptions lay in the fundamental philosophy of the age.

Certainly the prevalence of optimism in the French Enlightenment cannot be denied. Mankind had recently made great strides in the understanding of the world, and the optimism of science

[27] *Correspondance littéraire*, III, 328.
[28] *Correspondance littéraire*, III, 329.
[29] *Correspondance littéraire*, III, 330.

irradiated the realms of philosophy, politics, ethics, and even the arts. Projects of human advancement and reform multiplied on every side, and were seconded by a widespread confidence in the ultimate simplicity of the world's problems, once these problems were approached by an adequate method and an enlightened understanding. But other strains of eighteenth century thought were persistent, and time and again these gave pause to the optimism of the age. Some of these strains already have been summarized in this study; such for example was a disturbing skepticism concerning man's nature, together with a belief in immutable natural law. Such too were various forms of antirationalism; such were the historical spirit and growing relativism of the age, and the application of the analogy of the natural world. The concluding part of this work will explore in more detail the relevance of these and other bases of historical pessimism to the writings of several highly significant individual thinkers of the century, thinkers hitherto largely ignored in these pages.

Part V

The Men and the Doctrines

Chapter 18

Pessimism in Moderation— Montesquieu

> Almost all the nations of the world travel this circle: to
> begin with, they are barbarous; they become conquerors and
> well-ordered nations; this order permits them to grow, and
> they become refined; refinement enfeebles them, and they
> return to barbarism. (*Pensées et fragments*)[1]

The Foundations

One of the most familiar names in modern intellectual history is
that of the Baron de Montesquieu; to add yet another chapter to the
mass of commentary upon him may appear both redundant and
impertinent. But, as is also the case with Voltaire and Diderot and
the other writers yet to be treated in this study, Montesquieu's
thought is sufficiently complex to present an unending succession
of interpretative problems. Little need be said here concerning the
time-worn subject of Montesquieu's political theory, for it is elsewhere that lie the greater complexities and the more fruitful subjects
of investigation. In this first section attention will be given to those
elements of Montesquieu's basic philosophy which are relevant to
his doctrine of historical development, while the following section
will summarize his view not of governments alone, but of composite
cultures, their formation and their destiny.

Montesquieu's relationship with Vico has long been in dispute,
and even today it has not been conclusively demonstrated that
Montesquieu had read the "New Science." There are points of

---

[1] *Pensées et fragments inédits de Montesquieu* (Bordeaux, 1899, 1901),
I, 114.

similarity, though, between the two great contemporaries, just as there are points of similarity between Dubos and Montesquieu. In each case, however, the problem is not primarily that of direct and specific influence, but is one of greater subtlety and perhaps equal difficulty. What was it that made these three thinkers responsive to the same general current of ideas, and what was it that caused them to differ? The problem is of course too involved for full treatment here; this study must confine itself to only a few components of Montesquieu's fundamental world-picture.

Unfortunately, the pertinent segments of Montesquieu's philosophy are precisely those on which disagreement is most widespread among his interpreters. Disclaiming any pretensions to final answers, one can only hope to throw some light upon Montesquieu's complex philosophy through a re-examination of the original works themselves. And one of the first questions to be considered in any evaluation of Montesquieu's significance for his century is that of the relative roles of rationalism and historico-empiricism in his thought.

Doubtless Montesquieu's general intellectual interests would create a presupposition in favor of an empirical approach to world development. For he was primarily an investigator of historical and political phenomena, which by nature tend to be more concrete than those metaphysical problems which he noted only incidentally. Moreover, in his youth he had harbored a lively interest in the cultivation and progress of the sciences—an orientation which one might expect would have left in him a certain distrust for the purely rational and abstract. Yet rationalism may well remain a major factor in historical and political studies themselves, and was particularly likely to do so in the eighteenth century; it is only from a direct examination of Montesquieu's approach to these studies that any valid conclusions can be drawn concerning that approach.

Such an examination reveals a large infusion of abstract rationalism in Montesquieu's thought. Certainly his conceptions of right, of justice, and of natural law are essentially absolute and *a priori* in nature. For him, principles ordinarily come before the fact, as he himself notes. "I have posed principles and have seen particular instances submit to them automatically; I have found that the history of all nations has been the consequence of these principles."[2] Montesquieu's deductive method thus makes supplementary use of experience and factual studies, as a general guide and as an illustration and confirmation of his principles. Yet the distance is great between the investigative spirit of Montesquieu and that of Bayle, who took such joy in the ferreting out of isolated facts, often for the simple joy of research.

However, Montesquieu combines with this penchant for abstract thought a number of genuinely empirical strains. Such above all is his attention to the environmental factor in the formation of peoples —a factor which in its empirical complexity stands in sharp contrast to broad theoretical generalizations. If to the modern reader Montesquieu's grasp of the diversity and complexity of various civilizations may not seem impressive, the intellectual atmosphere of the eighteenth century should be recalled. In that century Montesquieu, like Dubos and Vico, possessed an unusual appreciation and sympathy for the diversity of those ages, peoples, and cultural currents which had gone into the making of history. His sense of the subtlety of historical causation was uncommon for his day, nor did he dismiss the historical picture as a mere crazy quilt of senselessness and evil. The urge to understand and to explain was always present in him, though it often led to precisely that abstract theorization which has already been noted. But on other occasions Montesquieu showed a real sympathy for the past; he possessed, for example, a feeling for the Middle Ages, and his private skepticism did not prevent a certain understanding of religious history and of the social value of Christianity.

Montesquieu's conception of the nature and freedom of the individual is also of importance in the formation of his historical philosophy, but is never treated systematically in his work. On the nature of man he writes in the most divergent terms: now on his passions and his malevolence and at other times on his aspirations and his tendencies toward reason and virtue. In the Troglodyte legend and elsewhere, Montesquieu seems to hold that man is inherently neither good nor evil but that these qualities are the product

[2] *De l'esprit des lois*, in *Oeuvres complètes* (Paris, 1875), III, 83.

of external circumstances. At the same time he points out that human passions remain the same throughout the years; he is very far from preaching the perfectibility of man through education. Education for Montesquieu is a method for raising men to the level of their civilization, but not necessarily an instrument for further progress. And the type of education to be offered under particular circumstances must depend upon those circumstances themselves. One must teach what it is necessary to teach; thus in a monarchy one must inculcate the feeling for that "honor" which is the monarchical principle.

Montesquieu's doctrine of determinism and liberty adds weight to the counter-optimistic strain in his thought. Here again his position is ill-defined, though on one point he is insistent: on the reality of human freedom of will. For him the moral world of human intelligence escapes the rigid determinism of the physical world; at times man may violate with some success the laws of the natural world. Moral obligation exists, and presupposes the reality of free will.

The correlation of free will and natural necessity however remains unsatisfactory in Montesquieu's system, for he seems to hold that man is a part of nature yet evades its laws. And, despite his formal abjuration of fatalism, he finds that these laws operate on a deterministic basis. This is true not only of the general physical laws of the universe, but also of the specific human environment. Montesquieu arrives in effect at an environmental determinism which would seem to be capable of reconciliation with only a limited freedom of individual action. If there appear to be accidents in history, Montesquieu writes that there are also general immutable causes which envelop and contain the particular accidents. "All accidents are submitted to these causes, and if the fortune of a battle, which is a particular cause, has ruined a state, there was at the same time a general cause which made it necessary that the state should perish by a single battle."[3]

The legislator, Montesquieu continued, is not at liberty to create or change all laws with impunity. He must hold the traditional ethical standards of his civilization in special respect; morality cannot

[3] *Considérations sur les causes de la grandeur des Romains et de leur décadence*, in *Oeuvres complètes*, II, 273.

be changed by legislation, but only by moral example. It is evident that Montesquieu retained a certain ethical idealism, that determinism, for him, never entirely ruled out ethical meliorism. It is even quite probable that he saw no incompatibility between his environmental determinism and his doctrine of moral freedom.

Typically enough, the source of Montesquieu's doctrine of determinism is double: it comprises both his rationalism and his historical empiricism. His determinism is rational when it is built up deductively from the principle of the invariability of natural law; it is empirical when it is founded upon an actual study of the influence of environment upon the constitution and development of peoples. For Montesquieu held that one can indeed subject to careful investigation those conditions of environment which make a nation what it is.

According to Montesquieu these conditions are of two sorts, the moral and the physical. The distinction had already been made by Dubos, but Montesquieu reversed the relative importance of the two, and held that climate plays only a secondary role, especially in the formation of the general character of a people. Thus for him the action of men and governments and the general environmental opportunities offered by a particular culture are ordinarily the deciding factors in the formation of human character.

And the type of government found in a given situation—that is, its cultural individuality—depends not only upon the climate but on such conditions as the social composition of the state and the personal qualities of the citizens. Of laws Montesquieu wrote: "They must be relative to the physical characteristics of the country: to the climate . . . , the quality of the soil, and the country's location and size. They must be relative to the occupations of the inhabitants— are the inhabitants hunters, shepherds, or tillers of the soil? In addition, laws must be relative to the degree of liberty which is constitutionally possible, to the religion of the people, and their number, their inclinations, their wealth, their commerce, their morality, and their manners."[4]

Is it true, as might appear at first glance, that Montesquieu for-

[4] *De l'esprit des lois*, in *Oeuvres complètes*, III, 99–100.

6*

sakes all absolute values for a thoroughgoing relativism? Such would indeed seem to be the case with governmental laws. "When citizens obey the laws, what does it matter whether they follow the same law?"[5] It was the stark relativism of such a statement that aroused the ire of later Enlightened philosophical absolutists such as Condorcet. At other times Montesquieu was more cautious, though without any real change of position: there are, he wrote, both "positive and relative qualities," and "when one says that there are no absolute qualities, one does not mean to say that there are none at all, but rather that there are none for us, and that our mind cannot determine them."[6]

It is a matter of considerable interest that in the one field in which Montesquieu formally upheld unchanging values he tended to see not progress but decadence across the years. This was the field of aesthetics. Here Montesquieu was clearly an amateur and in no respect a truly original thinker. Though he made a certain effort, as will be seen in the following section, to integrate artistic development with the general course of civilization, his aesthetic theory nevertheless appears as a rather irrelevant appendage to his general system, and illustrates that curious philosophical lag which is to be found so often in the thought of distinguished innovators. Yet, despite such amazing judgments as his parallel of Rembrandt and La Motte, Montesquieu was on the whole an intelligent, if uninspired, critic.

On the question of the imitation of nature, on *belle nature*, simplicity, and absolute literary rules, Montesquieu displays the usual symptoms of the Classical mind in aesthetic matters. However, like Dubos, he shows a distinct preference for the Ancients over the Moderns, and in his qualified admiration for Gothic art he is likewise a dissident from standard eighteenth century taste. In addition, his attempt to relate art and literature to the political unit gives his aesthetic theory a certain mark of originality.

Such are some of the more pertinent factors in the formation of Montesquieu's historical outlook. If the general impression is a bit

[5] *De l'esprit des lois*, in *Oeuvres complètes*, V, 413.
[6] *Pensées et fragments inédits*, II, 490, 477.

chaotic, so too was the historical philosophy which emerged from this background. But this very chaos was to lead to a measure of moderation and realism in Montesquieu's thought. Thus, for example, the strong element of historico-empiricism in his work was to make his developmental scheme less dogmatic and less rigid than that of Vico. This scheme of historical flux must now be examined in some detail.

THE ORGANIC CULTURE

History, as Montesquieu saw it, was the scene neither of linear progress or linear decadence on the one hand, nor of regular, independent, and preordained cycles on the other. Rather it presented a picture of organic cultures tending to follow a common basic pattern of development, yet growing and dying each in its own tempo and each related in some way to other cultures. For Montesquieu each cultural unit was a temporal and spatial entity existing within a national framework, and possessing a "general spirit" of its own.

This conception of the "general spirit" or genius of a nation was central in Montesquieu's historical scheme. His definition of this spirit was succinct: "I understand by the genius of a nation the manner [*mœurs*] and mental character of different peoples influenced by a single court and a single capital."[7] This character is formed, he noted in the "Spirit of Laws," from a synthesis of laws and governmental maxims, manners and morals, climate and religion, and historical example and tradition.

In his fragment "On Politics" he elaborated upon this conception. "Every society is a spiritual union [*union d'esprit*], and in it a common character is formed. This universal soul comes to express its thoughts in a particular manner—a manner which results from a chain of an infinite number of causes multiplying and combining from age to age. As soon as this tone is generally accepted it is it alone which governs, and all that sovereigns, magistrates, and peoples can do or imagine, whether seeming to follow or to violate

---

[7] *Pensées et fragments inédits*, II, 170.

this tone, is forever relative to it; it dominates until the total destruction of the society."[8]

This tone or spirit, Montesquieu continued, is not unchanging; it may fade away or be destroyed, and this by the same infinite accumulation of causes which created it in the beginning. It is subject, also, to modification by those general changes from age to age which cut across national boundaries. Thus Montesquieu's conception is by no means the static one which sometimes it has been supposed to be; the spirit of a nation, according to him, is constantly subject to change, for the worse as for the better.

And each cultural unit, as framework and expression of the cultural spirit, is a dynamic entity founded upon a vast complex of ever varying relationships, both internal and external. "Everything," Montesquieu once wrote, "is linked, and everything holds together."[9] Governments and societies are living, dynamic syntheses of men, institutions, and environment.

It is not necessary to deal here at length with the specific internal relationships which Montesquieu considered important in the growth and decline of nations, though mention may be made of several such relationships by way of illustration. Such, for example, was the influence of commerce and luxury upon the history of nations. On this subject Montesquieu took a moderate stand, recognizing that if luxury and commerce might lead to moral decay under certain circumstances, under others they might result in the perfecting of the arts and in the extension of a feeling for social justice. His general conclusion was that luxury tends to refine primitive peoples, and to ruin well-ordered states when carried to excess.

Here as throughout his work Montesquieu was concerned above all with the moral condition of the given nation. For him it was the decay of the national spirit, the ruin of public and private morality, which signaled the definitive decadence of civilizations. Laws, customs, and ethics, if separate entities, nevertheless were closely related. Moreover, Montesquieu did not neglect the multiplicity of

---

[8] *De la politique*, in *Mélanges inédits de Montesquieu* (Bordeaux, Paris, 1892), 160–161.

[9] *Pensées et fragments inédits*, I, 277.

vital interconnections among the arts and sciences, literature, and philosophy, or their various relationships with the cultural whole. The sciences and the mechanical arts, he noted, can serve society by contributing to such fields of endeavor as hygiene, commerce, and geographical exploration. The fine arts he saw as closely related to cultural development and to the spirit of the nation—witness the effect of Greek religion and athletics upon the art of that people.

Montesquieu also gave explicit attention to the correlation between the course of empires and that of literature, philosophy, and the fine arts. "The establishment of monarchical government," he wrote, "creates a certain refinement, but works of intellect appear only in the first period of monarchies, for the general corruption which follows affects the intellectual as well as other realms."[10] The prosperity of letters "is so intimately attached to that of empires that the first is infallibly the indication or the cause of the second. If we glance at the present world situation we shall see that Europe is prosperous and dominates the other three parts of the world while the rest of the globe suffers under the weight of poverty and slavery, and that in similar measure Europe is more enlightened than these other parts of the globe, buried as they are in deep darkness. If we look at Europe itself we shall see that those states in which letters are most cultivated have proportionately the greater power. And if we look only at our own France we shall see that the cultivation of letters has advanced or declined with the course of national glory. So it was that the light of letters shone dimly under Charlemagne and was then extinguished; so it was that it reappeared under Francis I and has since followed the brilliance of the monarchy."[11]

And Montesquieu felt that there was a similar correlation between the decay of the fine arts and that of nations. As examples he cited the decadence of sculpture and architecture in the decline of the Roman Empire and in the empire of the Caliphs, and the similar artistic decadence which was threatening contemporary France.

On the political, ethical, intellectual, and artistic influences of

[10] *Pensées et fragments inédits*, II, 28.
[11] *Pensées et fragments inédits*, I, 273.

one cultural unit upon the others, Montesquieu wrote little of an explicit nature. It is clear, however, that he did not regard these units as isolated altogether from the other nations of the world. Certainly he saw an extensive heritage in the modern age from classical antiquity, just as he spoke of the extraneous moral and artistic influences which helped mold Rome itself. Yet, if he rejected Vico's notion of hermetically sealed civilizations, the organic unity which Montesquieu saw in each individual nation could only lead to a system of considerable historical discontinuity.

If this conception of the dynamic individuality of civilizations restrained Montesquieu from seeing man's historical course in terms of a unitary and purposeful evolution, it encouraged a view of constant world movement and flux. In this further respect, then, it is quite incorrect to speak of Montesquieu's world-picture as static; all phenomena for him were being constantly modified in a continuous series of natural adjustments. Yet it is true that his application of this principle was faulty, that his actual treatment of history was often abstract, oversimplified, and completely non-historical.

Such was undoubtedly the case in his well-known theory of the growth, structure, and decay of the three forms of government—the republican, monarchical, and despotic. It must be noted, however, that at no time did Montesquieu consider these forms as stable and static; he viewed them, rather, as subject to constant modification both from within and from without. In a posthumous fragment he refers to the operation of internal and external causes of change, though over an extended period of time. "From time to time there occur inundations of peoples who impose their customs and their ethical code throughout the lands which they have occupied. The Mohammedan influx brought despotism along with it, while the northern peoples brought aristocratic government. It has taken nine hundred years for the abolition of this latter governmental form and the substitution of monarchy. And so the world will continue. It appears that as the ages pass we shall descend gradually to the lowest degree of civic servility, until some accident changes the disposition of men's minds and makes them as intractable as they were in earlier years. So it is that the world has always witnessed the flux and reflux of empire and of liberty."[12]

But it was upon the corruption of governmental principles, or internal decay, that Montesquieu wrote at greatest length. The perpetual lack of governmental equilibrium, the metamorphoses of republics and monarchies, both frequently inclining toward despotism—these points in his famous theory hardly require amplification here.

However, as has been seen already, Montesquieu recognized that the decline of governments involved much more than a mere change of political forms. He discussed ancient Rome at some length, as the type of a civilization in decline, and here as elsewhere he emphasized that decadence is inherent in progress itself, and that civic liberty is a frail plant indeed. Laws and principles are outgrown by an expanding state, and either their rigidity or their ill-advised modification will lead eventually to decadence, as in ancient Rome. Montesquieu went on to describe the moral and intellectual decay of the Romans. For the moral corruption of later Rome he found a variety of factors responsible, among them the inordinate growth of riches, the pernicious philosophy of the Epicureans, and Roman contact with the corrupt societies of the East. And, though the parallel was not specifically discussed by him, it may be presumed that often he was thinking not only of the decadence of the ancient world, but also of the decline which he believed was threatening France. Such too would seem to be the lesson taught by his legend of the Troglodytes.

The cyclical fluctuation of all cultural phenomena was considered by Montesquieu to be the inevitable accompaniment of political flux. Thus religion too, he wrote, can follow a cyclical course, within which the antitheses are piety and superstition. The arts likewise have their cycles, as well as their varying rates of development according to the nation in which they are found and the complex environmental situation of the moment. The exhaustion of the arts,

[12] *Pensées et fragments inédits*, II, 210.

like that of whole civilizations, may be the result of external circumstances, or it may derive from such internal causes as the necessary limitations upon all art forms. In literature as in empires Montesquieu concluded that prosperity is the immediate herald of decadence, and he added that the literary outlook for eighteenth century France was bleak indeed.[13]

Unlike Vico, Montesquieu tended to view his own day with both disapproval and alarm. To be sure, in his writings one may find occasional moderate praise for the growing common sense and humanitarianism of his century, as well as ridicule for the common tendency of all ages toward a belief in contemporary degeneration. But these passages run counter only to a theory of cosmic decay which was never held by Montesquieu, and not to his general theory of cyclical flux.

A complete catalogue of the criticisms which Montesquieu levelled against his century and his nation would be lengthy indeed, and a bit pointless. Leaving aside his specific grievances against the French political regime, one might consider, for example, a wide variety of commentary upon the moral decay of his age. Nor did he find the contemporary French world of intellect and letters without its serious failings. The acquisition of knowledge, he wrote, had taken on a deceptive air of facility which was encouraging false pride, *bel esprit*, and a neglect of fundamentals. Taste was corrupt, and, with the reign of satire and hasty judgment, criticism was preferred to serious study.[14]

In the "Persian Letters" and in the posthumous works one finds other judgments of the most miscellaneous nature, from passages on the decadence of established religion to those on the growing disrespect for noble rank and civic dignity. The extreme luxury and frivolity of the day he flayed severely, while the presumed depopulation of Europe was cited as a further indication of the fundamental decay of the century. And to complete this diverse list one might quote a curiously bilious passage from his fragmentary reflections. "I was asked," he wrote, "why there is no vogue today for Corneille,

[13] *Pensées et fragments inédits*, I, 275; II, 20-21.
[14] *Pensées et fragments inédits*, I, 275-276.

Racine, etc. I replied that it is because all those things for which intelligence is demanded have become ridiculous, and that indeed the evil lies even deeper than this. Men can no longer tolerate anything which has a fixed object: military men cannot tolerate warfare, officials cannot tolerate the office, and so on. We are coming to know generalities alone, and in practice these reduce themselves to nothing. It is our social intercourse with women which has brought us to this state, for they are dilettantes by nature. Today there is only one sex left; we have all become women as far as intellectual life is concerned. If one night our features were to change, no one would notice the difference." [15]

Montesquieu's plaints of contemporary decadence are often isolated in his writings, yet they occur frequently enough to indicate a genuine feeling for the lapses of his age. It is perhaps natural then that he should voice an interest in reforms of the most varied sort. But it is equally natural that his notions of reform should be sternly curtailed; both his personal spirit of conservative moderation and the implications of his philosophical ideas militated against his reformist tendencies.

Certainly his insistence upon environmental determinism played a vital role in his refusal to advocate wholesale reform. As has been seen earlier, this determinism was never an all-pervasive force; Montesquieu did not wish to deny altogether the efficacy of human choice and action. However, in his emphasis upon the complexities of the environment he had shown the great difficulty of reform. Government and its laws, he had written, were based largely upon the moral environment, and ethical behavior could be effectively reformed only by more desirable ethical behavior, not by legislation. Only after a long term of years could laws make themselves felt in the realm of morality.

For these and other reasons Montesquieu was far indeed from constructing any optimistic project for the descent of heaven upon earth. Growth and decay were the destiny of things earthly, and it seemed to Montesquieu both useless and positively dangerous to try to tamper extensively with destiny. In several brief sentences he out-

[15] *Pensées et fragments inédits*, II, 33.

lined a complete system of political conservatism. "A government resembles an arithmetic sum which is composed of several figures. When one takes away or adds a single figure, he changes the value of all the others. But since in arithmetic one knows the value and relationship of each figure, he can avoid error. It is not the same in politics; here one can never know what will be the result of the change which he makes. Such is the nature of things that the abuse very often is preferable to the reform, or at least that an established good is always preferable to a hypothetical amelioration."[16] The maintenance of the status quo in high civilizations thus tended to be Montesquieu's aim, for change could only hasten the inevitable decline.

So it was that in his most typical humor the keynote of Montesquieu's wisdom was conformity. Man does best, he felt, not to try to force the pace of nature, but rather to submit with good grace to its necessary and invariable laws. In this sense, and in this sense alone, one is justified in referring to Montesquieu's system as one of social statics. The world, he held, is in continual flux, but the forces which propel the general movement are largely outside the control of the human will. Man can remedy trifling evils and can even suspend or change for a time the inevitable course of a civilization, but man cannot brave forever the predetermined destiny of a nation.

Montesquieu's thought, to be sure, is complex and at times confused; to present a brief summary of his position is difficult indeed.[17] Yet one may safely characterize Montesquieu as a moderate and a conservative. Both in philosophy and in politics his great concern

---

[16] *Pensées et fragments inédits*, II, 365.

[17] An additional question is posed here: what relative weight should be given to the major published works of Montesquieu, as against the great mass of fragmentary material which became public property only a century and a half after his death? Is this latter material simply the insignificant by-product of Montesquieu's erudition, the ill-advised trivia which he himself did not deign to publish? Or is it not, rather, an important part of his work precisely because of its informality and spontaneity, because it was the intimate and uncensored expression of the author's mind? Certainly the material in the posthumous writings enriches his thought immeasurably, and in them much is revealed which otherwise could only be surmised.

was to avoid extreme solutions; he escaped, for example, both the rigidity and the absolutism of a Vico, and the extreme empirical relativism of a Dubos. His hopes for political reform were cautious, and never were they enlarged into a theory of progress—nor in fact were they ever specifically correlated with his doctrine of historical flux. Montesquieu was in no sense a genuine theoretician of progress, though by the same token he was perhaps not, consciously, an historical pessimist. But his pessimism, if often somewhat parenthetical, was none the less real. If in the last two centuries his work has sometimes served under the progressionist and even the revolutionary banner, this fact proves less concerning the original doctrines of Montesquieu than concerning man's eternal skill in forcing the past to do duty for a specific present.

Chapter 19

The Imperfect Dream—Voltaire

> The world is casting off its stupid simplicity at a furious rate. On all sides a great intellectual revolution is heralded. (Letter to D'Alembert)[1]

> The time will come when the savages of today will have their operas, and when we will be reduced to the dance of the peace pipe. (*Pensées, remarques, et observations*)[2]

PHILOSOPHY IN HISTORY

One of the most pressing problems which have confronted successive generations of students of Voltaire is the problem of the measure of consistency in his thought. The internal unity of Voltaire's basic philosophy now seems better established than in past years; certainly to designate his thought as a "chaos of clear ideas" is to do him a serious injustice. The greater amount of confusion is discernible not within but outside the fundamental philosophical or metaphysical problems treated by him—in those broader realms of application where momentary whims and polemical argument were likely to play an unusually important role. Such a realm was that of historical interpretation, with its questions of progress, decadence, and historical flux. Into Voltaire's treatment of these questions flowed a number of varying currents of ideas and emotions, from which could only come an eclectic result. Certainly a fully integrated synthesis of his historical philosophy can be attained only by an extreme forcing of his thought. This thought will be discussed here upon the pre-

---

[1] April 5, 1765, *Oeuvres complètes de Voltaire*, XLIII, 519–520.
[2] *Pensées, remarques, et observations de Voltaire*, in *Oeuvres complètes*, XXXI, 120–121.

sumption that in Voltaire the attitudes of historical optimism and pessimism were to a large degree discrete and irreconcilable.

The basis for Voltaire's historical optimism includes several currents common to many writers of the Enlightenment, notably the idea of the invariability of natural law, the psychological doctrine of sensationalism, and the belief in man's capacity both for goodness and for reason. If for Voltaire the invariability of natural law did not guarantee mankind against decadence, it did seem to offer the basis for eternal standards of moral and intellectual progress; it saved Voltaire from any thorough historical relativism and made possible the setting of fixed goals for human development. For if nature is ruled by invariable law, surely man, as a part of the natural world, must be similarly ruled; the ultimate uniformity of reason and morality in all ages and nations was among the first of Voltaire's philosophical assumptions.

Though he saw man as the vehicle of certain eternal and divinely sanctioned moral inclinations, Voltaire remained firm in his formal rejection of innate ideas, and in his belief in the sensations as the sole source of man's ideas. External circumstance, or experience, was for him the sole teacher of man. And upon this foundation Voltaire built that confidence which he often expressed in education as the force which would mold the individual and promote general progress.

To be sure, Voltaire often gave, in the application, a pessimistic turn both to his doctrine of sensationalism and to that of the invariability of natural law; moreover, a similar dualism entered into his consideration of the moral and intellectual condition of man. Leaving the exceptions to a later section, one may note for the moment Voltaire's great faith in human potentialities for goodness and for rationality. Here he imagined himself to be opposing the Christian dogma of the fallen nature of man; man, he asserted, is infinitely more good than bad. Man possesses the ability to reason, and it is this reason which must be the agent of progress.

Reason, for Voltaire, is that critical faculty which resists the promptings of the passions and the dictates of faith and authority. Reason and empiricism he saw as being in close alliance, though for pragmatic and polemical reasons he discussed and applied the two methods in rather erratic fashion. The habit of observation which he contracted from scientific and historical studies was to qualify in some ways his rationalistic optimism, but certainly in science itself Voltaire was an outstanding apostle of progress through a Newtonian union of reason and experimentalism. The complications and contradictions which arose when he tried to apply scientific method to other fields of human activity were accidental, and if in practice he was at times obliged to supplement rationalism with empiricism, a formal humiliation of reason was far indeed from his mind.

For it was the development of reason which Voltaire often considered to be the great and hopeful theme of history. Though he did not expect perfection to be the outcome of this development, certainly he did suggest that a trend toward this fleeting goal was possible, and indeed evident. Only God, he wrote, could be perfect, but it was for man to try to resemble God as far as his nature permitted. And God had endowed man with the seeds of universal reason, and with the power to conserve and to nourish these seeds.

Moreover, Voltaire always assumed that the Enlightenment was the expression of this universal reason, or at any rate of man's impulsion toward reason. Reason was philosophy, and philosophy reason. Thus the rational Voltairean view of history became an apology for the Enlightenment. History was the cosmic struggle of reason against unreason, and progress the gradual liberation of reason; the eighteenth century was witnessing many hopeful advances in this great struggle for liberation.

Voltaire at times perceived a compelling force in reason which was very nearly irresistible. Absurdity and evil would certainly vanish, he wrote, if men could see them rationally depicted. The world already was becoming wiser, and the growth of wisdom could only lead to a simpler and better religion, a saner politics, and a more prosperous economy. At worst, the universal diffusion of philosophy would "somewhat console human nature for the calamities experienced in all ages."[3]

---

[3] *Conclusion et examen de ce tableau historique*, in *Oeuvres complètes*, XXIV, 475.

All of this involves, unmistakably, a theory of progress. Yet Voltaire never made his idea of progress altogether clear and precise, perhaps because, as will be seen later, his observation of the world prevented him from envisaging progress as unitary and all-embracing. However, despite the continued prospect of human misfortune, Voltaire asserted again and again the reality of progress, however ephemeral this progress might appear to be. And even for bleak days his usual counsel was not one of passive despair, but of vigorous meliorative action. Certainly his own suggestions for reform were many, and extended over a broad area of human activity, from religion and ethics to politics and economics.

But Voltaire often did not limit himself to the simple hope for progress which was implied in his suggestions for reform; more categorical statements of the principle of progress may be found in his writings. Despite error and evil in the world, he wrote, men have progressed to a point midway between the night of ignorance and the noontide of reason. Freedom of conscience will come one day, and philosophy and reason will reign. "Everything that I see contributes to a great change [*révolution*] which will certainly occur, though I shall not have the joy of witnessing it. In all things the French move slowly, but move they do. The light has become so widely diffused that it will break out into the open when the opportunity first offers itself, and will cause a fine tumult indeed. The young people are fortunate—they will see great things."[4]

If this faith of Voltaire was in part, or even basically, an abstract optimistic construction, it was buttressed heavily by well-chosen facts. Progress, thought Voltaire in his more sanguine moods, was the lesson of history as well as the imperative of philosophy. There had been, he asserted, no golden age in the past, and contemporary conditions in all respects marked an improvement over the days of classical antiquity. The darkness of the Middle Ages was deep, and only with the Renaissance was lasting progress actualized. Finally with the "Age of Louis XIV"—a term which he applied to all of western Europe—Voltaire saw a tremendous acceleration in the pace

[4] Letter to the Marquis de Chauvelin, April 2, 1764, *Oeuvres complètes*, XLIII, 175.

of progress. In that great age England and Florence led the advance in philosophy, and France in the arts and in ethical science; together, and with the aid of other nations, they created the highest civilization which man had ever known.

His own century, he added, was in many respects the continuation of the preceding one. Reason and philosophy were making the greatest strides of all, and promised new triumphs, though perhaps at the expense of the more gracious arts of life. Religious toleration was increasing, and here and there might soon become complete. Several weeks before his death Voltaire wrote with deep satisfaction to Frederick the Great: "I have seen a score of similar proofs of that progress which philosophy has finally made in all walks of life. . . . It is true then . . . that men do eventually see the light, and that those who feel obliged to blind them are not always in a position to do so."[5]

However, it was not the progress of knowledge alone which Voltaire praised. He wrote at some length on economic progress; his arguments for the utility of luxury and against the depopulation theory of degeneration are too well known to require more than passing mention. Nor did he find that the various types of progress are produced wholly in haphazard fashion; there are rudiments of a theory of developmental relationships in his writings. Yet he never proposed an altogether unitary scheme of development; philosophy, for example, he saw as aiding morality while remaining indifferent or pernicious to the arts.

Despite his lack of system, Voltaire did remain, in his happier moods, a champion of general progress and of the French civilization of his own day. To celebrate the superior merits of the "good old days" seemed to him quite unreasonable; both as epicure and as citizen he found his century to be the most satisfactory of all thus far in history. But at the same time there were sobering considerations. Could this progress continue indefinitely? And were there not alarming cracks already visible in the structure? Here a completely

[5] April 1, 1778, *Oeuvres complètes*, L, 383–384.

different current of Voltairean thought came into play—a current which must be examined briefly before turning to the actual historical pessimism which it often induced.

THE GENESIS OF PESSIMISM

Voltaire never abandoned altogether the position of rationalistic optimism outlined in the preceding section. He did modify it, however, and at times very drastically. This was especially true in the later years of his life, when a shift in certain basic philosophical emphases made itself felt in his general world outlook. The result, let it be noted once again, was not an orderly synthesis, for the new infusions were not only in sharp conflict with optimistic rationalism but were not themselves always mutually compatible.

Of only indirect importance to the present study, Voltaire's change from the theory of the freedom of the will to a belief in its bondage nevertheless was perhaps the greatest single factor in the general reorientation which occurred in his thought near the mid-point of the century. This change, to be sure, was not as comprehensive as it has often been depicted. Both before and after the change Voltaire recognized two aspects of man's voluntary behavior: the moment of willing, and the carrying out of that willing into action. In both periods he recognized man's freedom in the latter respect. In the first period he saw possible only a limited freedom in the first field, that of willing; in the second period he denied categorically all such freedom. The change then was largely one of emphasis: his earlier belief that the ability to act according to one's will was most important and that it could therefore be identified with "freedom of will" was shaken by the recognition that the willing itself was more fundamental. And this freedom to will, properly speaking, he had never recognized. Man, he asserted, necessarily wills what he wills, and this necessity is external to him. Men are but thinking automata, atoms in movement, submitted to a chaos of events "which they can neither foresee, ward off, nor understand, yet which they sometimes fancy they can master."[6] "We are," he wrote to the Duc de Riche-lieu, "balloons pushed blindly and irresistibly by the hand of fate. Sometimes we collide with marble and sometimes with dunghills, and eventually we are destroyed forever."[7]

But would it not then follow that rewards and punishments are senseless, that men can only deliver themselves to passive resignation, and that general progress is simply fortuitous? To these questions Voltaire replied with a firm negative. Men will forever be active, he asserted, for such is their destiny. Crime will always be punished, for predestination toward crime implies predestination toward punishment. And neither progress nor any other historical movement is fortuitous, for the world is ruled by necessity.

Men in the mass, Voltaire continued, are guided as surely by the hand of fate as are individuals. "Chance" is but a word for man's ignorance of causes; nature and societies follow a necessary and pre-determined course. It is fate which ultimately governs the world, both in its progress and its regress; if world history follows a plan, it is a plan beyond the control of mankind. Moreover, it is, on the whole, a plan unfathomable and incomprehensible in its essence. "This then is the way of the world, ruled as it is by that fortune which is nothing but necessity and insurmountable fate. *Fortuna saevo laeto negotio*. Fortune forces us to play her terrible game like blind men: we never see the face of the cards."[8]

How can this inscrutable, autonomous fatality be reconciled with the molding of the universe by human reason? Voltaire does not in fact attempt a formal reconciliation, but rather calls upon the two theories in turn according to his current mood or the matter at hand. Perhaps, if pressed, Voltaire would have granted that even reason must act within the framework of determinism, and that man's proudest achievements are ultimately not the fruit of free will but of fate. Actually, though his determinism often hovered in the back-ground, Voltaire preferred to discuss most events as if they were

[6] Letter to the Comtesse d'Egmont, October 29, 1755, *Oeuvres complètes*, XXXVIII, 494.

[7] June 10, 1752, *Oeuvres complètes*, XXXVII, 437.

[8] "Théodose," *Dictionnaire philosophique*, in *Oeuvres complètes*, XX, 513.

discrete, independent phenomena, and man as if he were a free agent.

Certainly Voltaire's doctrine of the unchanging nature of man was less the fruit of a hypothetical deterministic outlook than of his study of history. For history and casual observation revealed to Voltaire many discouraging facts concerning human nature. First among these was the restriction of reason within certain bounds. Reason, if perfectible, was certainly not infinitely so, and final causes would remain forever mysterious. But more important as a counter-optimistic force was Voltaire's denial of the basic goodness of man. Human nature, for him, was neither fundamentally good nor fundamentally bad, but rather the product of circumstance and environment. In his more gloomy moods Voltaire had harsh words indeed for the human race, for its presumption, pettiness, passion, and vileness. But God, he reflected, had taken pity on mankind and had made it frivolous and vain so as to render it less miserable.

Such a view of humanity certainly could not encourage historical optimism. If Voltaire perhaps wrote some of these passages for literary effect alone, or under the influence of an ephemeral despair, not all of them can be dismissed as mere whims. On the whole they appear to be as authentic an expression of his mind as were those occasional extravagant paeans to reason which may also be found in his work; it is unfair to him to ignore either trend in favor of the other.

Voltaire's belief in the fundamental unchangeability of nature did not restrain him from granting to environment a considerable power over mankind and over the formulation of human values. While challenging Montesquieu's heavy emphasis upon climatic influences, he did see men as the product of religion, education, and governmental institutions. Though, for example, he upheld in general the universality of rational ethics, he found moral custom to be altogether arbitrary in certain aspects of sexual behavior. And on occasion he could even state that "virtue and vice, moral good and evil . . . in each country are what are useful or harmful to that society."[9] And he saw nations and historical ages as varying not

[9] *Traité de métaphysique, in Oeuvres complètes,* XXII, 225.

only in their moral standards but also in their general spirit and character. If environmental determinism always remained a somewhat exotic plant in Voltaire's philosophy, it was nevertheless present, and thereby offered a continual challenge to the conception of linear historical development.

The position taken by Voltaire on the question of philosophical or Leibnitzian optimism was equally ambiguous, for here again he neglected to establish a consistent system. In his earlier years, without actually embracing a strict philosophical optimism, he took an indulgent view of the ills of the world, and as late as 1746 he implied that if all was not well with the world, at least everything was passable. But the tone of *Candide* and of the "Poem on the Lisbon Disaster" is very different; to claim that everything is for the best in the best of possible worlds then seemed to him to be a cruel and heartless jest.

His attack on philosophical optimism took two divergent lines. On pragmatic grounds he opposed this optimism as preaching passive submission to fate and thus as deterring human progress through action. On empirical grounds he felt that philosophical optimism simply did not meet the facts squarely, that it could not satisfactorily account for the vast quantity of evil, error, and misfortune which obviously existed in the world. For Voltaire did not look at the world with the eyes of the rationalist alone; he never ceased to value highly the evidence of empirical observation. It is true that he lacked a strong sense for the great range of diversity among peoples, that he had little understanding of religious motivation, that his conception of historical causation was naïve, and that he often saw history less as an historian than as an artist and a polemicist. Yet he was not without a feeling for the complexities of scholarly research and for the rules of historical evidence. And as he confronted the historical scene he could only be impressed by the tragic and demonic current which it revealed all too clearly.

This current was to take a prominent place in his historical writing, where its persistence seems to indicate that he considered it more than a mere foil to the triumphant course of reason. One may dismiss such early poetic exercises as the ode of 1713 "On the Misfortunes of the Times," but it is impossible to do so with much of his mature production. Here again and again one finds the picture of the world as a pest-house of frightful ailments and perversions; the world frequently appeared to Voltaire as the eternal scene of crime and warfare, of folly and weakness, of misery and shattered illusions, and of the crushing of virtue by maleficence. There are, he granted, brief respites from the "bloody tragedy and ridiculous comedy of this world," but these are tiny oases in a vast desert of misfortunes.[10] Even the great ages of philosophy and the arts are not exempt from the follies and horrors of other times. To be sure, Voltaire acknowledged that the evils of mundane existence might be exaggerated, and now and then the exuberance in his nature revolted strongly against the restraints of his historical pessimism. Yet if at times Voltaire bore his pessimism lightly, the basic sincerity of his plaints can seldom be doubted.

Such then are some of the factors which seem to have caused Voltaire to modify his historical optimism. It appears unlikely that his denial of the freedom of the will had any direct repercussions upon his optimism, though at first glance it might be presumed to lead to a sort of fatalistic resignation. However, as a part of the theory of historical determinism, this denial of freedom seems to have created a certain presumption in favor of a continuing round of social sickness and health as the result of man's inability to control his own fate. At times the doctrine of the unchanging nature of man strengthened the same presumption, as did the contrary doctrine of environmental determinism. Finally, Voltaire's violent reaction against philosophical optimism emphasized the existence of a permanent factor of evil in world history, and the consequent barrier to extensive progress. Thus human perfectibility, if not altogether ruled out of history, became strictly limited, while its actualization became almost independent of man himself. The groundwork was laid for a broad doctrine of historical pessimism.

[10] Letter to the Comtesse de Lutzelbourg, November 1, 1758, *Oeuvres complètes*, XXXIX, 526.

The Limits of Perfectibility

Beset on all sides by hostile forces, Voltaire's rationalistic optimism often was hard pressed indeed. At times one even is tempted to see in this optimism a mere pragmatic dogma for vulgar consumption, while pessimism remained the authentic Voltairean attitude. Yet Voltaire was obstinate in his insistence upon a certain perfectibility inherent in man. This assertion of perfectibility, however, could not remain in a naïvely rationalistic form after the onslaughts of historico-empirical pessimism. Thus Voltaire, unwilling to relinquish altogether the optimistic dream, found himself forever qualifying his earlier sanguine statements.

Instances of such qualifications abound, especially in his later writings. Such was his emphasis on that malignant power of habit and custom which leads inevitably to political abuse. Such was his observation that general progress always lags far behind the enlightenment of the few. Such were his repeated categorical statements on the future continuation of international warfare and destruction. Barbarism, he concluded, was the natural condition of man; man could raise and maintain himself above this norm only by an extreme and sustained effort. And at times Voltaire could only question whether man had made any significant moral progress through the centuries. "Before daring to say that we are better than our ancestors we should have to prove that under their conditions of life we should abstain with horror from the crimes of which they were guilty—and it is not demonstrated that in such a case we would be more humane than they."[11]

Certainly the concept of decadence was familiar to Voltaire; as an historian of Western man he wrote extensively on the decadence of the medieval world, while as a literary critic he condemned unmercifully the artistic degeneration of his own day. With such lapses as these in mind, and with the mingled optimism and pessimism of his basic theory, he sometimes inclined toward a loose system of historical or cyclical flux which closely resembled that of Montes-

[11] *Des conspirations contre les peuples ou des proscriptions,* in *Oeuvres complètes,* XXVI, 15.

quieu. Like many of his contemporaries he saw four high-points in the philosophical and artistic record of mankind: Greece under Pericles and Alexander, Rome in the age of Caesar and Augustus, the artistic and humanistic Renaissance, and the Age of Louis XIV. History also revealed to Voltaire countless other fluctuations and revolutions, an eternal succession of barbarism and refinement. "After raising itself for a time from one bog, it [the world] falls back into another; an age of barbarism follows an age of refinement. This barbarism in turn is dispersed, and then reappears; it is a continual alternation of day and night."[12]

Thus Voltaire envisaged an uneven succession of progress and decadence in the world, an uneasy fluctuation of nations and ages, now in sickness and now in health. "We can note that in the course of many revolutions, both in Europe and in Asia, peoples which once were well organized have fallen into a state of near savagery."[13] Voltaire indicated, too, that he expected the fluctuating process to continue in the future. Civilization, he wrote, is forever susceptible to degeneration, while new cultures may rise from peoples at present barbarous or unorganized.[14] It is true that he did not develop this system extensively, and that many vital questions were left unanswered. But a Voltairean doctrine of historical flux does exist and must be taken into account whenever his philosophy of history is discussed.

Voltaire's diagnoses of decline in the Europe of his day are frequent, though their significance is often open to question. His general satisfaction with his own age has already been noted, and one may view with some skepticism a number of his extravagant condemnations of the contemporary scene. Did he really believe that his century was "not simply ridiculous, but horrible"?[15] One may be permitted to doubt it. Yet among other criticisms which he levelled against contemporary society are a number which cannot be dismissed so readily. Such were his attacks

[12] "Miracles," *Dictionnaire philosophique*, in *Oeuvres complètes*, XX, 85.
[13] *Essai sur les mœurs*, in *Oeuvres complètes*, XIII, 178.
[14] "Miracles," *Dictionnaire philosophique*, in *Oeuvres complètes*, XX, 85.
[15] Letter to the Comte d'Argental, August 30, 1769, *Oeuvres complètes*, XLVI, 427.

upon the persecution of philosophy and upon the dearth of talents in all fields.

But these and similar attacks do not weigh very heavily against the many praises which at other times he lavished upon his own age. If, as it appears, Voltaire believed that contemporary European civilization, like all civilizations, would finally decay, he commonly remained cheerful as to the present and the immediate future. On the more remote future one finds in his work a number of passages indicating a recognition of the possibility of decline. Late in life he put into the mouth of Reason the following words, addressed to Truth: "Let us enjoy these fine days and remain here on earth if they continue. But if storms arise let us retire to our caverns."[16]

Fanaticism, he admitted, forever threatens to destroy the painfully acquired progress made by philosophy.[17] It is true, he added, that "we have gradually perfected society—but we were destined to do so, and the conjunction of all world events was required in order to make possible the mere reverence of a dancing master. The time will come when the savages of today will have their operas, and when we will be reduced to the dance of the peace pipe."[18]

So it was that Voltaire, though often an apparent optimist concerning the potentialities of his own age, was at times a pessimistic skeptic on the ultimate destiny of the civilization which he knew. France and Europe, he implied, would not be exempt from the common fate of all nations, and even the Enlightenment did not mark the definitive stage of historical progress. Indeed, in moments of extreme disillusionment or of extreme tolerance Voltaire might renounce active social effort altogether, and preach instead the gospel of resignation and personal enjoyment. Such may or may not have been the intention of his celebrated injunction to cultivate one's garden, but other passages in his work are more explicit. Only resignation, he wrote, could sustain man against the misery and

---

[16] *Eloge historique de la raison*, in *Oeuvres complètes*, XXI, 522.

[17] "Heureux, heureuse, heureusement," *Dictionnaire philosophique*, in *Oeuvres complètes*, XIX, 346.

[18] *Pensées, remarques, et observations de Voltaire*, in *Oeuvres complètes*, XXXI, 120–121. This fragment is not authenticated beyond all doubt, but probably comes from the pen of Voltaire.

absurdity in the world. Like the angel Ituriel, Voltaire often seems wholly willing to accept man and the world as they are. With the arts and the social graces as consolation, the fated ills of the world may be forgotten, and the present moment enjoyed to the full.

Thus pessimism and even social indifferentism were integral parts of Voltaire's approach to world history; they were indeed the natural outcome of certain elements in his fundamental philosophy. And, though rationalistic optimism tended to prevail in his general historical philosophy, in one major field his pessimism was almost unchallenged—the field of taste and literature. Despite his slight attention to the fine arts, there are also indications that often he saw these as following a similarly discouraging course of development.

Voltaire never produced a systematic treatise on taste, but it is not difficult to piece together the fragments of such a treatise and thus to discover the general principles of his aesthetic theory. Such a synthesis reveals a system which, however gravely modified upon occasion, is unmistakably Classical in inspiration. Indeed, Voltaire embodied best of all among the writers of the French Enlightenment that literary orthodoxy which was threatened more and more seriously in the course of the century.

It is hardly necessary to discuss in detail Voltaire's system of aesthetics. On the nature and function of beauty, taste, and style he followed the most acceptable Classical teachings. Like most of his contemporaries he granted an aesthetic role both to pleasure and to ethical precepts, and like them he vacillated in his relative emphasis upon rules and genius. On the question of absolute standards of beauty he was similarly indecisive, though seldom in open revolt against Classicism. Frequently he asserted that absolute standards are impossible in a changing universe and that each people has its own unique genius of feeling and expression. Yet he never accepted completely the aesthetic relativism implied in these assertions, but rather maintained the coexistence of relative and eternal beauties. "Taste" was perhaps Voltaire's central aesthetic conception; he was adamant in upholding the reality of a fixed good taste, and a fixed bad taste, throughout the ages.

As with the other Classical aestheticians of the century, it was the

7+

literature of the Age of Louis XIV which was the model continually before Voltaire's eyes. He insisted that in that age literature had attained its most perfect, its most glorious expression; he could only hope that "the centuries to come might equal the great Age of Louis XIV, and that they might not degenerate while thinking they were surpassing it."[19] But throughout his work Voltaire made it quite clear that he considered such degeneration already a fact. Repeatedly he decried the growing literary decadence and barbarism of his day; his literary criticism, from as early as 1716, is a continued dirge. "The time of decadence," he stated flatly, "has come."[20] Nor did he altogether exempt his own work from the general trend, if one may judge from his frank admission of inferiority to Racine.

Since the Age of Louis XIV, France had, according to Voltaire, been living on its credit, "like a wealthy man who gradually ruins himself."[21] Criticism was replacing creation, and the subjects for literary treatment were being exhausted. Moreover, Voltaire extended his critique of contemporary literature into a general theory of literary decadence. In his writings one finds the familiar metaphor of the sterility of the thoroughly cultivated field; the epic poet, for example, who writes the work suitable to his subject, age, and nation, can only discourage all later writers in his field.

It is the same in the art of tragedy. One cannot hold that the great feelings, the great tragic passions, can vary infinitely and still remain new and striking. Everything has its limits.

Such too is the case with high comedy. In human nature there are at the very most only a dozen broadly marked characters.... Nuances, to be sure, are infinite, but striking colors are few, and it is these primary colors which the great artist uses.

Pulpit eloquence, and notably funeral orations, must share the same fate. Once the truths of morality have been eloquently announced, once the picture of human weakness and misery, vanity and death, has been painted by skillful hands, all of this becomes trite. One is left then with

[19] *Lettre de M. de Voltaire à l'Académie française*, in *Oeuvres complètes*, VII, 335.

[20] Letter to the Président Hénault, July 25, 1752, *Oeuvres complètes*, XXXVII, 456.

[21] Letter to Frederick of Prussia, May 27, 1737, *Oeuvres complètes*, XXXIV, 267.

the alternatives of imitation and senseless eccentricity. Since La Fontaine wrote a sufficient number of fables, all additional fables serve the same moral ideas and indeed re-create nearly the same adventures. So it is that genius has but one century, after which it must degenerate.

Achievement can be maintained more easily in those areas in which the subjects are ceaselessly renewed, such as history and physical science, and which require simply work, judgment, and a common approach. And the fine arts such as painting and sculpture can avoid degeneration when rulers follow the example of Louis XIV in employing only the best artists. For in painting and sculpture one can treat the same subjects countless times; the Holy Family is still painted though Raphael displayed his great superiority in the same subject. But one is not permitted to create another *Cinna, Andromaque, Art poétique,* or *Tartuffe.*" [22]

Thus to Voltaire his own age was no longer one of striking genius, but rather of mediocrity and voluminous productivity. The great example of the preceding century, he wrote, had not only made equal achievement impossible, but was serving to encourage a flood of literary production of the most indifferent and petty nature. Neologism was disfiguring the language, and the bizarre was replacing the beautiful. "Everything seems to concur in leading the French back to that barbarism from which Louis XIV and Cardinal Richelieu raised them." [23] Of his own century, Voltaire wrote: "So many laurels . . . quickly withered in exhausted ground; there remained only a very few with pallid fading leaves. Decadence came through facility and sloth, through sated tastes and an attraction to the bizarre. Vanity protected the artists who were re-establishing barbarism and, by persecuting genuine talent, drove many capable writers outside their native land. . . . With true art and genius nearly dead, merit came to be seen only in continued wrangling over the worth of the past century. . . ." [24]

Voltaire saw the new enthusiasm for mathematics and science as one of the factors in the decline of literature. In 1735 he complained bitterly that poetry was no longer in fashion in Paris, that every-

---

[22] *Siècle de Louis XIV*, in *Oeuvres complètes*, XIV, 553–554.

[23] "Epître dédicatoire à M. Falkener, marchand anglais," *Zaïre*, in *Oeuvres complètes*, II, 544.

[24] *La princesse de Babylone*, in *Oeuvres complètes*, XXI, 419.

body was turning to geometry, physics, and cold reason. "Feeling, imagination, and the graces are banished . . . ; belles-lettres are clearly declining."[25] He deplored the intrusion of scientific rationalism into poetry itself; "the geometric spirit, which today has invaded belles-lettres, has imposed a new restraint upon poetry."[26] Though statements such as these commonly date from Voltaire's earlier period, they do not run counter to the aesthetic doctrine even of those years when he was the patriarch of Enlightened philosophy.

And Voltaire saw, in the literary decadence of his own age, the same pattern of decline which history revealed in earlier times. Decadence, he noted sadly, "is the fate of all nations which have cultivated letters; each has shone brilliantly for a century and then languished for a millennium."[27] Voltaire saw the literary decadence of his own day paralleled by that of Greece and Rome and by that of Italy and Spain after the Renaissance. For this recurrent phenomenon in history Voltaire advanced not only the explanation by internal causes—the necessary exhaustion of literary forms—but also a variety of explanations involving external causes. Among the latter he included the state of the sciences, of government and patronage, and the general course of national development. Yet Voltaire obviously did not entirely integrate the arts with the general movement of civilization, as his divergent views on the literary decline and the general enlightenment of his century amply demonstrate. Not infrequently he noted the opposed character of the centuries of Louis XIV and Louis XV, the former being distinguished by literary talent and the latter by intellectual skill. As for the connection between literary and national development, he could only propose a very elastic rule: "It is always under the greatest princes that the arts have flourished, and the decadence of the arts has sometimes occurred during a time of national decadence."[28] Beyond this statement, and beyond certain embryonic attempts to link the develop-

[25] Letter to Cideville, April 16, 1735, *Oeuvres complètes*, XXXIII, 490.

[26] *Essai sur la poésie épique*, in *Oeuvres complètes*, VIII, 362.

[27] Letter to the Comte d'Argental, December 7, 1767, *Oeuvres complètes*, XLIV, 290. This comment arose from a reference to the definitive decadence of the contemporary theatre.

[28] Epître dédicatoire . . . ," *Zaïre*, in *Oeuvres complètes*, II, 545.

ment of literature with that of ethics and various intellectual disciplines, Voltaire did not venture.

There is a widespread tendency among students of Voltaire to ignore or to discount his statements on literary flux and decay as irrelevant to his work as an Enlightened philosopher. In justification for this attitude the words of Voltaire himself have sometimes been cited. Reason, he once wrote, "was agreeable and frivolous in the fine century of Louis XIV but in our day it begins to be solid. If perhaps this is at the expense of talent I believe none the less that we have gained a great deal by the exchange. Today we have no Racine, Molière, La Fontaine, or Boileau, and I think we shall never again have any of these—but I prefer an enlightened century to an ignorant century which has produced seven or eight men of genius."[29]

Do these words put the seal on the assumption that Voltaire's purely literary work was a relatively unimportant trifle in his life when compared to the polemical and philosophical aims to which he devoted himself? No perusal of his prolific production can lend support to such an assumption; his vital concern for things literary cannot be denied. If his verse and his theatre, as well as his literary criticism, are largely forgotten today, it must be remembered that during his lifetime they were the primary source of his fame. To attempt to determine his proportionate devotion to philosophy and to literature is the sheerest folly; one can only state that his affections fluctuated, and that neither aspect of his work can be dismissed as insignificant. One must not ignore his doctrine of the cyclical flux of literature simply because it does not fit neatly into the presumed "main current" of his thought.

In like manner, Voltaire's broader cultural pessimism has been generally underestimated, and often for a similar reason. Too frequently his jeremiads have been brushed aside as momentary whims or as literary devices. It would seem to be wiser to accept a fundamental inconsistency in Voltaire's philosophy and world outlook, and to abandon the attempt to integrate his whole work within a

[29] Letter to the Comte de la Touraille, May 12, 1766, *Oeuvres complètes*, XLV, 446.

neat and compact system. A reconciliation of Voltaire's rationalistic optimism and his historico-literary pessimism is possible and desirable in some instances; in others it can only lead to confusion and misrepresentation. Consistency, save in certain fundamental questions, was not a Voltairean virtue. An understanding of the complexities of his thought can only be based upon a recognition of this fact.

Chapter 20

Disillusionment and Diversity— Diderot

> I am of the opinion that it is a thousand times easier for an enlightened people to return to barbarism than for a barbaric people to advance directly toward civilization. (Letter to the Princesse Daskoff)[1]

FACT AND IDEAL IN THE ARTS

Diderot's philosophy is made difficult by a complexity which is even more marked than that of Voltaire's work. The diversity of Diderot's thought and personality is unmistakable, and has long been recognized by commentators on his writings; whether this diversity is the mark of profundity or of confusion is a question, however, upon which no general agreement is likely to be reached. The dualism of his approach to many intellectual problems is well exemplified by his discussion of the nature and historical destinies of literature and the fine arts.

In these fields Diderot symbolizes both the revolt from Classicism and the simultaneous survival of the old school of aesthetics. His opposition to the cold correctness which he felt was the aim of the Classicism of his day is a commonplace of French literary history; as a champion of emotion and feeling in the arts he is considered one of the initiators of Romanticism. It was as a Romantic that he protested against the impoverishment of the French language under the Classical regime, and that he attacked the narrow genre distinctions of the Classical theatre. More fundamentally, he some-

---

[1] April 3, 1771, *Oeuvres complètes de Diderot*, XX, 29.

times questioned the conception of a fixed, eternal beauty, and saw beauty not in terms of abstract rules but, in some degree, as the product of circumstance and of subjective aesthetic perceptions.

But there are also certain well-defined Classical elements in the aesthetic theory of Diderot. Thought for him kept its place beside feeling, and his most sanguine enthusiasm for the enrichment of the arts could not still his admiration for the great classics of the preceding century and of antiquity. There is sincerity in his insistence that the study of the Ancients would always have its value, and even his presentation of the doctrine of the imitation of nature has a Classical ring. For he did not preach the exact imitation of external nature, but rather the generalization of nature as expressed by an "interior model" within the artist—a model which scorned Romantic disorder and was in fact best formed by a study of earlier models. Even Diderot's injunction to see nature as did the Ancients, rather than to copy them, was a part of the most acceptable Classical doctrine.

If this Classical strain could not be readily reconciled with the Romantic notions which were held simultaneously by Diderot, it came into an even more violent conflict with the emotional nature of Diderot himself. The result could only be an aesthetic practice which avoided dogma and attempted to unite thought with emotion, and imagination with understanding. His aesthetic theory possesses the ambiguities of most transitional theory, yet, unlike the writings of Marmontel, it is perhaps more the product of originality than of bewilderment.

Before proceeding to Diderot's view of artistic and literary development, one must note an additional element in his aesthetics: his assertion of the pre-eminent role of morality in the arts. "To make virtue attractive, vice odious, and the ridiculous striking— these are the motives of the virtuous man who takes up pen, brush, or chisel."[2] It is not surprising that Diderot admired Richardson and adored Greuze, or that his own work reveals a strong moralizing tendency. This conception of the ethical function of art became the ally of Diderot's Classicism in his resistance to aesthetic relativism,

[2] *Essai sur la peinture,* in *Oeuvres complètes,* X, 502.

and it was one of the crucial weapons in his arsenal of positive criticism.

For in the arts Diderot was only secondarily a theorist; he was primarily a practising critic. As such he had standards, flexible though they might be. As to the fate of the arts in his own day, his judgments fluctuated considerably in detail but revealed several distinct trends. He was hopeful, for example, of continued progress in writing for the theatre, though alarmed by pernicious English influences, and sought to demonstrate the undeveloped potentialities of the stage by his own *drames*. On painting he was darkly pessimistic; this, he felt, was a lost art outside of France, and in France itself the most alarming symptoms of decline were evident. If the definitive decline was perhaps distant, it was none the less inevitable. And throughout the range of the fine arts and literature Diderot deplored the passing of the grand style. The petty and the frivolous, he believed, were replacing the broad and noble lines of earlier days; the verve, strength, and profundity of great art were giving way to feeble mannerism, and the insensitive touch of commerce and of analytic reason was smothering the flame of genius.

Diderot did not, however, limit himself to the passing artistic phenomena of the moment, but broadened his commentary into a general historical approach to the arts. He valued highly the element of creative freshness and originality, and postulated first of all the radical inability of any of the major arts to attain the perfection achieved by the Greeks. The Greeks alone, he wrote, had had no artistic precedents, and thus they saw the flowering of such fertile and original genius as could never be duplicated by their successors. All artists since the Greeks were fated to use Greek art as their model, and Diderot himself was among those who saw practical value in this use.

It was nevertheless evident to Diderot that the post-Grecian world had witnessed a number of cycles of progress and decadence in literature and the fine arts. Progress in these fields seems to have appeared to him natural enough, but decadence required explanation. For this decadence he saw, as did so many of his contemporaries, two categories of causes: the internal and the external. In

7*

both realms his approach differed considerably from that of Voltaire, though the two critics held certain views in common. Diderot rejected Voltaire's doctrine of the necessary exhaustion of the limited literary genre, but, from his general emphasis upon the value of originality, he did maintain that with the fixing of an artistic tradition decline must eventually take place in all nations. No race, he stated, can expect to maintain a high level of artistic achievement for more than a few centuries, and this rule applies not only to the fine arts, but to poetry, eloquence, and perhaps language itself.[3]

With the establishment of a literary tradition among a given people, wrote Diderot, there are only two courses left open to the creative artist, and both may be pernicious. The artist may turn to new genres—a procedure which is valid and desirable when properly controlled, but which harbors great potentialities for the bizarre, the mannered, and the eccentric. The alternative is to fall into a strictly mechanical and imitative pattern, and thus to abandon all hope of original, truly creative production. Significant imaginative literature may then die out altogether, to be replaced by the subtle refinements of the critics and the grammarians. From that day, the nation has seen the final breath of art in the grand style.

But Diderot did not explain decadence in literature and the fine arts solely in terms of natural exhaustion from internal causes. To study art, he wrote, one should examine carefully "an infinite number of questions relative to morality, customs, climate, religion, and government."[4] The decay of the arts is fully intelligible only when it is seen in the context of the cultural whole. Here, from the multitude of possible determining factors, Diderot chose to emphasize two external influences: the intellectual and moral state of the people or nation.

The decay of morality, he confessed, may serve as a challenge to literature, but such is not the normal path of development. It is true, for instance, that the subtle, delicate, and profound letters of Seneca

---

[3] *Salon de 1767*, in *Oeuvres complètes*, XI, 16.
[4] *Additions pour servir à quelques endroits de la Lettre sur les sourds et muets*, in *Oeuvres complètes*, I, 404.

were written in a dissolute age; it is also true that literature and the fine arts more often cannot meet the challenge and must sink into decay along with morality. As evidence for this assertion Diderot pointed primarily to the example of his own day, and to the work of Boucher and other artists in whom the decline of taste closely paralleled contemporary moral corruption. "Mannerism," he wrote, "is in the fine arts what hypocrisy is in morality. Boucher is the biggest hypocrite I have ever known...."[5] And Diderot added that moral decadence, if it does not touch the artist directly, will influence artistic production indirectly through the demands of corrupt patrons of the arts and of an economic system built upon the effete luxury of the few.

For Diderot thought the expansion of commerce and of a luxury economy to be the most important cause of moral decay. Though he defended that luxury which was the symbol of general prosperity, he saw only evil in the extreme luxury which opposed the ostentation of the few to the misery of the many. The first type of luxury, or general wealth, he considered indispensable to the advancement of the arts; the problem was to arrest the course of luxury before it became harmful. Frequently this could not be done. Even the relatively innocent ease of life prevalent under a generally prosperous economy could lead to a softening of the moral fibre, to a careless hedonism, and to a neglect of the true graces of life. Economic concerns would drive out genius, and the countinghouse would symbolically replace the artist's studio. This was the lesson of history, and the prospect before contemporary France.[6]

Diderot saw a similar danger to the arts from the intellectual development of a people. Philosophy, he wrote, must inevitably harm the arts; dissection, analysis, and rationalism can only deaden the inspiration and cool the impulse of genius. In poetry, "reason introduces an exactitude and precision, a methodology ... and a sort of pedantry which are fatal.... The philosophical spirit brings with it a dry and sententious style. Abstract expressions which cover a

---

[5] *Pensées détachées sur la peinture, la sculpture, l'architecture et la poésie*, in *Oeuvres complètes*, XII, 121-122.

[6] *Salon de 1769*, in *Oeuvres complètes*, XI, 450-451.

vast number of phenomena multiply and take the place of imagery of language."[7]

The understanding of natural law, Diderot added, robs the external world of its terror and much of its poetry, and a rational social life removes the occasion for that grand and heroic action which once inspired so much great art. Such art is often distinctly harmed by the progress of prosperity, peace, and public happiness; it is tribulation and disaster which cause the first flowering of genius. Then, "in proportion to the quelling and outdistancing of a nation's violent troubles, spirits become calm, the image of danger is forgotten, and letters are silenced. Men of great genius are nurtured in difficult times, they flourish immediately after these days of trial, they follow the decline of nations and are extinguished with those nations. However, since it is rare for a nation to disappear without a long succession of disasters, enthusiasm may be reborn in certain privileged souls, and the productions of genius are then a bizarre mixture of good and bad taste. One can discern in this period both the richness of past days and the misery of the moment. The work of these men of genius may be compared to the last pulsations of a dying man. Frenchmen, feel your pulse."[8]

Thus on the historical destiny of literature and the fine arts Diderot arrived at a comprehensive pessimism. Not even the occasional expansive hopes of the new Romanticism could stand against the gloomy teaching of history. By temperament Diderot perhaps inclined toward optimism, but disillusionment was often the fruit of his observation of men and of history. Somewhat the same pattern, less clearly defined, may be found in his broader philosophical synthesis and in his view of the course of nations and civilizations in general.

THE GREATER SYNTHESIS

The incongruities to be found in Diderot's writings extend farther than a mere dualism between fact and ideal, between cold observation and expansive emotion. His philosophical synthesis itself con-

---

[7] *Salon de 1767*, in *Oeuvres complètes*, XI, 131.
[8] *Fragments politiques*, in *Oeuvres complètes*, IV, 43–44.

tained several marked divergencies of method and theory, and these divergencies were reflected in his historical views. Certainly, for example, his treatment of the roles of rationalism and empiricism had its wider repercussions, just as did the continuous struggle within him between feeling and reason.

The thorny problem of Diderot's rationalism is one of those most likely to remain unresolved by historians. Doubtless there was a real conflict in Diderot's own mind between the not altogether compatible claims of rationalism and empiricism in the realms of science and philosophy. Clearly he was distrustful of most of the grand philosophical abstractions of the past; clearly too he was tempted by the dream of an ultimate scientific synthesis which would arise primarily from hypothesis rather than from facts alone. Yet he never held that scientific observation or experiment was fruitless, and at times he seems to have felt that description rather than final explanation was the true goal of science and philosophy. Man, he could assert, was fated to see not reality but forms and shadows; the attainment of absolute knowledge was a pure chimera. Diderot, in moods such as this, unmistakably suggested the impossibility of an indefinite expansion of knowledge, and floated between intellectual agnosticism and pragmatic meliorism.

In historical and sociological studies, at any rate, Diderot was usually the empiricist. Like Dubos and Montesquieu, Diderot had, for his century, a keen eye for the diversity of earthly phenomena. Yet, even here, disturbing intrusions of a basically rationalistic temper were not lacking. What, for example, could be the fate of an abstract ethical system in an historical context? Diderot's ethics rested upon the assumption of certain eternal laws governing human relationships, yet he never evolved a fully integrated ethical system. Indeed, the very basis of his ethics, the doctrine of the goodness of human nature, was by no means firmly established.

Nature, Diderot maintained, had established eternal laws which were essentially good and which would necessarily prevail; men were not born naturally bad, but were made evil by a vicious environment. Nevertheless, even with the artificial restraints of a corrupt society removed, man could hardly be considered exclusively and inevitably good by nature. Virtue, Diderot decided, is not the result of an effortless release of human goodness, but is the fruit of conscious and painful effort. Rousseau had dreamed of progress as the almost inevitable unfolding of natural goodness, once unfettered; Diderot was not so sanguine.[9]

Certainly in his own day Diderot saw evil and vice coexisting with goodness and virtue; more significantly, he did not think their eradication in sight. Indeed, he seems to have believed in an eternal equation of good and evil in the world, with the augmentation of one factor leading to a corresponding augmentation of the other.[10] "The world," he wrote, "does not profit from its advance into old age: it does not change. It is possible that the individual perfects himself, but the race becomes neither better nor worse in the mass. The sum of evil passions remains the same, and the enemies of the good and the useful remain as numerous as ever."[11]

Diderot's examination of the respective claims of natural law and human freedom is hardly more favorable to an exclusive affirmation of human perfectibility and progress. Here again his doctrine is not altogether clear, for he vacillates between liberty and determinism. At one point at least, Diderot believed in man's perfectibility through reason; moreover, such a belief would seem to be buttressed by his cautious defense of free will in the *Encyclopédie*. He granted a certain efficacy to education and legislation in perfecting men, though he thought this efficacy much overrated by Helvétius and others. Men differ, he believed, in their native abilities; it would be absurd to presume their equal perfectibility.

All men, added Diderot, are a part of nature, and thus they are subject to the complex network of causation which determines the course of nature. At times he did attempt to distinguish between

[9] Diderot no more preached primitivistic historical regress than did Rousseau; his advocacy, like Rousseau's, of a general elimination of artificial accretions within civilization is a progressive, not a reactionary principle. Any attempt to return to a fancied presocial state seemed to Diderot pure madness. See "Luxe" (*Encyclopédie*), *Oeuvres complètes*, XVI, 28.

[10] *Supplément au Voyage de Bougainville*, in *Oeuvres complètes*, II, 248.

[11] *Avertissement du VIIIe volume de l'Encyclopédie*, in *Oeuvres complètes*, XIII, 171.

physical and moral causation, and to assert the independence of the latter; at other times he seemed to embrace a thoroughgoing determinism. "All of us," he wrote to Mlle Jodin, "are puppets in the hand of a fate which moves us at will...."[12] His most explicit defense of determinism is contained in a letter of 1756: "Look carefully at the matter, and you will see that the expression 'freedom of will' is meaningless, that there are and can be no free beings, and that we are simply what follows from the general order, from our organization, our education, and the whole chain of events in the universe. There is only one sort of necessity; it is the same for all beings...."[13]

Clearly there is to be found a real doctrine of environmental determinism in Diderot's work, though with less emphasis than in the writings of Montesquieu or even Voltaire. Among the external circumstances which Diderot granted are influential in molding nations, ages, and individuals are climatic conditions and population density. Nations, he wrote, differ from other nations, and ages from other ages. Each century has its peculiar intellectual atmosphere which determines inexorably the forms of expression which must prevail, and which presumably determines also the progress or decadence of these forms. "The course of knowledge and literature is a charted one, from which the human mind finds it almost impossible to stray. Every age has its own genre and its own type of great men. Woe to those who, destined by their natural talents to distinguish themselves in that genre, are born in the following century and are carried by the torrent of reigning studies to literary occupations for which they do not have a natural aptitude. They might have made names for themselves; instead, they work laboriously and unfruitfully and die in obscurity."[14]

By such fatal forces, then, is mankind moved in its historical course. And "movement" is a key word in Diderot's historical outlook, as in his view of the natural world. The world as he saw it is in a state of dynamic flux; the world transforms itself constantly.

---

[12] February 10, 1769, in *Oeuvres complètes*, XIX, 408.
[13] Letter to Landois, June 29, 1756, in *Oeuvres complètes*, 435–436.
[14] "Eclectisme" (*Encyclopédie*), in *Oeuvres complètes*, XIV, 345.

Human history, itself a part of nature, must submit to the same process. "Everything is in perpetual flux"; "all things change, all things pass, and only the whole remains."[15] Diderot's theory of the biological transformation of species was not primarily a doctrine of natural progress but simply of growth and decline, or flux. Such too was his typical philosophy of human history.

If Diderot was "by nature" an optimist, the point can scarcely be proven conclusively. It is wiser to state simply that, as in the case of Voltaire, his moods were contradictory and his thought complex. The ideas of progress and decadence, and of a flux comprising both of these, are to be found in his work; the historian remains on secure ground only when he summarizes Diderot's recorded views of these phenomena, without wandering unduly into psychological analysis.

Unlike the usual eighteenth century conception of progress, Diderot's view seems to have dispensed at times with fixed standards of measurement and to have involved a definition of progress simply in terms of increasingly skillful methods and techniques. Could a progress measured so vaguely be considered true progress? Fortunately the issue may be evaded, for Diderot seldom envisaged progress strictly in these terms. His projects of reform indicate a belief in the efficacy of human action, and it is evident that he retained his own standards of intellectual, artistic, and social life—standards against which he might measure his own day and the past history of humanity. Thus he saw the current progress of learning, the refinement of manners, and the decrease of superstition and of submission to faith and authority as unquestionable indications of advance. As to the future he had high hopes for a continuation of progress in the experimental sciences, though not in geometry.

Yet Diderot was hesitant in his suggestions of reform, and his hopes for the coming progress of humanity were limited. Even scientific progress, he wrote, would be slow, and would be arrested within a few centuries when it reached the limits of useful applications. Moral and social progress could be only temporary and provisional, for the equilibrium between good and evil could not be

[15] *Rêve de d'Alembert*, in *Oeuvres complètes*, II, 132, 138.

upset permanently. The masses were intellectually incapable of absorbing any significant advances, and the general diffusion of scientific, philosophical, and artistic progress would never be realized.

Diderot's philosophical outlook and his vision of history made him see decadence, like progress, as necessary and unavoidable. Decline, he insisted, must inevitably follow growth, and to halt its momentum is practically impossible.[16] It is in the nature of governments and of religions to become corrupt in the course of time; despotic authority becomes established and is fatal to the whole civilization. "With a people in slavery, everything becomes corrupt." "All civil and national institutions eventually degenerate and consecrate themselves as supernatural and divine laws. Similarly all supernatural and divine laws strengthen and maintain themselves by degenerating into civil and national laws. This reciprocal degeneration is one of the metamorphoses most fatal to the happiness and instruction of the human race."[17]

Economic decadence too, according to Diderot, is a common phenomenon, and is most notably exemplified by the undue favoring of industry over agriculture. Agriculture is the foundation of the state and cannot be too much encouraged, while the disproportionate development of industry and commerce can only harm a people. For the commercial spirit is incapable of inspiring the arts and can only lead, in time, to moral corruption.

The history of the world, then, follows a succession of periods of growth and decay, a system of loose cultural cycles though not of exact repetitions. "The fate which rules the world wills that everything should pass away. The happiest state of an individual or of a nation has its limits. Everything carries within itself a hidden germ of destruction."[18] The true potentialities of the human race can never be determined, for again and again it is stopped short in its progress toward enlightenment. These revolutions or periods of decay are

[16] *Fragments politiques,* in *Oeuvres complètes,* IV, 44.

[17] *De la poésie dramatique,* in *Oeuvres complètes,* VII, 370; *Voyage autour du monde ... sous le commandement de M. de Bougainville,* in *Oeuvres complètes,* II, 202.

[18] *Salon de 1767,* in *Oeuvres complètes,* XI, 93.

necessary; "they have always occurred and will continue forever. There even is a fixed maximum interval of time between revolutions, and this fact in itself limits the extent of our labors. In the sciences there is a point beyond which one is scarcely permitted to advance."[19] And these necessary revolutions, again, are by no means limited to the course of man's intellectual development. In reference to the American Revolution Diderot expresses the hope that the Americans may "ward off the extreme growth and unequal distribution of wealth, the rise of luxury, softness, and moral corruption, and that they may maintain their liberty and their government. May they postpone, at least for a few centuries, the decree pronounced upon all earthly things—the decree which condemns all things to follow a succession of birth, vigor, decrepitude, and destruction."[20] As to Diderot's opinion of his own nation and age, one may cite his wistful hope that some day, in some isolated part of the globe, a society might be maintained in a civilized state midway between "the childhood of the savage and our decrepitude."[21]

Thus the enlightened projects of the rationalistic philosopher, the enthusiasm of the literary reformer, the generous hopes of the man of feeling all were ultimately engulfed in an inclusive view of inescapable historical flux. Yet Diderot's writings impart no feeling of bleak despair, for within the framework of historical flux he saw room for much temporary improvement. It is only natural that as a vigorous and practical thinker he preferred to dwell not upon the eventual destruction of those ideals and institutions for which he labored, but rather upon their realization here and now, however ephemeral they might prove to be. For even the intermittent deterministic philosophy of Diderot, like that of Voltaire, was by no means a counsel of inaction. Men, he seems to say, must attempt to profit from the potentialities of the moment; only then may they be permitted to reflect that decay and destruction are the inescapable larger framework of their historical destiny.

[19] "Encyclopédie" (*Encyclopédie*), in *Oeuvres complètes*, XIV, 427.

[20] *Essai sur les règnes de Claude et de Néron*, in *Oeuvres complètes*, III, 324.

[21] *Réfutation suivie de l'ouvrage d'Helvétius intitulé "l'Homme,"* in *Oeuvres complètes*, II, 432.

Chapter 21

Ethical Pessimism—Vauvenargues

> That which pertains to the soul alone is not favored by the
> light of the mind; it is in vain that we perfect our know-
> ledge. (*Discours sur le caractère des différents siècles*)[1]

Montesquieu, Voltaire, Diderot—these are great and familiar names
in the history of the French Enlightenment. Yet one does not exhaust
the variegated thought of the century by studying them, or even
by studying those lesser figures who, preceding or following the
great men, added detail to the main current of the Enlightenment.
How complex this current actually was and how arbitrarily it has
often been defined have already been noted. It is true, nevertheless,
that through the prestige of its protagonists this current has achieved
a certain unity. If one should attempt to define the norm of Enlightened philosophy in France one would presumably study, first of
all, the thought of Voltaire and Rousseau, Diderot and Montesquieu
—and even in such diversity the Enlightenment would have some
meaning as a unit; even from the work of these thinkers one might
establish a rough practical norm of Enlightened thought. However,
it would soon be evident that many thinkers partly or wholly
nurtured by the Enlightenment are not a part of this main stream;
they form rather the extreme wings of conservatism and radicalism,
and comprise groups at least as inconsistent within themselves as is
the main body of *philosophes*. It is the purpose of these final chapters
to examine the thought of several of these atypical but significant
writers.

Luc de Clapiers, Marquis de Vauvenargues, was one of those who,
without entering the clerical camp, most clearly belonged to the

[1] *Oeuvres* (Paris, 1857), 158.

conservative wing of eighteenth century French thought. If his work marked a partial revolt from the values of the Enlightenment, the motivation of this revolt lay largely in a yearning for former times. In his deism, in his indifference to Christianity, Vauvenargues was of the eighteenth century, but his true spiritual home was an earlier age. A classicist and a humanist, he might have felt quite at ease in the seventeenth century or during the Renaissance. Literature, not science, was his guide—a literature which was nourished upon the principles of classical antiquity. In questions of aesthetics Vauvenargues was unequivocally a champion of French Classicism, and a critic of contemporary decadence. French literature, he felt, was decaying both because it was neglecting the Classical rules of sound writing and because it was losing the warmth of past years.

But what of the philosophical assumptions of Vauvenargues—the assumptions relevant to his ultimate world outlook? If by no means a rationalist in the Cartesian sense, Vauvenargues was not, on the other hand, altogether scornful of the rational faculty. He insisted, for example, upon the existence of absolute and eternal truths, though he doubted the power of reason to discover them. The proper role of reason was to be the analysis of facts gleaned from the observation of oneself and of others; this type of empiricism, primarily introspective, was Vauvenargues' primary source of knowledge. The moral truths so revealed were to him more certain than the facts of science, for they were simpler and more immediately perceived than the complex phenomena of the external world. But man's actual contact with moral truth came through an intuition which Vauvenargues, unlike Descartes, differentiated from reason itself, and which in practice came to be identified with emotion or feeling. "Knowledge by feeling," he wrote, "is ... the highest degree of knowledge ... ; reason does not know the interests of the heart."[2]

Such was one of the routes which led Vauvenargues to his attempt to rehabilitate the instinct and the passions, and to formulate the most famous of his maxims: "The great thoughts come from the

[2] *Réflexions sur divers sujets*, in *Oeuvres*, 112; *Réflexions et maximes*, in *Oeuvres*, 385.

heart."[3] His view of goodness in nature provided yet another basis for the same conclusion. Nature, he felt, contained vast potentialities for goodness, and at times he tended to favor the universal harmony of philosophical optimism. Yet all, he admitted, was not well in the world; a mixture of good and evil characterized not only the external environment but also human nature itself. This belief was to temper Vauvenargues' incipient optimism on the future course of mankind, while leaving sufficient room for confidence that the emotions were at least as reliable a guide to action as was any other human faculty.

Vauvenargues' ethical system, then, was founded upon instinct, emotion, and feeling, rather than upon knowledge and reason. And in this system human action relied upon feeling as a motive force rather than upon the rational operations made possible by freedom of will. For Vauvenargues was a proponent of the bondage of the will. The laws of nature, he wrote, are fixed and inalterable; they allow for no true independence in man or in any other created being. Man is free only in that he may follow his own desires without restraint, for his desires are determined irrevocably by the general order of nature and the plan of God.

This infusion of determinism did not prevent Vauvenargues from setting up ethical ideals and from hoping to influence human conduct in certain practical ways. Emphasizing pleasure and duty, action and glory as the vital ethical injunctions, he attacked indefatigably the moral conditions of his own time. Grandeur he felt to be the prime characteristic of a distinguished code of human behavior, and it was precisely this quality which he thought supremely lacking in the world about him. Everything, he sighed, was becoming petty, and not least the virtues themselves. Pleasantry, frivolity, and *bel esprit* were invading all realms of life, and were but subterfuges to conceal a radical emptiness and indecision of soul. Vauvenargues held the growth of luxury partially responsible for these conditions, and at times gave himself over to nostalgia for the simplicity of antiquity and other early ages. He was, however, well aware of the impossibility of returning to the life of primitive centuries now long past, and in his more sober moments he recognized

[3] *Réflexions et maximes*, in *Oeuvres*, 386.

the imperfections of primitive existence, and those potentialities for good which were contained in highly developed civilizations.

Armed with this ethical system and convinced of its central importance in the course of human development, Vauvenargues was provided with a measure for the general progress or decadence of civilized man. He granted the tremendous strides recently made in science and in the intellectual mastery of the world; in knowledge the modern world was indubitably far in advance of the ancient civilizations. "Heirs of the centuries before us, we can only be richer than our predecessors in things of the mind; this fact can hardly be contested without injustice to us."[4] Yet, unlike the majority of his Enlightened contemporaries, Vauvenargues saw little cause for rejoicing in this progress of knowledge. Neither scientific advance nor the material comforts ensured by that advance could rightly be adduced in support of a theory of general progress. For were men less happy, less worthy or less great in those ages preceding the introduction of the modern amenities of life? Modern man is less ignorant than his savage ancestors and than the citizens of Greece and Rome, but is he basically better than any of these? To these questions Vauvenargues replied with a categorical negative; "the learned ages," he asserted, "are scarcely more significant than the others, except that their errors are more useful."[5]

Not only, wrote Vauvenargues, does the progress of science and knowledge not bring with it the moral betterment of mankind: such progress may often be positively harmful to man's ethical development. The injury done to morality by the advance of science and knowledge is effected through several channels, among them the neglect of ethically useful knowledge through the pursuit of irrelevant scientific chimeras, and the growth of vanity, ambition, and presumption. Worst of all, the accumulation of extraneous knowledge in men's minds may confuse their native judgment. "Very few people are able to make good use of the minds of others; knowledge increases, but good sense is always rare." "The effect of a great multiplicity of ideas is to cause soft minds to fall into contradictions;

---

[4] *Discours sur le caractère des différents siècles*, in *Oeuvres*, 151.
[5] *Réflexions et maximes*, in *Oeuvres*, 446.

the effect of science is to shake certainty and to confound the most obvious principles."[6] Thus men fall into a universal doubt, into a Pyrrhonism which eventually can only paralyze all thought and all action.

Such, continued Vauvenargues, was precisely the intellectual trend of contemporary Europe. The reigning maxims presented all things as uncertain and problematical, and this being so "both authors and readers were agreed that the only matter worthy of effort was the display of wit...."[7] Men, despite their subtle wit and intellect, were perhaps as far from attaining truth as had been their most ignorant ancestors. Never before had men been burdened with as many useless and superficial bits of knowledge as in the current century. This was the age of the new barbarism, of scorn for truth and simplicity.

But Vauvenargues went well beyond the passing scene in his critique of historical optimism. Nature, he wrote, is continually active and changing; the manners and morals of peoples are transformed from age to age and from nation to nation. Philosophy itself has its momentary fashions, as do music, architecture, and dress. Even science does not progress unhesitatingly, for men stray in their senseless search for novelty. All advanced centuries, including the finest, degenerate rapidly and sink into barbarism. In this confused picture only one factor is of true significance: the moral condition of the population at a given time and in a given place. For this condition does change, and it is notorious that "morals become corrupt more easily than they reform themselves."[8]

But in Vauvenargues' opinion, ethical conditions, despite fluctuations from year to year and even from age to age, do not change markedly across the whole course of human history. Man raises himself above brute instinct only with the greatest difficulty, and then not in proportion to the increase of enlightenment. Nature has prescribed a limit to moral perfection and to the elevation of men's souls. Ethical progress is not as obviously cumulative as is

[6] *Discours sur le caractère des différents siècles*, in *Oeuvres*, 152, note 1; 152.
[7] *Fragments: Plan d'un livre de philosophie*, in *Oeuvres posthumes et œuvres inédites* (Paris, 1857), 70.
[8] *Réflexions et maximes*, in *Oeuvres*, 442.

scientific progress, for nature spoke as insistently to the first men as it does to modern peoples. This voice of nature, Vauvenargues insisted, has grown fainter as that of reason has increased in intensity. At best, man can hope to return momentarily to his earlier, more natural, state; in no event can he expect to advance morally beyond that state.

Substantial and lasting progress, then, is impossible in that one field in which Vauvenargues saw it to be of real significance. To be sure, it is likely that, as a moralist, Vauvenargues harbored certain hopes of contributing to the ethical betterment of man. Yet one must also note such passages as this: "I do not wish to blame, to change, or to improve [*perfectionner*]; that would not be my proper role. I simply want to warn men against expecting too much of our philosophy and our arts. . . ."[9] And even in his more sanguine moods Vauvenargues did not seem to expect more than fleeting ameliorations in matters of detail. His message is essentially one of stoicism and of individual betterment, and not of general progress even in matters of morality. What gives this doctrine its peculiar significance, and what raises it above a careless and selfish hedonism, is the fact that it is the fruit of a careful weighing of alternatives. Vauvenargues considered the ideals of the Enlightenment and found them wanting; he rejected the dream of progress through knowledge and social action because he saw the basic human values elsewhere.

[10] *Discours sur le caractère des différents siècles*, in *Oeuvres*, 162.

Chapter 22

Social Pessimism—Linguet

Society makes the world a vast prison in which only the
guards are free. (*Théorie des loix civiles*)[1]

In his day a brilliant lawyer, a caustic journalist, and a striking critic
of social institutions, Simon Nicolas Henri Linguet today is scarcely
more than a name even to students of history. His neglect is easily
enough explained though not altogether deserved. It is true that
most of his writing is of mediocre quality, and that it is often
polemical in tone and ephemeral in interest. Yet, as an example of
nonconformity and as a conservative whose originality verges on
paradox, Linguet remains one of the more fascinating figures of the
eighteenth century.

At first glance Linguet seems to have stood far apart from the age
of the Enlightenment into which he was born, for both his religion
and his sociology were opposed to the doctrines of the reigning philosophy. Professing to be a faithful son of the Roman Catholic Church,
he hailed religion as the indispensable support of the state and of the
whole social structure. But closer examination reveals a strong taint
of indifferentism and of skeptical rationalism in his theological
conceptions; private freedom of judgment, together with outward
conformity, emerges as his true ideal. Similarly, his political and
social theory, far though it is from predominant Enlightened conceptions, firmly rests, at least in part, upon such typical shibboleths
of the day as nature, reason, utility, and even humanitarianism.

Yet Linguet, doubtless partly for personal reasons, became an
outspoken enemy of the liberal philosophy of his day, and saw in its

[1] *Théorie des loix civiles, ou principes fondamentaux de la société* (London,
1767), II, 517.

spread a sure sign of contemporary decadence. As a Christian he condemned the *philosophes* for their pride and lack of self-discipline. As a moralist he saw the new philosophy to be a negative doctrine, incapable of inspiring positive virtue. As a political and social theorist he attacked the *philosophes* for their advocacy of personal independence and civic freedom—ideas which could only lead to internal disturbances and revolutions within states.

Moreover, in his opinion, the utopia fondly envisioned by the *philosophes* was illusory; Linguet had only irony for this dream of heaven on earth. "When philosophy has spread its wings over this desolate globe, when the world is saturated with its beneficent influence, the golden age will be reborn, and in the ecstasy of a firmly established happiness men will kiss the hands of the sages to whom they owe this happiness. Nothing can equal the beauty of this picture. Religion itself, purified of those accretions deriving from the weakness and passion of men, could scarcely paint one so seductive. But the more this picture might give rise to pleasant ideas, the more painful it would be to learn one day that it was an illusion."[2]

Linguet took this position against the dream of progress not only because of his dislike of the *philosophes* but also because such a conception ran counter to that broader social theory which was his most startling contribution to eighteenth century thought. This theory postulated, first of all, an idyllic primitive existence in mankind's earliest years. Society, Linguet held, was not inaugurated by a contract, for it is improbable that the masses should have enslaved themselves voluntarily. The social state, rather, was born among hunters, born of the violence excited by hunger and by envy. Property, too, was founded upon usurpation and injustice, but is none the less inviolable. For society is inconceivable without property; the overthrow of property would entail the disintegration of the whole social structure. Any idea of a return to nature is absurd, for there has been only one true "natural law"—the spirit of primitive life, that spirit of liberty which is incompatible with society. The original nature of man was destroyed when society

---

[2] *Le fanatisme des philosophes* (London, Abbeville, 1764), 6.

began, and all subsequent history has been the record of humanity irretrievably fallen, with no practical means of salvation in sight.

The contemporary social structure appeared, then, to Linguet as "a pyramid in which the pressure upon each layer gradually increases down from the peak which supports nothing and weighs upon all."[3] Inequality is the real bond of society; the world is "a vast prison in which only the guards are free."[4] Poverty and misery are inevitable, especially among the day laborers of town and country, and to try to achieve universal happiness is to pursue a chimera. If the mass of the people are "free," they are free only to be neglected and left to starvation. This freedom then is a curse, not a blessing, of modern refinement, and can be remedied in only one way—by a return to that state from which historically the laborer has sunk: slavery.

Slavery, Linguet admitted, is in some respects deplorable, but it does bring mankind the great advantage of security. Indeed, its reestablishment in the Western world is inevitable through revolution. But even this step will be a mere palliative, and a step as painful as it is inevitable. Any true social regeneration of mankind is quite out of the question. Linguet's social and political theory is the glorification of authority, stratification, and immobility; Europe's future, he asserted, must regrettably fall into a pattern of Asiatic autocracy.[5]

Yet within the exigencies of this social and political framework Linguet granted that certain ages and nations had been more fortunate than others, and that one might properly speak of the progress and decadence of mankind in restricted fields. In his own day, for example, progress had been made in certain arts and in technology.

---

[3] *Annales politiques, civiles et littéraires du dix-huitième siècle* (London, Lausanne, Paris, 1777–1792), XV, 36–37.

[4] *Théorie des loix civiles*, II, 517.

[5] Inevitably the question arises as to the true motives of Linguet's work. It would be not unnatural for the liberal to find in Linguet more irony than sincerity—an interpretation based upon the assumption that Linguet's main thesis is too monstrous to have been advanced altogether seriously. I find no convincing support for such an interpretation, and much to indicate Linguet's literal intent, qualified at most by the fact that he was a journalist, fully conscious of the publicity value of a striking paradox. In short one should, I feel, take Linguet at his word, and as his contemporaries understood him.

But in morality and in civic relations mankind, he believed, had deteriorated. Intellectual advances had been made here and there, "but have the people derived any real advantage from these advances? With manners which are more polished, writings which are more methodical, and a sense of enjoyment which is more delicate . . ., are governments more considerate, legislation more enlightened, wars less bloody, or state finance less destructive?" And Linguet thought the expanding military establishments of his time a "fearful symptom of decadence."[6]

As Linguet contemplated the historical vicissitudes of the human mind, he could only see an erratic process of limited advance and of decline, forever bound by that "fatality which demands that in all things activity should be followed by languor, and movement by repose."[7] The flowering of the arts and sciences, for example, would invariably be accompanied by effete luxury and moral corruption; such a flowering might well be the first sign of the decline and fall of a civilization. "It seems then that the arts and the sciences are a compensation, a salutary remedy which nature prepares for an exhausted human race."[8]

But it is Linguet's extreme social pessimism which gives his work its main mark of originality. The world as he saw it must suffer unendingly and irreparably for the creation of human society, since the golden age of primitive life is irrevocably past. Though himself an individualist, Linguet preached discipline and conformity; resignation and stolid conservatism were his counsel for mankind, and into this discouraging social pattern all advance and decline in intellectual life must fit. It is in this sense that Linguet is one of the more striking opponents of the eighteenth century notion of progress.

[6] *Annales politiques, civiles et littéraires*, I, 58; XIII, 63.
[7] *Annales politiques, civiles et littéraires*, I, 65.
[8] *Histoire du siècle d'Alexandre* (Paris, 1769), 11.

Chapter 23

Materialistic Optimism—Holbach

> Is not Reason permitted to hope that one day she will regain
> those powers so long usurped by error, illusion, and trickery?
> (*Le christianisme dévoilé*)[1]

In its broadest sense, materialism was a doctrine espoused within a very extended circle of eighteenth century liberal thinkers. Certainly there existed among the *philosophes* a general belief that the universe could be explained intelligibly only in terms of matter, and not of spirit. But there was a vast distance between the materialistic thought of Voltaire and that of Diderot, and an even vaster distance between that of Diderot and that of Sade. Materialism as a term is more fruitfully applied only to those systems which fulfill two requirements: the frank acceptance of a materialistic universe as the basic postulate of philosophy, and the forthright proclamation of atheism. By these standards materialism appeared but rarely in eighteenth century France; among the leading figures of the age only Diderot came near this rigorous system. Yet the materialistic writings attracted an attention disproportionate to their number, and in the intellectual life of the day they were of great significance.

In these concluding chapters three of the most important contributions to this movement will be examined: the work of Holbach, La Mettrie, and Sade. Each of these writers took a different position upon the obligations and the fate of mankind; only Holbach, the genial host of the *philosophes*, arrived at an ethical and social synthesis which approximated that of his most noted philosophical contemporaries. Though Holbach was essentially an optimist, his work

---

[1] *Le christianisme dévoilé, ou examen des principes et des effets de la religion chrétienne* (Paris, 1767), 218.

well deserves discussion in a study of historical pessimism, for from it one may perhaps discover why much the same philosophical assumptions led in one case to optimism, yet in other instances led to historical indifferentism or to a perverted cultural pessimism.

Neither a profound nor a refined thinker, the Baron d'Holbach rather was a practical social crusader. The arts apparently did not arouse his sympathies in the least, and the abstract subtleties of metaphysics only excited his scorn. Yet his philosophical system, if not a subtle one, had the virtue of honest bluntness: Holbach wrote what many a liberal thinker, but for pusillanimity, might have written long before. Materialism, determinism, and atheism lurked in the philosophy of nearly all the authors of the French Enlightenment, but it was La Mettrie and Holbach, above all, who brought these doctrines, together with several rather startling implications, fully into the open air of debate.

Holbach's primary goal was the destruction of superstition and authority, of priestcraft and governmental tyranny. For him all religion, and not simply the abuse of religion, was superstitious; religion, he wrote, invariably had its origin in ignorance of the true nature of the world. Religion in turn had become the source of all human prejudice, and the firm support of tyrannical rulers. "Everything proves to us that it is religious ideas which have the greatest capacity for tormenting and dividing men, and for making them unhappy...." These ideas "have obscured ethics, corrupted politics, retarded the progress of the sciences, and rooted out happiness and peace from the hearts of men."[2]

But destruction of prejudice and obscurantism, wrote Holbach, must be supplemented by the construction of a new order of things. Confidently he proclaimed that man could discover certain infallible principles of social and political behavior, and that upon these a whole new world might be built. Holbach was convinced that his own philosophy was the embodiment of these absolute and invariable principles—principles founded, of course, upon human reason.

And Holbach's faith both in reason and in scientific fact was im-

[2] *Systéme de la nature, ou des loix du monde physique et du monde moral* (London, 1770), II, 257, 285.

plicit, though he was tempted to slight historical fact. It was, doubt-less, largely his rationalism which led him to view nature and history as an uninterrupted chain of causes and effects based upon invariable and uniform natural law. The universe, he wrote, is composed of matter and movement alone, and man is a part of the natural world. Nature is a continuing course of creation and destruc-tion and of the alteration of relationships, and in this everlasting movement chance has no part whatsoever. "Fate is the eternal, immutable, and necessary order established in nature, or the neces-sary liaison between cause and effect." Man's actions, similarly, are the result of a strict determinism; man is but "a passive instrument in the hands of universal necessity." "Education is . . . but necessity shown to children. Legislation is necessity shown to the members of a political body. Morality is the necessity of human relationships shown to reasonable beings."[3]

The keystone of Holbach's social reconstruction was his system of ethics. Like his various contemporaries who faced the same prob-lem, he saw no contradiction between determinism and a doctrine of moral imperatives. The combination of outright atheism and of a neo-Christian ethics was one of the most striking features of Holbach's thought. From the simple facts of man's rationality, sensi-tivity, and sociability, Holbach constructed a single moral code, a system of social obligation, binding upon all ages and all nations. "Morality must be founded on invariable rules . . ."—rules which form "a system capable of being as rigorously demonstrated as arith-metic or geometry."[4] Men and nations vary in their externals, and ethical customs vary from place to place, but there is a basic morality which should be the same for all peoples, and basic standards of utility which are applicable to all social groups.

Much of Holbach's work consists of an attempt to trace the out-lines of this absolute and universal morality. Clearly he believed that human progress must be measured according to the degree to which men followed this enlightened code. And their capacity for doing

[3] *Système de la nature*, I, 220, 75, 216.
[4] *Le christianisme dévoilé*, 128; *Système social, ou principes naturels de la morale et de la politique* (London, 1773), I, 88.

so was guaranteed, he thought, by the sensationalist doctrine of Condillac. Men, according to Holbach, are born neither good nor bad, but only with certain passions and needs; sense experience alone imparts knowledge and molds character. Yet, unlike many of his less sanguine contemporaries, Holbach granted only a minimal role to the action of an uncontrollable environment upon mankind. He saw the effect of climate as slight, and preferred to emphasize the influence of governmental forms and of education and legislation— that is, of those forces most clearly modifiable by the human will.

Perfectibility through education and legislation became the central theme of hope in Holbach's historical optimism. The advance of knowledge, he believed, is the criterion and the bulwark of progress, for ignorance and prejudice cause not only intellectual error but indeed all human misery and degradation. Men do evil, and escape happiness, only because their reason has not been properly developed. It is for the philosophers, educators, and legislators to show men their true interests, to teach them not to mistake the evil for the good. Legislation is to be the fundamental agent of progress, especially insofar as it establishes adequate educational facilities.

In writing of human perfectibility, Holbach did not forget the system of rigid determinism which he had outlined elsewhere. It is one of the notable peculiarities of his system that his philosophical determinism did not enter into alliance with a pessimistic theory of environmental action, but rather with the idea of perfectibility through enlightenment. Perfectibility, for Holbach, is not an accident, but a necessary law of human development. "It is evident," he wrote, "that nature has made man susceptible to experience and consequently more and more perfectible. Thus it is absurd to want to stop him in his course, in the face of an eternal law which pushes him forward."[5]

Truth indeed, according to Holbach, is essentially invincible; the triumph of reason is insured. "One day the conjuncture of countless rays of light will form a tremendous illumination which will warm all hearts, enlighten all minds, and even surround those who seek

[5] *Essai sur les préjugés, ou de l'influence des opinions sur les mœurs et sur le bonheur des hommes* (London, 1770), 97.

to extinguish it. If truth, now restricted to the minds of a few men, makes only slow progress, this progress is none the less sure. Truth is spreading step by step and eventually will produce a general conflagration in which all human errors will be consumed."[6]

Thus Holbach, like Voltaire in his more optimistic moments, came to envisage an almost automatic progress outside of human control. Here then is a problem which was to torment all later progressionist theory: how is one to reconcile progress through purposeful human action with progress which is in some sense fatal and pre-determined? Some writers have emphasized the one, and some the other, of these two modes of action, but nearly all progressionist theories contain at least a suggestion of both doctrines. Holbach certainly did not solve the problem, and perhaps did not even recognize its existence.

For Holbach did not limit himself to pronouncements on the inevitability of progress; man's progress, he suggested, depends to a high degree upon his constant endeavor to better himself and to fight error and evil in the world. Holbach himself proposed a number of specific reforms, and felt that his own writings would help lead men to nature and to reason. But whether founded upon conscious struggle or upon inevitability, progress remained very real to Holbach, both as a present fact and as a future certainty. "Whoever cares to look attentively at most of the European nations cannot fail to recognize the most obvious effects of the progress of enlightenment. . . . The human mind, paralyzed for centuries by superstition and credulity, has awakened at last." "Despite the obscurity of the early dawn in which the nations still are groping their way, there are frequent flashes of light which presage the sunrise and the coming of full daylight."[7] The light of reason will break forth inevitably and may even cast reflected rays, one day, upon the general mass of mankind.

Such is the general tone of Holbach's prediction of future progress —the tone most typical of his historical philosophy. Yet it is true that at times Holbach qualified somewhat his world optimism. Progress,

[6] *Essai sur les préjugés*, 384.
[7] *Système social*, III, 228; *Essai sur les préjugés*, 388–389.

8+

he admitted, can only be painful and slow, and the millennium may, after all, be distant. "Let us not flatter ourselves . . . that reason with a single stroke can deliver mankind from the errors with which it is poisoned by so many concurrent forces. It would be vain indeed to hope to cure in an instant those epidemic and hereditary errors which have been ingrained for centuries and which are continually nourished and strengthened by the ignorance, passions, customs, interests, fears, and repetitive calamities of the nations. Ancient revolutions in the natural world brought forth the first gods, and new revolutions will produce new gods if the old have been forgotten. Ignorant, unhappy, and fearful men will always create gods, or credulity will make them accept those gods which imposture and fanaticism proclaim."[8]

It is not often that Holbach's historical optimism extended to the great mass of men; the full effects of progress, he wrote, are limited to an intellectual and a moral élite. Nor, in his opinion, is progress unbroken, for decadence, whether religious, economic, or political, will often interrupt its course. Empires and whole societies have their revolutions, for invariably they nurture within themselves the potentialities of dissolution and death. "Like sick men, societies have their crises, their moments of delirium, of decline and recovery. A deceptively healthful appearance often conceals internal weakness, and death itself may quickly follow a period of the most robust health."[9] Though Holbach saw no magic antidote for this perpetual fluctuation of ill health and well-being, he made it clear that the duty of enlightened men is to act as physicians to the world's ills, and thus to postpone sickness and death. The happiness of nations as of individuals cannot be permanent, but one can profit from such favorable moments as come one's way.

Does Holbach then suffer from the same pessimism, the same painful perplexity which often characterizes the work of Voltaire? The similarities between the two systems of thought are obvious, yet there are differences. There is, first of all, a clear shifting of emphasis

---

[8] *Système de la nature*, II, 314.
[9] *La politique naturelle, ou discours sur les vrais principes du gouvernement* (London, 1773), II, 224.

in these systems. If Voltaire's faith in progress remains vigorous to the end of his career, it is shaken more often and more drastically than is the parallel faith of Holbach. More significantly, Voltaire, though perhaps the less rigorous determinist of the two thinkers, at times emphasizes the blind action of natural and social forces, while Holbach insists upon the molding power of education and legislation, more surely within human control. In addition, Holbach's writings convey a greater feeling of the historical continuity between civilizations than does the Voltairean philosophy. Often Voltaire sees progress only within the framework of a given national or cultural unit, whereas Holbach almost invariably views developmental cycles within the context of that human reason which is eternally expanding somewhere on the earth's surface.

Thus Holbach succeeded in creating an optimistic synthesis comprising the idea of social, ethical, and intellectual progress. Perhaps the structure is not sound, but its mere erection is an unusual feat. For its ultimate avowed foundations, one must remember, are no more than sensationalism and social obligation, and a universe which is but a mass of atoms moved in rigorously deterministic fashion. The doctrine of progress which caps this structure in Holbach's work is precariously established and precariously maintained. Other materialists perceived an incongruity between structure and superstructure, and proceeded to do away with the idea of progress altogether.

Chapter 24

Indifferentism—La Mettrie

Some cry out, others declaim, and I laugh. (*Anti-Sénèque*)[1]

The written production of Julien Offray de la Mettrie was much less voluminous than that of the Baron d'Holbach, and his materialistic philosophy less fully developed. Yet two decades before the appearance of Holbach's work La Mettrie's philosophy was the scandal of his century, and for far more solid reasons than those which caused Holbach's atheistic diatribes to be widely condemned. Holbach, despite his frank godlessness and materialism, contrived an ethical and social system acceptable to the most conventional deists and liberals; La Mettrie, on the other hand, revealed a maddening indifference to those social and ethical values which the Enlightenment held sacred. And the new philosophy could no more tolerate indifference than could the old religion.

Indicative of this indifference toward accepted standards was La Mettrie's scant inclination to discuss the matter of progress. It is true that he noted now and then an occasional instance of progress, or of decadence, but these are merely passing references outside the essential body of his thought. A note here on the philosophical progress of the seventeenth century, a note there on the decadence of contemporary literature—these do not weigh heavily in the balance against his utter silence on the central question of the general course of mankind in the past and in the future. The reasons for this silence merit examination.

La Mettrie remained throughout his career a doctor; his philo-

[1] *Anti-Sénèque, ou discours sur le bonheur*, in *Oeuvres philosophiques de mr. de la Mettrie* (Berlin, 1775), II, 140.

sophical method, by and large, was that of the clinical specialist. It was not the ideal or the abstract which aroused his interest, but rather the close observation of natural phenomena. Against "the vain opinions of the philosophers" he sought to oppose experiment and observation.[2] Distrusting all principles which he could not test empirically, he could only be a complete skeptic in many branches of philosophy. The question of essences and of final causes, notably, seemed to him both meaningless and futile. Scornful of attempts to discover the undiscoverable, he held that men should resign themselves to knowing only what their senses revealed to them, and that they should cease tormenting themselves with the problems of the unknowable.

But La Mettrie's Pyrrhonism was not all-embracing. He was fully convinced of the validity of several philosophical tenets, among them atheism, materialism, determinism, hedonism, and the relativity of morality and of taste. It was upon these general principles that he built his view of man and the world. His atheism was blunt and uncompromising, and his materialism was a doctrine equally forthright. The universe, he asserted, is composed of a sole substance, matter, which is diversely molded and transformed. Nature is a vast, continuous chain of beings in which man is but one link. Men are machines, like other animals. Moreover, they are machines which, at least by general standards, are essentially not good but evil, and which only in time are modified to meet the rules of the reigning moral pattern.

The character and actions of men, according to La Mettrie, derive entirely from external circumstances, and from that disposition of the internal organs which is formed by external circumstances. "Man," he wrote, "is a machine governed imperiously by an absolute fatalism."[3] And not only is man's will not free: man has almost no true values to serve as guides to action. Virtue, in La Mettrie's view, is wholly relative to the circumstances in which man finds himself, to the public interest in a given situation. There is then no absolute virtue, nor is there any true vice, justice, or in-

---

[2] *L'Homme machine*, in *Oeuvres philosophiques*, III, 22.
[3] *Discours préliminaire*, in *Oeuvres philosophiques*, I, 18

justice. "Everything is arbitrary, and made by man's own hand."[4]
And if this is true, it is hardly fair to punish those who now are
called criminals. La Mettrie does not preach crime; he simply notes
that since morality is relative to the given society, those who do
not conform to that morality must not be allowed to go abroad pub-
licly, for they are sick and abnormal.

Man then, in La Mettrie's system, is the sole measure of all
values. This, he held, is no less true in the aesthetic than in the
ethical realm; taste, like virtue, is a purely relative quality. Good
taste, as it is popularly understood, is nothing but those "sensations
which most often flatter all men and which are, so to speak, the
most generally accredited and the most in vogue. . . . If there are
tastes which are better than others, the comparison can be made
only in reference to the sensations of one person. . . ."[5]

So it was that in ethics and aesthetics—two of those fields most
discussed by contemporary theoreticians of progress and decadence
—La Mettrie denied the possibility of establishing any absolute
values. His private exceptions to this rule, notably in metaphysical
philosophy, do not bulk very large against his general skepticism.
It is scarcely surprising that La Mettrie, for whom nearly all truth
was relative, should have become indifferent to the attainment of
truth.

Happiness, according to La Mettrie, is much more important to
the individual than a truth which is largely illusory. Though no
happiness which is absolute and complete can be achieved, this
limitation does not decrease its attraction. Happiness and pleasure
are demonstrable realities, however ephemeral they may sometimes
prove to be. "He who has found happiness has found everything."[6]
In this vital quest for happiness there is no place for the hesitancies
and the irrelevancies of reason and academic learning. Men must
devote themselves wholeheartedly to the satisfaction of the senses;
the truly wise man is the voluptuary.

It can only follow from this conception of human goals that tradi-

---

[4] *Anti-Sénèque*, in *Oeuvres philosophiques*, II, 13.
[5] *Traité de l'âme*, in *Oeuvres philosophiques*, I, 146, 147.
[6] *Anti-Sénèque*, in *Oeuvres philosophiques*, II, 98.

tional morality must yield to hedonistic imperatives when the two forces come into conflict. Man does not become more happy, more keenly alive to the sensuous pleasures, by attempting to better himself according to the moral standards of his society. The good man is often bitterly unhappy, while the evildoer, if he can escape remorse, may enjoy a life of the most pleasant sensuous indulgence. To be sure, at this point La Mettrie seems to draw back from the full consequences of his theory; he is unwilling to state in outright fashion that the social good must be subordinated to personal pleasure. Indeed at times he seems to approve of regional ethical codes, as useful to a particular society. Yet the trend of his ethical philosophy is clear enough, and the withering scorn which he displays toward the mass of mankind only accentuates the anti-social implications of his thought.

It is upon such grounds as these that La Mettrie is indifferent to the course of the external world. Progress does not concern him. The history of the world is the record of an eternal and meaningless flux, and as such is quite unworthy of serious attention. History is but one other instance of eternal return, of atomic interplay, of relentless transformation and recurrence. "In the morning man and the rose appear, and in the evening they are no more. Everything disappears and is replaced; nothing perishes."[7]

To La Mettrie the pretensions of mortal man could only seem comic when placed against the senseless phantasmagoria of history. "The chagrin, adversity, evils, and minor mortifications of life scarcely touch me at all," he wrote. "Some men cry out, others declaim, and I laugh."[8] Glory and honor, scholarship and learning, progress and decadence—these, in the long run, were irrelevant and ridiculous trifles to La Mettrie.

Is it possible that La Mettrie underestimated his own powers, that his occasional self-effacement as the court fool of the Enlightenment was overmodest? Whatever one's verdict may be, and even if one dismisses La Mettrie's writings as an extravagant expression of mere wit and paradox, it can hardly be denied that these writings

---

[7] *Système d'Epicure*, in *Oeuvres philosophiques*, I, 278.
[8] *Anti-Sénèque*, in *Oeuvres philosophiques*, II, 140.

came as an invigorating current to a century which, with all its intellectual ferment, remained essentially smug and self-satisfied. But it was not yet enough that the Enlightenment should have its puckish jester; it must also have a private demon sprung from its own flesh and blood. To fulfill this role the Marquis de Sade blazed a unique trail across the final decades of the century.

Chapter 25

Perversion—Sade

> The laws are egotistical, and we too should be egotistical. They serve society, but the interests of society are not our interests. (*La nouvelle Justine*)[1]

The years of the Directory saw a wide and public circulation of the works of the Marquis de Sade. The French eighteenth century by then had already learned much concerning the political potentialities of the Enlightenment, and now in its final years, with the decay of rigorous republican morality, the century was permitted to examine freely the demonic ethical iconoclasm which it had long nurtured within itself. By any moral standards current then or now the work of Sade was the product of a diseased mind, yet this mind was itself clearly the product of the eighteenth century. Sexual perversion—even those peculiarly elaborate and unpleasant brands of perversion described by Sade—is presumably of all ages, but the intellectual basis, or rationalization, of that perversion in Sade's writings is specifically a fruit of the Enlightenment.[2]

Unfortunately the unattractive nature of much of Sade's literary production, together with the extravagance of his more carnal

[1] *La nouvelle Justine* ("Holland, 1797"), III, 177.

[2] Primarily a writer of fiction, Sade seldom speaks directly and unequivocally of his own feelings; probably on no writer has there been more violent disagreement as to motivation and basic philosophy. The intellectual synthesis assigned to Sade in this chapter is that expressed, throughout his work, by the demonic monsters who people his dream world. It is this synthesis which is presented most forcefully and consistently in his writings, and which has generally, if perhaps erroneously, been taken to represent the authentic attitude of Sade himself. There can be little doubt, in any case, that it is this synthesis which has longest survived as typical of Sade, and which will continue to survive all attempts to clear his personal reputation.

sectaries, has obscured the true significance of his work. Whether beast or Divine Marquis, Sade was a serious thinker. It is difficult, undoubtedly, to determine the extent of this seriousness, but to ascribe his thought solely to lechery and paradox is impossible. Sade was a lineal descendant of both the earnest and virtuous Holbach and the amiable La Mettrie, and his ethical code was perhaps no less rigorous and no more fanciful a deduction from materialistic principles than was the neo-Christian code of the excellent German baron. In his repeated emphasis upon nature and reason, and upon philosophy itself, Sade falls even within the main current of the Enlightenment. One is more amused than startled to note, in the midst of the most lurid obscenity, a passage such as the following: "Our orgies were punctuated with philosophical discussions; we had no sooner committed a horror than we sought to legitimate it."[3]

The attack of Sade upon religion resembled that of Holbach in its virulence and in its failure to confine itself to mere anti-clericalism. For Sade as for Holbach all religion was gross superstition and should be replaced by the imperatives of reason and of nature. Sade was convinced that the universe operates by strictly mechanical forces, and that these forces are blind. Man, wrote Sade, is inextricably a part of nature and must act within its restrictive framework. Man is wholly the product of his heredity and his environment; his every move is fatally determined by powers outside his control. And since he is not responsible for his own acts, punishment for crime is senseless. Education and laws are powerless against man's moral behavior, for man is born with certain tastes and dispositions which cannot be consciously altered. Eventually, however, each climate, age, and nation comes to possess its own moral standards, and Sade proclaimed the non-existence of that universal morality to which his century had often clung so tenaciously.

But if Sade rejected the uniform ethical codes of the *philosophes*, he was no less insistent upon the reality of certain other absolute standards of morality. The new morality, like the more conventional ethical code of a Voltaire or a Holbach, was to be based upon natural and rational foundations. It is immediately evident, however, that

[3] *La nouvelle Justine*, III, 45.

the "nature" and "reason" of Sade were not the nature and reason of his Enlightened predecessors. Sade was to erect an ethical system which was the utter antithesis of the liberal ideals of his age.

With bitter scorn Sade confronted Holbach's assertion that virtue is pragmatically justified. Virtue, he insisted, does not triumph on this earth; ingratitude has been the recompense given by virtue to its devotees, while vice has richly rewarded its own practitioners. In the definitive version of *Justine* Sade establishes his guiding principle: "We ... shall paint crime as it is—always sublime and triumphant, contented and prosperous—and virtue likewise as it can only appear to men—always sad and sulking, pedantic and unfortunate." And Sade concludes that "it is infinitely better to enroll oneself among the evildoers who prosper than among the virtuous who fail in all their enterprises."[4]

A hedonistic ethics had long been accepted, to a greater or lesser degree, by the Enlightenment; Sade merely extended and perverted a doctrine already prevalent in non-Christian circles. There is, he wrote, only one ethical goal, "that of attaining happiness, no matter at whose expense.... Nature, which brought us alone into the world, nowhere orders us to show respect toward our fellows; if we do show respect it is only because it is politic to do so."[5] Man need pursue his personal pleasure alone—and it is sexual pleasure which is uppermost in Sade's mind. The sex act, he wrote, is the heart of philosophy.

But Sade carried much farther his doctrine of selfish hedonism. One's happiness, he held, is relative to the unhappiness of others; "happiness is not a state of the soul but a comparison of that state with the state of other souls. And what comparison can be made when all other people are like ourselves? ... My happiness can only exist through the misfortunes of others."[6] Clearly then it is to one's interest to make as many other people as unhappy as possible.

Thus it is that Sade came to preach war to the death between the individual and society. The interests of society are not the interests

[4] *La nouvelle Justine*, I, 4, 3.
[5] *La nouvelle Justine*, I, 195.
[6] *La nouvelle Justine*, III, 173, 174.

of the individual, nor can the former be understood as directly and
as thoroughly as the latter. One's own feelings, which are immediate
and reliable, must not cede to social compunctions, which are confused and misleading. Sade refers throughout his work to the individual not as one of the general mass of the population, but as
the man who is unusual, strong, and remorseless. Nature, he notes,
is the constant scene of the victory of the strong over the weak, of
the survival of the fittest. Men are not born equal; there has always
been a great slave caste, and surely the law of the weak cannot
apply to the strong. It is for the elite to break the general laws, to
rebel against mediocrity and against the social pact which per-
petuates that mediocrity. The absurd despotism of the weak must
give way to the cruel despotism of the strong.

Perpetual movement, continued Sade, is the law of the universe.
Similarly, "happiness is only in that which excites, and . . . it is
crime alone which excites. Virtue is simply a state of inaction and
repose, and can never lead to happiness."[7] The movement of the
universe comprises an eternal succession of creation, growth, and
destruction; nature can only re-create itself by a series of crimes.
It follows then that he who is most adept at destroying other beings
is best serving the interests of nature. The criminal is the man best
attuned to the general world harmony. Murder is the most useful,
and also the finest, the grandest, the most delectable, of all human
actions. The strong man cannot compromise with virtue: he must
be evil wholeheartedly. The pursuit of crime lifts him above the
misery of the multitude, and should mass morality apprehend and
condemn him, the scaffold can only deliver him forever from misery.

But it is here that Sade recognizes a terrifying fact: it is impossible even for the most vicious of men to be truly criminal. The
man who outrages society and its laws is utterly incapable of out-
raging nature, for all that is is natural. "The impossibility of out-
raging nature is . . . the greatest anguish man can know."[8] It is
this recognition which is the heart of Sade's satanic pessimism—a
pessimism well documented by the following passage from *Justine*.

"The sole aim of all our actions [declared D'Esterval] is the

---

[7] *La nouvelle Justine*, II, 228.   [8] *La nouvelle Justine*, II, 112.

transgression of morality and the smashing of religion. It is only on the rubble of these chimeras that we can establish our earthly felicity."

"That is quite true," said Bressac, "but I know of no crime which fully expresses that degree of horror which I feel for morality, and no crime which can destroy... all religious superstitions. What is it that we actually do in this life? The answer is simple. All our petty crimes against morality may be reduced to a few perversions and murders, an occasional rape or incestuous act, while our religious crimes are no more than a blasphemy here and a profanation there. Is there one of us here who can honestly say that these miserable acts are truly satisfying?"

"No indeed," replied the fiery Madame D'Esterval. "I suffer perhaps even more than you from the mediocrity of the crimes which nature permits me. In all our actions it is only idols which we offend, and not nature itself. It is nature which I yearn to be able to outrage; I want to throw its plans into disorder and block its ordained movements, to arrest the stars in their course and shake the globes which float in cosmic space, to destroy what serves nature and give protection to what irritates it—in a word, to insult nature and to suspend its great effects. And I can do none of these things."

"This," interposed Bressac, "is precisely what proves that there are no crimes. The word can apply only to such actions as Dorothy has mentioned, and you can see that these actions are impossible. Let us then take our vengeance in such ways as we can; let us multiply our horrors since we cannot improve upon them."[9]

Such is the terrible and irremediable despair at which Sade eventually arrives. Even the most violent and elaborate of crimes can bring neither purgation of the interior demon nor its satisfaction. So it is that not only the virtuous and the weak but also the vicious and the strong are condemned to ultimate futility. The external world in itself is nothing; it is the scene of a meaningless and irrelevant flux.[10] Man is everything, but even he cannot escape the nothingness which engulfs him. Man does not grow in virtue through the years, nor can he progress significantly in criminality. The earth is a vast enclosed maze in which impotent men blaspheme and murder in a desperate and vain struggle to escape.

The world picture of the Marquis de Sade was unique in his cen-

[9] *La nouvelle Justine*, IV, 39–40.
[10] *Histoire de Juliette* (Sceaux, 1948–1949), IV, 79–80.

9+

tury. His work presumably aroused little more than prurient curiosity during his lifetime, and it would be a mistake to assign to it any widespread intellectual influence in those years.[11] Yet Sade is too much a part of the eighteenth century to be dismissed as a mad eccentric. Like La Mettrie he was indifferent to the ideas of general progresss and decadence, for with him as with his precursor it was the happiness of the individual rather than the welfare of society which was the central goal of man's life. Indeed the progress of society, as then understood, could only hamper the development of the exceptional individual. Here as elsewhere, if one may take him seriously, Sade embodied not only a revolt from his own age, but the deliberate rejection of all that a Christian and liberal Western society has stood for over a period of many centuries. His abilities were perhaps not those of a Voltaire, a Montesquieu, or a Diderot, but surely he does not merit the virtual oblivion to which conventional history has prudishly confined him. With such other nonconformists as La Mettrie and Holbach, Vauvenargues and Linguet, he deserves a prominent role in the reconstructed pageant of eighteenth century French thought.

[11] His influence was considerable in the nineteenth century. See Mario Praz, *The Romantic Agony* (London, 1933), 93–186.

Conclusion

This study has recorded a great gamut of opinion on the problem of man's historical destiny. In the century and a half preceding the great Revolution, French thought on this problem was of a complexity today generally underestimated. Though the idea of progress acquired a considerable vogue in that period, it was an idea met at times by indifference or by countercurrents of a positive nature. From a vast wealth of published material the present writer has sought to extract some of the more significant conceptions of decadence and historical flux, and to identify certain philosophical foundations of those conceptions. If the choice of material has necessarily been somewhat arbitrary, an effort has been made both to collect as wide a range of opinion as possible and to give some attention to all the major thinkers of the age. Yet these pages can only afford an intimation of the great challenges to scholarly research which still remain.

An investigation of the genesis of eighteenth century French ideas of decadence and flux, a topical analysis of these ideas and of their intellectual prerequisites, and an examination of the relevancy of historical pessimism to the work of several outstanding authors of the Enlightenment—such have been the major concerns of this study. Final answers have been available to few questions, but in the intellectual world a tentative and provisional interpretation of significant phenomena is preferable to ignorance or neglect.

It is clear that the ideas of decadence and historical flux were widely discussed in eighteenth century France, and that in certain instances they challenged directly the common notion of historical progress. Though no quantitative measure of the extent of these disturbing ideas is possible, their presence, or indeed their prominence, in the philosophical syntheses of such writers as Condillac, Diderot, Voltaire, and Montesquieu is witness to the genuine importance of the trend. Nor was this trend limited to a handful of advanced thinkers, for a general diffusion is evident among minor writers of all persuasions. Historical optimism and pessimism alike cut across the boundaries between radicals and reactionaries, clerics and *philosophes*.

How then is the critic to account for the appearance of historical indifferentism and of the ideas of decadence and flux in eighteenth century France, and notably within the Enlightenment itself? Here he must face the inevitable, and perhaps insoluble, problem of historical correlation. Even granting the philosophical validity of the principle of causation, how is he to be assured of a causal connection between ideas? In most instances he must have recourse to a probability sanctioned by repetition, and to the analogy of his own logical processes. Both methods may be deceptive. The present study simply suggests a number of factors which seem to have entered into the formation of certain conceptions of progress, decadence, and flux in the eighteenth century. A degree of correlation has been noted, for example, between rationalism, progress, and decadence, and between historico-empiricism and historical flux. Relevance to the development of historical philosophies has also been seen in the questions of determinism, of the nature of man, of relative values, and of individual as against social preoccupations.

If the explanations suggested here have been tentative, it is nevertheless evident that the ideas of decadence and flux did infiltrate nearly all realms of historical speculation in the eighteenth century. Decadence, involving an abandonment of certain values which were more or less fixed and absolute, was often diagnosed not only in contemporary life, but was sometimes thought to be a constant potentiality throughout human history. And flux, whether involving frequent repetitions of progress and decadence according to rationalistic standards, or envisaged simply as a process of historical change made difficult of evaluation by relativistic considerations, was a conception familiar to thinkers of the most diverse schools.

With all these reservations, the French Enlightenment clearly retained much of that generous belief in progress which could only be the result of its broader intellectual orientation. Science had opened up great vistas before the eighteenth century, and confidence in scientific progress irradiated other realms of activity. As in science, so elsewhere technique came to be considered a major agent of amelioration. Here was a concept which could readily cooperate with rationalism and humanism in the foundation of a great system of world optimism. So it was that the idea of progress grew and throve, and so it was that many later historians neglected to note that this idea, central as it is to the understanding of the eighteenth century, was not unchallenged in that century.

The notion of progress has forever been a principle of action as well as an intellectual belief, whereas the ideas of decadence and flux often do not contribute directly to action. In eighteenth century France the belief in decadence might lead to projects of reform, or simply to an attitude of resignation; it might, on the other hand, be a mere intellectual reservation, irrelevant to problems which were immediate and concrete. There have been few men who have not cherished certain ideals, and the idealist forever must hope and work for progress even in the face of the eventual defeat of his ideals. Holding firmly to earthly goals, the Enlightenment inevitably strove for earthly progress and sought to justify its striving by the historical record.

Thus the belief in progress grew during the eighteenth century—yet powerful influences were continuously at work against this belief. The Enlightenment was characterized by a heightened sense of earthly destiny, and if it was conscious of progress so too was it conscious of decadence and historical flux. In force and attraction these pessimistic doctrines could not compete on even terms with the greater lure of historical optimism, but the notions of decadence and flux stubbornly resisted destruction by progressionist imperatives. The strength of this resistance, moreover, was not an accident. Historical pessimism was by no means an obscure and irrelevant reaction against the ideals of the Enlightenment; it was firmly rooted in the thought of the age.

An Essay on Bibliography

The work of scarcely a single writer during the Old Regime in France, of scarcely a single modern critic of that period, has failed to impinge at least momentarily upon the subject of this volume. A "complete" bibliography of the field would therefore be not only staggering in size but also negligible in usefulness. Thus, as is true in varying degrees with nearly every major research project, the difficulty here has been one of a superfluity, not a dearth, of riches. The problem, in other words, has been one of choice.

In the following pages, then, will be found only a few bibliographical guideposts, not an exhaustive bibliography. Here will be found an indication, at least, of the general nature of the materials which I have used in preparing this study, and which still offer opportunities for research. Secondary sources are represented more sparingly than are primary sources, for it is necessarily upon the latter that nearly all the conclusions of this volume must ultimately rest. At times, inevitably, the selection here has been somewhat arbitrary; certainly every specialist in the seventeenth and eighteenth centuries—perhaps even every general historian—will find favorite and standard works omitted from this discussion. For a fuller, but still incomplete, bibliographical listing of works used, the student may refer, in the Harvard University Library, to the typescript of the doctoral dissertation which forms the basis of the present study: *Decadence and Historical Flux: French Anti-Progressionist Thought in the Eighteenth Century*.

The sequence of treatment employed in this essay follows that in the text, with two exceptions. First, there is a brief consideration of general works which overlap the major divisions of the text. Secondly, Parts III and IV in the text are represented by four bibliographical sections, one (IV) devoted to general and topical studies of the eighteenth century, and the others (V–VII) to individual thinkers.

1. *General Works*

The historian, the literary critic, the student of ideas need only recall the vast production of books and essays of a general as well as of a specific nature in their respective fields to realize how many of these touch, whether briefly or at some length, upon the concepts of historical philosophy treated in this study. The general works—often works of sound scholarship and real insight—can undoubtedly have great value as introductions to the question of historical pessimism in the seventeenth and eighteenth centuries: they are, however, simply introductions, and as such will not be emphasized here.

From the considerable number of general discussions of historical philosophy I will mention only three which are particularly enlightening. One is fairly recent: Friedrich Meinecke's *Entstehung des Historismus* (Munich, 1936), the first volume of which includes a perceptive analysis of the historical mentality of the Enlightenment. The other two works are older but still useful: Robert Flint's *Historical Philosophy in France and French Belgium and Switzerland* (Edinburgh, 1893), and Charles Renouvier's four-volume *Philosophie analytique de l'histoire* (Paris, 1896–1897). Both works antedate the major wave of historical interest in the idea of progress, and tend, I feel, to be more balanced in their consideration of historical optimism and pessimism than are many later studies.

On the idea of progress itself countless books and articles have been written from the most various analytic, philosophical, and historical viewpoints. The best historical studies remain the pioneer works of J. B. Bury and Jules Delvaille: *The Idea of Progress* (London, 1924) and *Essai sur l'histoire de l'idée de progrès jusqu'à la fin du XVIIIe siècle* (Paris, 1910) respectively. Both, of course, exemplify the obverse of my concern with historical pessimism, the present study being indeed conceived in part as an antidote precisely to such works as these. Delvaille, especially, is often overzealous in seizing upon any literary scrap of evidence which may enlist a given thinker in the progressionist tradition. Other useful studies of the idea of progress include John Baillie's *Belief in Progress* (London, 1950), Wilson D. Wallis's *Culture and Progress* (New York, 1930), and a brief but judicious essay by René Hubert, "Essai sur l'histoire de l'idée de progrès," *Revue d'histoire de la philosophie et d'histoire générale de la civilisation*, new ser. VIII (1934), 289–305; new ser. IX (1935), 1–32.

Among the many specialized monographs relevant to historical philosophy are several which, because they cut across temporal or topical boundaries, may best be noted at this point. These include, first of all, Arthur O. Lovejoy's excellent *Great Chain of Being* (Cambridge, Massachusetts, 1936). A doctoral dissertation by John A. Kleinsorge, *Beiträge zur Geschichte der Lehre vom Parallelismus des Individual- und Gesamtentwicklung* (Jena, 1900), analyzes a question highly relevant to historical pessimism, as does Walter Rehm's study, *Der Untergang Roms im abendländischen Denken*, in *Das Erbe der Alten*, ser. II, vol. XVIII (1930).

II. *Seventeenth Century Philosophies of History*

For Descartes the most valuable sources are of course his own works: *Discours de la méthode* (Evreux, 1927), and *The Philosophical Works of Descartes*, 2 vols. (Cambridge, 1931–1934). Among the most useful secondary sources are André Cresson's *Descartes* (Paris, 1942), S. V. Keeling's *Descartes* (London, 1934), and Emile Rideau's *Descartes, Pascal, Bergson* (Paris, 1937).

On Pascal, the *Pensées et opuscules*, L. Brunschvicg, ed. (Paris, 1923) is basic. Good general studies include *L'esprit humain selon Pascal* by Ed. Benzécri (Paris, 1939), and *La philosophie et l'apologétique de Pascal* by E. Janssens (Louvain, 1906). Régis Jolivet contrasts Pascal's philosophy with Cartesianism in "L'anticartésianisme de Pascal," *Archives de philosophie*, vol. I, cahier III: *Etudes sur Pascal, 1623–1923* (1923), 54–67. In *La cité de Pascal* (Paris, 1928) Charles Droulers argues unconvincingly that Pascal presents a broad theory of progress; in *La pensée politique de Pascal* (Saint-Amand, 1931) Etiennette Demahis offers a more cautious affirmation of Pascal's historical optimism.

Most of the pertinent passages from Bossuet may be found in the following works: *Discours sur l'histoire universelle*, P. Jacquinet, ed. (Paris, 1886); *Bossuet moraliste*, P. Bonet, ed. (Paris, 1912); *Choix de sermons de Bossuet, 1653–1691*, A. Gazier, ed. (Paris, 1883); and *Traité de la connoissance de Dieu et de soi-même*, M. U. S. de Sacy, ed. (Paris, 1864). Georges Hardy emphasizes Bossuet's optimism in *Le "De Civitate Dei" source principale du "Discours sur l'histoire universelle"* (Paris, 1913). General works include Emile Baumann's *Bossuet* (Paris, 1929), and Gustave Lanson's *Bossuet* (Paris, 1891).

For a survey of the Quarrel of the Ancients and the Moderns, see the solid monograph by Hubert Gillot, *La querelle des anciens et des modernes en France* (Nancy, 1914). Boileau is best studied in the four volumes of *Oeuvres complètes*, A. C. Gidel, ed. (Paris, 1870–1873). Other works include René Bray's *Boileau* (Paris, 1942), Gustave Lanson's

9*

Boileau (Paris, 1892), and Marcel Hervier's *L'Art poétique de Boileau* (Paris, 1936). For Perrault, see *Oeuvres choisies de Ch. Perrault* (Paris, 1826), and *Parallèle des anciens et des modernes*, 2 vols. (Amsterdam, 1693). The twelve volumes of Fénelon's *Oeuvres* (Paris, 1826) are indispensable; Moïse Cagnac's *Fénelon* (Paris, 1910) and Ely Carcassonne's *Fénelon* (Paris, 1946) are secondary sources of moderate interest.

The libertine school which Saint-Evremond represented is the subject of a work by François Perrens, *Les libertins en France au XVIIe siècle* (Paris, 1896). Saint-Evremond's writings are available in the ten volumes of *Oeuvres* edited by P. Des Maizeaux (Paris, 1740). These may be supplemented by two dissertations: Ernest Mollenhauer's *Saint-Evremond als Kritiker* (Greifswald, 1914), and K. Spalatin's *Saint-Evremond* (Zagreb, 1934).

The work of Bayle is to be found in Beuchot's sixteen-volume edition of the *Dictionnaire historique et critique* (Paris, 1820), and in the four volumes of *Oeuvres diverses* (The Hague, 1737). Jean Delvolvé's *Religion, critique et philosophie positive chez Pierre Bayle* (Paris, 1906) is a solid general study. Bayle's historical pessimism is noted by Howard Robinson in *Bayle the Sceptic* (New York, 1931), and by Horatio E. Smith in *The Literary Criticism of Pierre Bayle* (Albany, 1912).

The eight volumes of *Oeuvres de Fontenelle* were published in Paris during the Revolution (1790–1792). The best secondary source for Fontenelle is J.-B. Carré's *La philosophie de Fontenelle ou le sourire de la raison* (Paris, 1932)—an admirable, comprehensive work which very nearly makes my own pages on Fontenelle superfluous, except as a brief survey. Also to be consulted is H. Linn Edsall's essay, "The Idea of History and Progress in Fontenelle and Voltaire," *Studies by Members of the French Department of Yale*, A. Feuillerat, ed. (New Haven, 1941).

III. *Eighteenth Century Optimism*

Supplementing such general works as those of Bury and Delvaille already cited, Carl L. Becker's *Heavenly City of the Eighteenth Century Philosophers* (New Haven, 1932) offers a sprightly introduction to the historical optimism of the Enlightenment. Charles Frankel has written a scholarly monograph on the same subject: *The Faith of Reason* (New York, 1948).

Reserving for a later section of this essay any mention of general works dealing with eighteenth century clericals and *antiphilosophes*, one may proceed directly to the three thinkers given more than passing reference in the first chapter of Part II. For the Abbé Le Gros, see his *Examen des systêmes de J. J. Rousseau de Genève, et de M. Court de Gebelin, auteur du "Monde primitif"* (Geneva, 1786). Of the works of the Abbé de Lignac, the following are most important: *Elémens de métaphysique tirés de l'expérience* (Paris, 1753); the five-volume *Lettres à un Amériquain, sur "l'Histoire naturelle, générale & particuliere" de monsieur de Buffon*, and varying titles (Hamburg, 1756); and the two-volume *Examen serieux & comique des "Discours sur l'esprit"* (Amsterdam, 1759). There is also a study of Lignac by F. Le Goff, *De la philosophie de l'abbé de Lignac* (Paris, 1863). By Bonnet there are eighteen volumes of *Oeuvres d'histoire naturelle et de philosophie* (Neuchâtel, 1779–1783), and on his philosophy two monographs may be consulted: *Charles Bonnet* by Georges Bonnet (Paris, 1929), and *La philosophie de Charles Bonnet de Genève* by Raymond Savioz (Paris, 1948).

On Deschamps, Morelly, and Mably a useful secondary source is André Lichtenberger's *Le socialisme au XVIIIe siècle* (Paris, 1895). For the words of Deschamps himself, see *Le vrai système* (Paris, 1939), and for further commentary on his work, Emile Beaussire's *Antécédents de l'hégélianisme dans la philosophie française: Dom Deschamps, son système et son école* (Paris, 1865). The two major works of Morelly are *Code de la nature* (Paris, 1910), and *Naufrage des isles flottantes, ou Basiliade du célébre Pilpai*, 2 vols. ("Messina," 1753). For Mably, see the *Collection complète des oeuvres de l'abbé de Mably*, 15 vols. (Paris, 1794–1795). Ernest A. Whitfield's *Gabriel Bonnot de Mably* (London, 1930) is an adequate general treatment; one may also refer to Edgard Allix, "La philosophie politique et sociale de Mably," *Revue des études historiques*, XLV (1899), 1–18, 120–131, and to L. Michoud, "Les théories sociales et politiques de Mably," *Bulletin de l'Académie delphinale*, ser. IV, vol. XV (1901), 89–147.

The actual writings of Jean Jacques Rousseau, as many a hasty commentator on his thought should have remembered, are the best source for understanding the man. See the *Oeuvres complètes*, 13 vols. (Paris, 1885–1905), and the *Correspondance générale*, 20 vols. edited by T. Dufour (Paris, 1924–1934). From the vast secondary bibliography I would choose, first of all, two general works: Albert Schinz's *La pensée de Jean-Jacques Rousseau* (Paris, 1929), and Ernest H. Wright's shorter *Meaning of Rousseau* (London, 1929). F. C. Green, in *Rousseau and the Idea of Progress* (Oxford, 1950), sees Rousseau as an advocate of moral, if not intellectual, progress. Robert Derathé, in *Le rationalisme de Jean-Jacques Rousseau* (Paris, 1948), helps explode the hallowed belief that Rousseau can be adequately explained as a man of emotion. Two competent studies of Rousseau's doctrine of natural goodness are in essay form: George R. Havens, "Rousseau's Doctrine of Goodness According to Nature," *Publications of the Modern Language Association of America*, XLIV (1929), 1239–1245; and Albert Schinz, "La théorie de la bonté naturelle de l'homme chez J. J. Rousseau," *Revue du dix-huitième siècle*, I (1913), 434–447.

The histories of progress noted earlier are often the best secondary sources concerning Chastellux, Mercier, Terrasson, Volney, the Abbé de Saint-Pierre, and even Turgot and Condorcet. Of course the five-volume *Oeuvres de Turgot*, G. Schelle, ed. (Paris, 1913–1922) and the twelve-volume *Oeuvres de Condorcet*, A. C. O'Connor and M. F. Arago, eds. (Paris, 1847) are basic. Douglas Dakin's *Turgot and the "Ancien Régime" in France* (London, 1939) has a relevant section. Two full-length studies of Condorcet are worthy of note: Franck Alengry's *Condorcet, guide de la révolution française* (Paris, 1904), and J. Salwyn Schapiro's *Condorcet and the Rise of Liberalism* (New York, 1934).

IV. *Eighteenth Century—General and Topical Works*

Of the many general works bearing upon eighteenth century thought I will note only three. Ernst Cassirer's *Philosophy of the Enlightenment* (Princeton, 1951) is a brilliant survey. Paul Hazard's three-volume study, *La pensée européenne au XVIIIème siècle de Montesquieu à Lessing* (Paris, 1946), is more thorough; typically, it overestimates the historical optimism of the age. In Emile Faguet's much older work, *Dix-huitième siècle* (Paris, n.d.), there may be found many acute observations, including several on the limitations of eighteenth century optimism.

On the natural sciences in eighteenth century France Daniel Mornet's *Les sciences de la nature en France, au XVIIIe siècle* (Paris, 1911) may serve as an introduction. On the role of empiricism in the sciences and in philosophy, see such general essays as Charles J. Beyer's "Du cartésianisme à la philosophie des lumières," *The Romanic Review*, XXXIV (1943), 18–39, and also Gustave Lanson's "Le rôle de l'expérience dans la formation de la philosophie du XVIIIe siècle en France," *Etudes d'histoire littéraire* (Paris, 1929), 164–209.

On the historical and sociological theories of the Enlightenment, several titles may be mentioned in addition to those more comprehensive works earlier noted. Of a general nature are the following: Roman L. Bach, *Die Entwicklung der französischen Geschichtsauffassung im 18. Jahrhundert* (Bruchsal, 1932); R. N. Stromberg, "History in the Eighteenth Century," *Journal of the History of Ideas*, XII (1951), 295–304; René Hubert, *Les sciences sociales dans "l'Encyclopédie"* (Paris, 1923); and Nelly N. Schargo, *History in the "Encyclopédie"* (New York, 1947). Climatic theory in the early decades of the century is reviewed in a recent essay by Roger Mercier, "La théorie des climats des *Réflexions critiques* à *l'Esprit des lois*," *Revue d'histoire littéraire de la France*, LIII (1953), 17–37, 159–174. Primitivistic theories and cyclical conceptions are considered in Auguste Le Flamanc, *Les utopies prérévolutionaires et la philosophie du 18e siècle* (Paris, 1934).

On aesthetics these general works are perhaps especially valuable: Wladyslaw Folkierski, *Entre le classicisme et le romantisme* (Paris, 1925); André Fontaine, *Les doctrines d'art en France de Poussin à Diderot* (Paris, 1909); and Theodore M. Mustoxidi, *Histoire de l'esthétique française, 1700–1900* (Paris, 1920). From the many studies of eighteenth century literary theory, the following titles may be chosen to represent the whole: John R. Miller, *Boileau en France au dix-huitième siècle* (Baltimore, 1942); Daniel Mornet, "La question des règles au XVIIIe siècle," *Revue d'histoire littéraire de la France*, XXI (1914), 241–268, 592–617; J. Rocafort, *Les doctrines littéraires de "l'Encyclopédie" ou le romantisme des Encyclopédistes* (Paris, 1890); Daniel Mornet, *Le romantisme en France au XVIIIe siècle* (Paris, 1932); and Werner H. Luschka, *Die Rolle des Fortschrittsgedankens in der Poetik und literarischen Kritik der Franzosen im Zeitalter der Aufklärung* (Munich, 1926).

V. *Eighteenth Century—Critics and Aestheticians*

In this section I shall do little more than note the titles, mostly of primary sources, which were most useful to me in studying individual critics and aestheticians of the eighteenth century. Though in the preparation of this study many other authors were scanned, I realize that my final choice was at least in part arbitrary, and that a great wealth of material remains for the student.

For Aquin de Chateaulyon, see *Satyre sur la corruption du goût et du style* (Liège, 1759). For the Abbé Batteux there are the six volumes of *Principes de la littérature* (Lyon, 1802), and *Les beaux arts réduits à un même principe* (Paris, 1747). Three works of Bricaire de la Dixmerie are particularly relevant: *Les deux âges du goût et du génie français, sous Louis XIV & sous Louis XV* (The Hague, 1769); *Lettres sur l'état présent de nos spectacles* (Amsterdam, 1765); and *La sibyle gauloise* (London, 1775). Chabanon contributes an essay *Sur le sort de la poésie en ce siècle philosophe* (Paris, 1764), and Charpentier the two-volume *Causes de la décadence du goût sur le théâtre* (Amsterdam, 1768).

Of the many valuable works by Clément, several fall more properly into a later bibliographical section. Among his more strictly critical works the following are especially significant: *Essais de critique sur la littérature ancienne et moderne*, 2 vols. (Amsterdam, 1785); *Observations critiques* (Geneva, 1771); *Nouvelles observations critiques* (Amsterdam, 1772); *Première lettre à monsieur de Voltaire* (The Hague, 1773); *Quatrième lettre à monsieur de Voltaire* (The Hague, 1773); and *De la tragédie*, 2 vols. (Amsterdam, 1784).

One of the more important works of the eighteenth century, and one of the most useful in my own study, is the three-volume *Réflexions critiques sur la poësie et sur la peinture* by the Abbé Dubos (Paris, 1755). On Dubos two monographs may be cited: Armin H. Koller, *The Abbé DuBos: His Advocacy of the Theory of Climate* (Champaign, 1937), and Alfred Lombard, *L'abbé Dubos* (Paris, 1913).

In the field of art criticism Dupont de Nemours is represented by *Lettres de Du Pont de Nemours à la margrave Caroline-Louise de Bade sur les Salons de 1773, 1777, 1779* (Paris, 1909). *L'année littéraire*, edited by Fréron (Amsterdam and Paris, 1754–1789) is not only a record of Fréron's own literary criticism but also an important guide to many forgotten works of the century, some of them now unavailable. The *Oeuvres complètes de Gilbert* (Paris, 1823) contains that author's "Satire I: Le dix-huitième siècle." Rémond de Saint-Mard contributes *Réflexions sur la poésie en general, suivies de trois lettres sur la décadence du goût, en France* (The Hague, 1734). Finally, for Marmontel there are the two volumes of *Poétique françoise* (Paris, 1763), the eighteen volumes of *Oeuvres complètes* (Paris, 1818–1819), and two doctoral dissertations: Heinrich Bauer's *Jean-François Marmontel als Literarkritiker* (Dresden, 1937), and S. Lenel's *Un homme de lettres au XVIIIe siècle: Marmontel* (Paris, 1902).

VI. *Eighteenth Century—Antiphilosophes*

Again, for the *antiphilosophes* as for the critics and aestheticians of the century, my bibliographical selection must be very limited and somewhat arbitrary. A useful introductory study is Robert R. Palmer's *Catholics & Unbelievers in Eighteenth Century France* (Princeton, 1939). Also applicable is a work by Kurt Wais, *Das antiphilosophische Weltbild des französischen Sturm und Drang, 1760–1789* (Berlin, 1934).

A number of works by Caraccioli are highly pertinent: *Le Chrétien du temps, confondu par les premiers Chrétiens* (Paris, 1766); *Le cri de la vérité contre la séduction du siècle* (Paris, 1765); *Dialogue entre le siècle de Louis XIV et le siècle de Louis XV* (The Hague, 1751); *La jouissance de soi-même* (Utrecht, 1759); *Lettres récréatives et morales, sur les mœurs du temps*, 2 vols. (Paris, 1767); and *Voyage de la raison en Europe* (Compiègne, 1772).

By Chaudon there are the two volumes of the *Anti-dictionnaire philosophique* (Paris, 1775), and the two volumes of *Les grands hommes vengés* (Amsterdam, 1769). *Les ridicules du siècle* by Chévrier (Paris, 1752) is a typical example of superficial criticism of the manners, morals, and literature of the age. Clément contributes a *Petit dictionnaire de la cour et de la ville*, 2 vols. (London, 1788), a *Satire sur la fausse philosophie* (n.p., 1778), and a collection of *Satires* (Amsterdam, 1786). For the Abbé Coyer, see his *Oeuvres complettes* in seven volumes (Paris, 1782–1783).

The Marquis de Pompignan is represented by four volumes of *Oeuvres* (Paris, 1784), and by a *Discours et mémoire* (n.p., 1760). On Pompignan a dissertation is also available: Fr.-Albert Duffo, *J.-J. Lefranc, marquis de Pompignan* (Paris, 1913). Two rather ponderous works by Rigoley de Juvigny and Sénac de Meilhan, respectively, round out this tentative listing: *De la décadence des lettres et des mœurs, depuis les Grecs et les Romains jusqu'à nos jours* (Paris, 1787), and *Considérations sur l'esprit et les mœurs* (London, 1787).

VII. *Eighteenth Century—Miscellaneous Philosophes*

Far more important than the *antiphilosophes*, more important even than the critics and the aestheticians, are the *philosophes*, dreamers and architects of the Enlightenment. In subsequent sections more detailed attention will be devoted to each of those thinkers given an individual chapter in the text; in the present section may be found a few guideposts to the study of other, but still important, writers.

A prime source for any study of the Enlightenment, embodying as it does nearly the whole *philosophe* movement, is the great *Encyclopédie, ou dictionnaire raisonné des sciences, des arts et des métiers*, 17 vols. (Paris and Neuchâtel, 1751–1765), together with its *Supplément*, 4 vols. (Amsterdam, 1776–1777).

For D'Alembert, see the five volumes of *Oeuvres* (Paris, 1821–1822), and the *Oeuvres et correspondances inédites*, C. Henry, ed. (Paris, 1887). The best critical study is that by Maurice Muller, *Essai sur la philosophie de Jean d'Alembert* (Paris, 1926).

Buffon is best studied in the imposing *Histoire naturelle, générale et particulière*; sixty-four volumes of the Sonnini edition (Paris, 1799–1808) are by him. See also the two volumes of *Correspondance inédite*, H. N. de Buffon, ed. (Paris, 1860), and two secondary works: Henri Lebasteur, *Buffon* (Paris, 1889); and Louis Roule, *Buffon et la description de la nature* (Paris, 1924).

The *Oeuvres de Condillac* in twenty-three volumes, Arnoux and Mousnier, eds. (Paris, 1798) are basic to any comprehensive understanding of the century. Three critical studies may also be noted: Raymond Lenoir, *Condillac* (Paris, 1924); Baguenault de Puchesse, *Condillac* (Paris, 1910); and Georges Le Roy, *La psychologie de Condillac* (Paris, 1937).

For Grimm the first source is of course the sixteen-volume *Correspondance littéraire, philosophique, et critique*, M. Tourneux, ed. (Paris, 1877–1882). One may also consult André Cazes, *Grimm et les Encyclopédistes* (Paris, 1933), and Edmond Scherer, *Melchior Grimm* (Paris, 1887).

Helvétius is represented by the ten volumes of *Oeuvres complettes* (Paris, 1793–1797), and by two good secondary works: Mordecai Grossman, *The Philosophy of Helvetius* (New York, 1926), and Albert Keim, *Helvétius* (Paris, 1907). For the Marquis de Mirabeau, see *L'ami des hommes* (Paris, 1883), and for Raynal the *Histoire philosophique et politique des éstablissements et du commerce des Européens dans les deux Indes*, 10 vols. (Geneva, 1780–1781).

VIII. *Montesquieu*

The E. Laboulaye edition of the *Oeuvres complètes*, 7 vols. (Paris, 1875–1879) contains Montesquieu's best known works. Of the many additional primary sources published since Laboulaye's day, the following are most significant for my study: *Cahiers, 1716–1755*, B. Grasset, ed. (Paris, 1941); *Mélanges inédits*, A. de Montesquieu, ed. (Bordeaux, 1892); *Pensées et fragments inédits*, 2 vols., G. de Montesquieu, ed.

(Bordeaux, 1899–1901); and *Voyages de Montesquieu*, 2 vols., A. de Montesquieu, ed. (Bordeaux, 1894–1896). The fragments in these more recent volumes were not written by Montesquieu for publication, and often reveal more of the man than do the major published works.

Among the general studies of Montesquieu the most useful to me were these: H. Barckhausen, *Montesquieu, ses idées et ses oeuvres d'après les papiers de la Brède* (Paris, 1907); Joseph Dedieu, *Montesquieu* (Paris, 1913); Victor Klemperer, *Montesquieu*, 2 vols. (Heidelberg, 1914–1915); and Albert Sorel, *Montesquieu* (Paris, 1889).

From among the countless specialized monographs and essays concerning Montesquieu only a few will be singled out here. Edwin P. Dargan's *Aesthetic Doctrine of Montesquieu* (Baltimore, 1907), for example, contains an exhaustive treatment of its subject.

On the historical methodology and philosophy of Montesquieu there are a number of provocative essays. Gustave Lanson, in "Le déterminisme historique et l'idéalisme social dans *l'Esprit des lois*," *Etudes d'histoire littéraire* (Paris, 1929), 135–163, holds that Montesquieu offered his conservatism to the cause of idealistic reform, and thus was an historical optimist. Gilbert Chinard attempts to refute Lanson in a highly pertinent article, "Montesquieu's Historical Pessimism," *Studies in the History of Culture: The Disciplines of the Humanities* (Menasha, 1942), 161–172; here Chinard concludes that Montesquieu thought of human societies as living organisms, thriving and then declining, and that the main trend of his work is pessimistic. An essay by Charles J. Beyer, "Le problème du déterminisme social dans *l'Esprit des lois*," *The Romanic Review*, XXXIX (1948), 102–106, stresses Montesquieu's "social determinism," which is seen as less founded upon observation than upon logic. Finally, René Hubert, in "La notion du devenir historique dans la philosophie de Montesquieu," *Revue de métaphysique et de morale*, XLVI (1939), 587–610, emphasizes the dynamism of Montesquieu's world-view, and that sense of pluralism and discontinuity in history which could only thwart any theoretical vision of progress.

IX. *Voltaire*

Le sottisier de Voltaire (Paris, 1880) and the *Oeuvres inédites*, F. Caussy, ed. (Paris, 1914) add but slightly to the Moland edition of the *Oeuvres complètes de Voltaire* (Paris, 1877–1885). Here, in fifty-two bulky volumes, is perhaps to be found quite adequate material for a reasoned judgment of this giant among *philosophes*.

There is, of course, a plethora of critical studies of Voltaire; a few of these are good. For example, there is something of value in the following general treatments: André Bellessort, *Essai sur Voltaire* (Paris, 1925); Jean F. Nourrisson, *Voltaire et le Voltairianisme* (Paris, 1896); Edme Champion, *Voltaire: études critiques* (Paris, 1892); Léon Crouslé, *La vie et les oeuvres de Voltaire*, 2 vols. (Paris, 1899); Raymond Naves, *Voltaire* (Paris, 1942); and Paul Sakmann, *Voltaires Geistesart und Gedanken-welt* (Stuttgart, 1910). The last four of these, incidentally, deny, with varying degrees of vehemence, that Voltaire maintained a true doctrine of progress.

Two studies give some special insight into Voltaire's general philo-sophical methodology: Robert E. Fitch's *Voltaire's Philosophic Pro-cedure* (Forest Grove, 1935), and J. R. Carré's *Consistance de Voltaire le philosophe* (Paris, 1938). The latter work argues convincingly that Voltaire's philosophy was not as inconsistent as it is often portrayed.

Three important studies of Voltaire's position as critic and aesthetician may be cited: Robert Lowenstein, *Voltaire as an Historian of Seventeenth Century French Drama* (Baltimore, 1935); Raymond Naves, *Le goût de Voltaire* (Paris, 1938); and Paul Sakmann, "Voltaire als Aesthetiker und Literarkritiker," *Archiv für das Studium der neuren Sprachen und Literaturen*, CXIX (1907), 110–138, 383–398; CXX (1908), 99–120.

On Voltaire's historical philosophy the following essays may be noted as possessing some merit: Alfred v. Martin, "Motive und Tendenzen in Voltaires Geschichtsschreibung," *Historische Zeitschrift*, CXVIII (1917), 1–45; K. Rockett, "An Optimistic Streak in Voltaire's Thought," *The Modern Language Review*, XXXIX (1944), 24–27; and Paul Sak-mann, "Universalgeschichte in Voltaires Beleuchtung," *Zeitschrift für französische Sprache und Literatur*, XXX (1906), 1–86. The first two of these emphasize Voltaire's historical optimism, the last his pessimism.

X. *Diderot*

Though there are other published works of Diderot, these do not add significantly, for the purposes of my study, to the material in the twenty volumes of *Oeuvres complètes*, J. Assézat and M. Tourneux, eds. (Paris, 1875–1877).

Among the best general studies of Diderot are Hubert Gillot's *Denis Diderot* (Paris, 1937), Daniel Mornet's *Diderot* (Paris, 1941), and Franco Venturi's *Jeunesse de Diderot, 1713–1753* (Paris, 1939). Mornet, particularly, emphasizes the contradictions within Diderot's thought, his historical philosophy included.

So too does Lester G. Krakeur, in "Diderot and the Idea of Progress," *The Romanic Review*, XXIX (1938), 151–159. This brief essay is an admirable sketch, without attempting to cover Diderot's notions of artistic decadence, or the intellectual substructure of his historical philosophy. Georges May's essay, "Diderot pessimiste: la crise de mélancolie des années 1760–1762," in *Quatre visages de Denis Diderot* (Paris, 1951), sees pessimism as a temporary phase in Diderot's outlook.

Useful monographs on Diderot's ethical theory include Pierre Hermand, *Les idées morales de Diderot* (Paris, 1923); J. Robert Loy, *Diderot's Determined Fatalist: A Critical Appreciation of "Jacques le fataliste"* (New York, 1950); and Lester G. Crocker [Krakeur], *Two Diderot Studies: Ethics and Esthetics* (Baltimore, 1952). Aram Vartanian's *Diderot and Descartes: A Study of Scientific Naturalism in the Enlightenment* (Princeton, 1953) offers a fresh approach to Diderot's general philosophical methods; its placement of Diderot in the rationalistic, Cartesian tradition is provocative, if open to debate.

Several interesting treatments of Diderot's aesthetics are available: Felix Vexler, *Studies in Diderot's Esthetic Naturalism* (New York, 1922); Yvon Belaval, *L'esthétique sans paradoxe de Diderot* (Paris, 1950); and Lester G. Krakeur, "Aspects of Diderot's Esthetic Theory," *The Romanic Review*, XXX (1939), 244–259 (see also the same author's monograph mentioned in the preceding paragraph). Belaval finds much coherence in Diderot's aesthetics, and Krakeur much confusion.

XI. *Vauvenargues and Linguet*

The rather slight literary production of Vauvenargues is contained in two volumes edited by D. L. Gilbert: *Oeuvres* and *Oeuvres posthumes et oeuvres inédites* (both Paris, 1857). Secondary sources include: Antoine Borel, *Essai sur Vauvenargues* (Neuchâtel, 1913); Gustave Lanson, *Le marquis de Vauvenargues* (Paris, 1930); Paul Souchon, *Vauvenargues, philosophe de la gloire* (Paris, 1947); Fernand Vial, *Une philosophie et une morale de sentiment: Luc de Clapiers, marquis de Vauvenargues* (Paris, 1938); and May Wallas, *Luc de Clapiers, Marquis de Vauvenargues* (Cambridge, 1928). Most of these, perhaps rather understandably, do not consider the idea of progress.

From the voluminous writings of Linguet several may be chosen as particularly valuable for his views on history and society: *Théorie des loix civiles*, 2 vols. (London, 1767); *Le fanatisme des philosophes* (London, 1764); *Histoire du siècle d'Alexandre* (Paris, 1769); and the nineteen volumes of *Annales politiques, civiles et littéraires du dix-huitième siècle* (London, Lausanne, and Paris, 1777–1792).

The only full-length study of Linguet is Jean Cruppi's *Un avocat journaliste au XVIIIe siècle: Linguet* (Paris, 1895); it is largely devoted, however, to biographical narrative, and carries his life only to 1775. The one attempt to give a rounded presentation, though cursory, of Linguet and his works is by Henri Martin: "Etude sur Linguet," *Travaux de l'Académie Impériale de Reims*, XXX (1859), 341–425; XXXI (1860), 81–149. The best analysis available of Linguet's social theory is in André Lichtenberger, *Le socialisme utopique* (Paris, 1898).

XII. *Holbach, La Mettrie, and Sade*

On Holbach, two critical studies deserve mention: Pierre Naville, *Paul Thiry d'Holbach et la philosophie scientifique au XVIIIe siècle* (Paris, 1943); and W. H. Wickwar, *Baron d'Holbach: A Prelude to the French Revolution* (London, 1935). The best sources are of course Holbach's own works, of which the following are most useful: *Le bon-sens* (London, 1772); *Le christianisme dévoilé* (Paris, 1767); *Essai sur les préjugés* (London, 1770); *Ethocratie* (Amsterdam, 1776); *La morale universelle*, 3 vols. (Amsterdam, 1776); *La politique naturelle*, 2 vols. (London, 1773); *Système de la nature*, 2 vols. (London, 1770); and *Système social*, 3 vols. (London, 1773).

La Mettrie's writings require only three slender volumes: *Oeuvres philosophiques de Mr. de la Mettrie* (Berlin, 1775). One may also consult Raymond Boissier, *La Mettrie* (Paris, 1931), and J. E. Poritzky, *Julien Offray de Lamettrie* (Berlin, 1900).

The bibliography of Sade, though large, presents peculiar problems, most of them related to considerations of propriety and censorship. Of the two full-length studies worthy of mention, neither is particularly enlightening for present purposes: C. R. Dawes, *The Marquis de Sade* (London, 1927); and Geoffrey Gorer, *The Marquis de Sade* (New York, 1934). Other studies tend to be either vague, clinical, or otherwise irrelevant to the theme of my work.

Sade's own writings, with certain innocuous exceptions, are not readily accessible. For this reason, and this reason only, one may recommend the *Selected Writings*, edited by L. de Saint Yves (New York, 1954), to the casual student. Of the major works by Sade—if the scholar is fortunate, or unfortunate, enough to find them—by far the most valuable are *La nouvelle Justine*, 4 vols. ("Holland, 1797"), and *Histoire de Juliette*, 5 vols. (Sceaux, 1948–1949).

Index

Absolute values, 15, 33, 46, 86–87, 89–91, 95, 156–57, 159–60, 183, 195, 202, 212–13, 219–20; breakdown, 109–15; relevance to philosophy of history, 3, 13, 56, 58, 61, 66, 68, 71, 76–80, 83, 85, 230. *See also* Rationalism.

Aesthetics, 23–30, 86–95, 109–21, 160, 183–87, 189–94; importance in eighteenth century, 4, 187. *See also* Classicism; Romanticism.

Ancients and Moderns, Quarrel of, 23, 25–30, 34–35, 38–39, 42, 76, 88, 121

Aquin de Chateaulyon, 89

Arts. *See* Aesthetics; Authority; Nature; Relativism; Rules.

Augustine, 10, 18, 139

Authority, in arts, 24–25, 29–30, 46, 95

Bacon, F., 11
Bacon, R., 10
Batteux, 87, 90, 114
Bayle, 36–39, 46, 100
Bel esprit, 28, 91
Bernard of Morlas, 10
Bodin, 11
Boileau, 23–25, 27–28; compared with Fénelon, 28–29; compared with Perrault, 29–30; compared with Saint-Evremond, 34; influence on eighteenth century, 30; on criticism, 94; on naïveté. 91
Bonnet, 52–53, 83
Bossuet, 18–22, 46
Bouhours, 28
Bricaire de la Dixmerie, 116, 124
Buffon, as empiricist, 103; criterion of progress, 77; on climate, 136; on decadence of philosophy, 78; on decadence of states, 143; on feeling in arts, 111; on flux, 147, 151; on irregularity of progress, 105; on nature, 83; on nature of man, 104

Caraccioli, 79–80, 135, 140, 146
Cartesianism, compared with Classicism, 24–25, 27
Causation, historical, 18, 20
Charpentier, 89, 117
Chastellux, 62
Chaudon, 88, 128, 135
Christian philosophy of history, 2, 9–11, 14–22, 46, 50–53, 146
Classicism, 23–30, 34, 86–95, 160, 183–87, 189–94, 202; breakdown, 109–15. *See also* Authority; Exhaustion of arts; Nature, Rationalism; Rules.
Clement, on *bel esprit*, 91; on decadence of literature, 89, 93; on decadence of painting, 88; on luxury, 127; on philosophy in literature, 92; on reading public, 94
Climate, theories, 29, 32–33, 43, 56, 58, 64, 114, 136–37, 159, 177, 197
Compensation, theories, 43, 129–30, 196
Comte, 65
Condillac, criteria of progress, 77; historical emphasis, 106; psychology, 99; on barbarism, 149; on climate, 136; on compensation, 130; on cycles in arts, 120; on determinism, 102; on empiricism, 102; on exhaustion of arts, 117–18; on flux, 148–49, 151; on history as teacher, 106; on influences on cultural development, 124; on irregularity of progress, 104–5; on

Harvard Historical Monographs

* Out of print

18. A Cistercian Nunnery in Mediaeval Italy: The Story of Rifreddo in Saluzzo, 1220–1300. By Catherine E. Boyd. 1943.
19. Vassi and Fideles in the Carolingian Empire. By C. E. Odegaard. 1945.
20. Judgment by Peers. By Barnaby C. Keeney. 1949.
21. The Election to the Russian Constituent Assembly of 1917. By O. H. Radkey. 1950.
22. Conversion and the Poll Tax in Early Islam. By Daniel C. Dennett. 1950.*
23. Albert Gallatin and the Oregon Problem. By Frederick Merk. 1950.
24. The Incidence of the Emigration during the French Revolution. By Donald Greer. 1951.*
25. Alterations of the Words of Jesus as Quoted in the Literature of the Second Century. By Leon E. Wright. 1952.*
26. Liang Ch'i Ch'ao and the Mind of Modern China. By Joseph R. Levenson. 1953.*
27. The Japanese and Sun Yat-sen. By Marius B. Jansen. 1954.
28. English Politics in the Early Eighteenth Century. By Robert Walcott, Jr. 1956.*
29. The Founding of the French Socialist Party (1893–1905). By Aaron Noland. 1956.
30. British Labour and the Russian Revolution, 1917–1924. By Stephen Richards Graubard. 1956.
31 RKFDV: German Resettlement and Population Policy. By Robert L. Koehl. 1957.
32. Disarmament and Peace in British Politics, 1914–1919. By Gerda Richards Crosby. 1957.
33. Concordia Mundi: The Career and Thought of Guillaume Postel (1510–1581). By W. J. Bouwsma. 1957.
34. Bureaucracy, Aristocracy, and Autocracy. The Prussian Experience, 1660–1815. By Hans Rosenberg. 1958.
35. Exeter, 1540–1640. The Growth of an English Provincial Capital. By Wallace T. MacCaffrey. 1958.
36. Historical Pessimism in the French Enlightenment. By Henry Vyverberg. 1958.